C000134157

The Return of

High Inflation:

Risks, Myths, and Opportunities

Wolfgang H. Hammes, Ph.D.

The Return of High Inflation © Copyright 2016 by Wolfgang H. Hammes

All rights reserved. No part of this book may be reproduced in any form or by any electronic or mechanical means including information storage and retrieval systems without the permission in writing from the publisher, except by a reviewer, who may quote brief passages in a review.

Published by The Vangi Group.

For information about permissions to reproduce selections of this book, please write to the publisher: The Vangi Group, 4400 North Federal Highway, Suite 210-19, Boca Raton, FL 33431.

For information about hiring the author for workshops or keynote speeches, please contact the publisher at info@vangiconsulting.com

Library of Congress Control Number: 2016901046

Includes bibliographical references and index

ISBN: 978-1-944614-00-3 (paperback)

LIMIT OF LIABILITY/DISCLAIMER OF WARRANTY: THE PUBLISHER AND THE AUTHOR MAKE NO REPRESENTATIONS OR WARRANTIES WITH RESPECT TO THE ACCURACY OR COMPLETENESS OF THE CONTENTS OF THE WORK AND SPECIFICALLY DISCLAIM ALL WARRANTIES, INCLUDING WITHOUT LIMITATION WARRANTIES OF FITNESS FOR A PARTICULAR PURPOSE. NO WARRANTY MAY BE CREATED OR EXTENDED BY SALES OR PROMOTIONAL MATERIALS. THE INFORMATION AND STRATEGIES CONTAINED HEREIN MAY NOT BE SUITABLE FOR EVERY SITUATION. THIS WORK IS DISTRIBUTED WITH THE UNDERSTANDING THAT NEITHER THE PUBLISHER NOR AUTHOR IS ENGAGED IN RENDERING LEGAL, ACCOUNTING, TAX, FINANCIAL, INVESTMENT, OR OTHER PROFESSIONAL SERVICES OR ADVICE. IF PROFESSIONAL ASSISTANCE IS REQUIRED, THE SERVICE OF A COMPETENT PROFESSIONAL PERSON SHOULD BE SOUGHT. NEITHER THE PUBLISHER NOR THE AUTHOR SHALL BE LIABLE FOR DAMAGES ARISING HEREFROM. THE FACT THAT AN ORGANIZATION OR WEBSITE IS REFERRED TO IN THIS WORK AS A CITATION AND/OR A POTENTIAL SOURCE OF FURTHER INFORMATION DOES NOT MEAN THAT THE AUTHOR OR THE PUBLISHER ENDORSES THE INFORMATION THE ORGANIZATION OR WEBSITE MAY PROVIDE OR RECOMMENDATIONS IT MAY MAKE.

To my parents

To my wife Angela and my children Claudia and Maximilian

PREFACE

The day this book is published, the vast majority of people will not be overly concerned about inflation risks. In fact, many of them may worry about the opposite: deflation. Politicians, central bankers, and business people—everybody seems to be preoccupied with deflation risks.

Following the majority view rarely has been an effective strategy to escape financial and nonfinancial catastrophes. The reader should be aware that most so-called experts or authorities regularly fail to anticipate major risk events. You can see this important point when looking at expert opinions voiced just before the Great Depression of 1929, the October 1987 stock market crash, the new economy bubble, the U.S. housing bubble, the last financial crisis, and many more extreme risk events. If there is an inflation crisis in the future, do not expect the majority of people or even experts to ring the alarm bells in time. You will be on your own to protect yourself.

High inflation is a very severe risk event. The last inflation crisis in the developed world during the 1970s put severe stress on companies and individuals. The stock market within a short period lost about half of its value, unemployment rates skyrocketed, interest rates shot above twenty percent. History suggests that high inflation is not only a financial risk event, but a social one as well. Very often, countries that live through a period of excessive inflation have become socially and politically destabilized as extremists of either political spectrum use the pain and frustration of the general public to gain popularity. Some of the worst historic events were preceded by periods of high inflation.

A return of high inflation to the developed world should not surprise us. Judging from historical analogies, inflation is a likely outcome of the economic malaise we are in and the policies we have chosen to address economic weaknesses. More specifically, irresponsible fiscal behavior, excessive levels of government and private sector debt, and ultra-loose monetary policies are very likely to be followed by a period of excessive inflation. While we cannot exactly time the occurrence of such an inflation risk event, we can quite well assess its general probability of occurrence.

There are two key issues of which the reader should be aware. First, the vast majority of companies and individuals are not prepared to deal with a return of high inflation. We know from risk management history that unpreparedness can aggravate substantially the consequences of any risk event. Second, our understanding of how inflation works and what needs to be done from a risk management perspective is still incomplete and insufficient. There is very little practical research out there that could help managers or individuals prepare for such a risk event. This is an inexcusable omission.

The situation is even worse. Our modern economic and financial systems and processes are based on the assumption of low inflation. They have never been stress-tested for a different scenario. Therefore, it is quite possible that a return of high inflation to the developed world will lead to a much more severe financial crisis than the one we experienced a few years ago.

Inflation requires a different set of skills than those taught to us in western business schools. In fact, some of the most widely accepted management paradigms in the developed world will not only become ineffective during times of high inflation, they may also become quite dangerous and create substantial harm in the future.

While I address these issues, I will not close the research gap on this important topic. Therefore, you should view this book only as a first step in addressing some of the research and experience gaps. Also, you should not believe that reading one book will enable you to immunize you or your company against inflation risks. Instead, you should engage in a continuous learning process and seek the help of qualified professionals when crafting your inflation strategies.

There is one substantial issue that no book can address and that you must be aware of. Inflation is a social phenomenon. It simply means that institutions and individuals lose faith in paper money. As they do so, they will change their behavior and make a range of rational and irrational decisions to deal with the problem. Some of these irrational decisions are predictable as they have occurred in many past inflation cycles. For example, politicians like to introduce select price controls to the economy to "protect" the consumer (i.e., voter). This ineffective strategy has been practiced since the inflation days of Roman Emperor Diocletian in the third century. Almost always, it made things worse, but politicians use it to restore calm among the people in the short term. The next inflation cycle in the developed world will most likely lead to many more examples of irrational decisions and outcomes that are impossible to anticipate in this book. These challenging situations must be dealt with by analyses of the respective situational context.

This leads me to an important topic: how to use this book. Reading this book should be the start of an important journey that hopefully will put you in a position to protect yourself from the risks of inflation. Maybe the journey will take you a step further and enable you to turn inflation risks into a big opportunity as Warren Buffett did during the 1970s. This, however, will require a substantial amount of additional work and research. Ideally, you get together with other people and share your thoughts and strategies regarding rising inflation. To be most effective, you should include people with relevant experience in your discussion or working groups. A person who relocated from Venezuela or Argentina may add a lot of "street smart" inflation experiences to your discussions. A relative, friend, or acquaintance who experienced the U.S. or U.K. inflation periods of the 1970s as a manager is likely eager to share his perspective. The goal of this book is to alert you to a dangerous threat and to motivate you to start a journey to mitigate and preempt these risks. This book will not take you to the end of the journey. It will only be a first step that has to be followed by many other steps.

The first part of the book is an overview and a summary of some of the most important ideas presented later. It is lengthier than typical overviews. I chose this structure to enable time-pressed readers to gain quickly a basic understanding of my concerns and ideas. This structure may also help you understand the foundations of my thinking and my theories before going into a detailed analysis. The second part highlights the issues and risks I see for our future and provides some historic perspectives. As a lot has been published about past inflation cycles, I chose not to repeat detailed descriptions of these past periods of inflation. Instead, I wanted to focus on applying past experiences and lessons learned to the situation of the modern world and its future. Chapter 4 seeks to explain why society repeatedly fails to anticipate major risk events. It argues that certain conditions are likely to precede major risk events and describes how these conditions exist when it comes to inflation risks.

Part III offers a selection of the frameworks, concepts, and ideas that I have developed for my clients and that may help prepare both companies and individuals for the next inflation cycle. Obviously, these basic concepts need to be tailored to the reader's specific situation. Also, situational judgment is necessary to adjust for inflation risks that deviate from past patterns. While these concepts may prove helpful for a start, they cannot replace professional advice that is necessary to develop recommendations for your specific situation. Please consider them as unproven ideas and theories that need to be tested and refined by the next period of high inflation.

Part IV discusses possible implications of inflation on financial markets and on your personal situation. This is not investment advice. Instead, possible issues that should be considered when drafting a personal inflation strategy for you and your family are discussed. Again, this book does not provide any form of advice. Professional advice must be sought to develop recommendations that suit your specific needs.

The book would not be complete if I did not offer some ideas on how to avoid the mistakes that led to the current economic malaise. Part V provides a framework to authorities for establishing a more robust economy and for achieving sustainable and high-quality economic growth. Since a detailed description of these issues goes beyond the scope of this book, I will focus on the three key pillars for an alternative economic paradigm: absolute price stability (accepting mild deflation), robust systems and processes, and high-quality economic growth.

The sole purpose of this book is to alert the reader to substantial risks we are facing and motivate him to consider preparatory work to address these potential risks. The focus of the analysis is on the developed world, which I assume is grossly underprepared to deal with a return of high inflation. This does not mean that other countries will be safe regarding inflation risks. However, they face a different situation that requires a different analysis and different strategies. I do believe that some emerging market countries are better equipped to deal with high inflation than most developed countries. In fact, some emerging market countries might be able to turn inflation risks into an opportunity that will let them leapfrog into a much advanced competitive position. It is quite possible that the next inflation cycle will lead to a reversal of roles between developed and emerging market countries.

Finally, for full disclosure purposes, I should inform the reader about two pieces of background information. First, I am German. Many people feel that Germans, particularly the German central bank, suffer from an excessive phobia of inflation. The German Bundesbank, the country's central bank, is one of very few central banks in the world that takes a critical stand on current and past ultra-loose monetary policies. This critical view, which is shared by many Germans, makes the Bundesbank and the German people targets for criticism and mockery. In my view, German concern about inflation and the stability of paper money systems is simply rooted in monetary history in general and German history in particular. Germans have, unfortunately, unique experiences with the problems of inflation. It is not uncommon for a German of my parents' or

9

grandparents' generation to have experienced six or more different currencies and substitute currencies (e.g., "Notgeld") over their lifetime. Many of these currencies later became practically worthless. This is an experience British and American central bankers and people have not lived through. If any developed nation accumulated hands-on expert know-how on inflation and monetary decay, it is Germany. Maybe our fears are exaggerated, but they are unfortunately rooted in very uncomfortable first-hand experiences.

The second disclosure relates to my business background. I am not an economist, but a management consultant and former investment banker who is focused on strategy formulation for my clients. More specifically, my mission is to help clients to relate strategy to risk and future management issues. This requires a screening of economic developments, trends, risks, and opportunities. My research and theories are based on observation, system analysis, critical thinking, and scenario analysis. I focus on reality and the positive and negative paths it may take in the future and try to translate this into proactive and anticipative strategies for my clients. I am not at all interested in theoretical models that are based on assumptions that do not reflect economic and practical reality. My goal is to protect my clients from negative surprises and to help exploit attractive opportunities. As you will see, the return of high inflation can be both a risk for the unprepared and an opportunity for the prepared. To me, surprises are typically signs of a neglect of risk management issues in your strategy. Fortunately, there are very few risk events that come as a total surprise to us, and if you believe that the last financial crisis was one of them, then you need to rethink your risk and future management approaches. As credible experts warned as early as 2000 of the possibility of a major credit risk event threatening the banking system, you should have had such a risk event on your strategic risk radar screen. If you did not, do not repeat the same mistake by ignoring the risk of a return of high inflation to the developed world.

We are now at a stage in history when the economic, fiscal, financial, and social situation in many developed countries resembles terrifying parallels to past periods of history prior to major outbreaks of high inflation or other severe disruptions. I sincerely hope that the developed world is spared a return of high inflation and I also hope that my fears and concerns prove to be exaggerated. However, hope does not have a legitimate place in responsible risk management. You should not bet your financial and social well-being on hope. In risk management, it has always been a good strategy to hope for the best, but nevertheless prepare for the worst.

I wish my readers good luck in this challenging endeavor.

Wolfgang Hammes, Ph.D.

December 2015, Boca Raton, Florida

TABLE OF CONTENTS

PART I: OVERVIEW

CHAPTER 1: THE RETURN OF HIGH INFLATION—A SEVERE RISK FOR THE UNPREPARED, A GREAT OPPORTUNITY FOR THE PREPARED

Over one hundred years ago, in early 1914, few in Germany were worried about inflation risks. Why should they have been? Germany was one of the biggest economies in the world, it had a track record of economic and social solidity, and its workforce was considered highly educated and productive. German companies were admired for their innovativeness and entrepreneurship. Germany's currency was strong and its financial markets were stable and working well. Ignoring inflation, however, was a fatal mistake for Germans at that time. Less than a decade later, excessive debt, prolonged fiscal deficits, and ultra-loose monetary policies led to a period of hyperinflation that crippled Germany's economy, destroyed its currency, and made savings and fixed income investments practically worthless. Even worse, the German hyperinflation destabilized Germany's social and political order. Within less than ten years, Germany went from boom to bust.

In December 1972, few in the U.S. were worried about inflation risks. Why should they have been? Did not the S+P 500 stock market index just reach a new all-time high? Was not the economy growing again at a healthy rate? Were not demographic developments promising an attractive future, growth, and prosperity? Was not its central bank successful in fine-tuning business cycles? Were not politicians and central bankers equally confident about the U.S.'s immediate future? Were not most top managers predicting bright prospects for the years to come? Ignoring inflation risks in early 1973, however, turned out to be a fatal mistake for companies and individuals. Just twenty-one months later, the S+P 500 stock market index had lost about half of its value, interest rates skyrocketed, and the economy fell into a deep recession. Inflation had its grip on the U.S. for the next decade. Anyone who was caught unprepared suffered tremendously.

On the day this book is released, few people in the developed world will be worrying about inflation. In fact, many people, financial experts and leading central bankers among them, will be worrying about the opposite risk event: deflation. The media is full of articles about deflationary threats to our economy. Do not be fooled by this. It is common that the vast majority of people and experts fail to anticipate major risk events. And when it comes to inflation, many people, including experts, have an extremely poor track record of anticipating it, even though there are many obvious warning signs out there.

It is surprising that very few people are concerned about inflation and that even fewer actually do something to protect themselves. The developed world currently fulfills almost all requirements for high inflation to return. Situations in which extreme levels of indebtedness, low economic growth, and fiscal imbalances were addressed with ultra-loose monetary policies led more often than not to high inflation rates. With this came dangerous volatility and disruptiveness in the economy, financial markets, and society. Why do most of us expect this time to be different? Einstein is said to have defined insanity as doing the same thing over and over again and expecting different results. Is it a sign of insanity that many of us believe that we will get away with it this time?

The developed world is at risk of severe instability and disruptiveness that will be caused by the return of high inflation rates and all the second and third order effects that will come with it. As I describe in this book, there is a chance that we will experience economic, financial, and social disruptiveness that goes beyond the levels we experienced during the last financial crisis. The current situation is much more serious, and the fact that so few companies and individuals are prepared for it will most likely increase the damage to society once inflation rates start to rise.

Therefore, not preparing yourself, your family, or your company for this risk event is like gambling or naively hoping that the world will always turn out to be fine. However, risk management strategies based either on gambling or hopes are very dangerous and irresponsible choices.

This book seeks to explain how a return of high inflation can damage and derail the economy, financial markets, businesses, and society in developed countries. The myths, the risks, the dangers, and also the opportunities of living in a world of high inflation are discussed. You will learn that for the unprepared company or individual high inflation is a painful and brutal experience. For the very few people who understand how to deal with it, however, it can open up exceptional opportunities. Therefore, you should use the ideas in this book first to protect your downside and then to develop strategies that may turn inflation risk into an opportunity.

Inflation is a nice-sounding word for a process that is actually quite nasty, grossly unfair, and dangerously destructive: the decay of money. People who have not actually experienced the ugly reality of high inflation might be tempted to view inflation as something that just raises the cost of living a bit. Many economists and central bankers still believe they can gamble with inflation rates to improve short-term economic growth and employment levels. They fail to see that inflation once ignited is very difficult to contain and can easily spiral out of control. They also fail to understand that the economic and financial systems that are the foundation of the developed world cannot deal with even moderately high inflation rates. The economic, financial, and social systems that we created over the past three decades in the developed world have been designed under the assumption of low inflation. We never stress-tested them for periods of high inflation, as we have assumed that these times are behind us. If we had done so, we would have quickly realized that they simply cannot cope with extended periods of high inflation, and politicians, central bankers, and top managers would immediately put high inflation on the top of their risk management agendas.

For people who lived through periods of excessive inflation (although there are few among today's decision makers in the developed world) inflation has a different meaning. I always remember the fear in the faces of my grandparents in Germany when the term "inflation" was mentioned in the media. They knew that once inflation is in motion, it is extremely difficult to contain. They also knew that it can easily derail an economy and deteriorate living conditions for all people, as Germany experienced during the 1920s or as the people of Venezuela witness at this moment. But high inflation does not stop there: It can lay the foundation for the destabilization of society as it presents a chance for political extremists to gain influence.

Inflation always means the decay of money, regardless of whether inflation rates are high or low. You love inflation and the decay of money if you are highly indebted, as inflation eats up the value of your debt. Inflation can miraculously eliminate excessive debt levels (at the expense of conservative savers). For example, excessive inflation reduced the value of all domestic government debt piled up by Germany during World War I (i.e., until 1918) to the equivalent of the cost of about half a gallon of milk at the end of 1923. Roughly 155 billion German paper marks of debt in 1919 were practically eliminated five years later.

Inflation rewards the indebted speculator, the fiscally irresponsible government, and the greedy profiteer and arbitrageur, but not the conservative saver or ordinary person. Tax laws in most developed countries support this wealth transfer from the saver to the speculator as interest expenses on loans are tax deductible, while interest income on savings is often highly taxed.

Since high inflation has not been present in the developed world since 1982 (the year when the last inflation cycle ended in the U.S.), few people today are concerned about inflation. Most people are more concerned about deflation. This is a common mistake in risk management. We do not worry about things that did not happen for an extended period of time. Instead, we focus on risk events that just happened or threats that are presented powerfully by the media.

I do not state that it is impossible for deflation to occur. In fact, deflation could result from deteriorating demographics, outsourcing of manufacturing to low-cost countries, forced deleveraging of consumers'

22

balance sheets, or technological progress. My point is, however, that in contrast to deflation worriers I believe that deflation would occur only for a short period of time and would then make way for even more vicious and aggressive inflationary trends. I also believe that the situation in Japan is uniquely different from the situation in other developed countries and that therefore it is unlikely that developed countries experience similar deflation issues as in Japan.[1] The misperception of Japan's real problems has ignited some sort of deflation mania in the developed world that is neither helpful nor relevant.

Deflation increases the real value of debt. In an over-indebted environment, central banks and politicians will do anything possible to prevent deflation. Otherwise, governments (and other highly indebted entities or households) run the risk of default as their (nominal) income streams fall with deflation and will be insufficient to service the debt. High levels of indebtedness and long periods of deflation are not compatible.[2] Therefore, counter-intuitively, short periods of deflation may even increase future inflation risks.

When I warn of a return of excessive inflation to the developed world, I am not (yet) concerned about a hyperinflation comparable to the one seen in Germany during the 1920s. I would not say that it is impossible for a hyperinflation to occur in one or several countries in the developed world. It is possible that the extreme pro-growth initiatives put in place in many developed countries could spiral out of control.

What concerns me most is that even more moderate levels of inflation could cause a catastrophic shock to our economy, financial markets, and society. In my view, inflation levels observed during the 1970s in the U.S. would be sufficient to push the developed world into a new banking and financial crisis that would easily top the damage caused by the last one.

Unfortunately, central banks in developed countries continue to pursue their ultra-loose monetary policies with great conviction. They are unimpressed by historic analogies or the concerns I voice in this book.

They continue to implement tools and policies that are not that different from the ones implemented by German officials during the time preceding the period of hyperinflation. Back then, there was a similar conviction that the economic malaise following World War I had to be addressed by debt-financed infrastructure investments and entitlements accompanied by ultra-loose monetary policies.

It is ironic that Germany today opposes those strategies of more debt-financed spending and ultra-loose monetary policies while the U.S. (and many other countries) enthusiastically embraces them. It seems that many countries have switched sides compared to their conduct after World War I. Back then, while Germany was pursuing its inflationary policies, the U.S. adopted exactly the opposite strategy: an aggressive reduction of government spending and restrictive monetary policies. The U.S. strategy proved to be successful, while Germany ended up in hyperinflation and chaos. After a brief (but admittedly severe) recession in 1920 and 1921, the U.S. economy recovered strongly from its bitter medicine and boomed during most of the 1920s (i.e., the "roaring twenties"). Today, Germany adopts the successful U.S. strategy of the late 1910s, and the U.S. (and most other developed countries) experiment with policies that brought down Germany during the 1920s.

While high inflation is a serious and dangerous risk, this book is not about doom and gloom. Any event that causes high levels of volatility and disruptiveness presents both risks and opportunities. This is equally true for high inflation. Companies and individuals who understand the new rules of the game enforced by high inflation cannot only address most of the severe risks; they can also turn high inflation into an attractive opportunity. Vast fortunes have been created during past periods of high inflation by companies and individuals who understood the new rules of the game before anyone else.

HOW DID WE GET HERE? FINANCIAL ENGINEERING VERSUS REAL ECONOMY

Many people blame the banks solely for the current economic malaise. Such an interpretation of history is dangerously incomplete and fails to identify the root causes of our problems. We must learn our lessons to prevent making the same mistakes over and over again. Let me therefore share with you my view of the root causes of our current economic problems, as I believe it is crucial to understand them in order to enable you to devise appropriate inflation strategies.

First, we must go back to 1982, the end of the last inflation cycle in the U.S. At that time, decision makers missed an exceptional chance to create sustainable wealth and prosperity by leveraging low debt levels, attractive demographics, technology, engineering, and innovation.

Instead, the developed world chose a different strategic paradigm. Most developed countries pursued a strategy that aspired to achieve maximum short-term economic growth based on aggressive use of debt. The discipline of financial engineering helped to create the mechanisms and tools to absorb the increasing volumes of debt.

Debt was used to pull forward future consumption. Debt levels not only increased steadily from the early 1980s in absolute terms, they also increased in relative terms. Today, many countries experience a total debt-to-GDP ratio of close to 300 percent or more. For many developed countries, relative indebtedness measured by the total debt-to-GDP ratio has increased close to three times or more compared to the early 1980s.

Normally, any economy would have choked on such levels of indebtedness. However, financial engineering provided new ways and tools to absorb these high volumes of debt. It also helped banks to move loans off their balance sheets and free up capital for new loans. Banks moved from an "originate and hold (loans) paradigm" to an "originate, repackage, and sell" paradigm. Strategically, they transformed themselves from storers of risks to movers of risks. Repackaged loans were sold as investments to new domestic and international investors, including investment funds, insurance companies, foreign banks, and hedge funds. Intermediaries were so successful in selling repackaged debt products that they ran out of sufficient new loans to create new investment products. Synthetic structures were created to satisfy the strong demand from investors. Financial innovation accelerated during the 1990s and early 2000s. For example, credit derivatives were introduced to separate the credit risk element from a fixed income investment and make credit risk separately tradable. Complexity of those investments and structures increased rapidly.

An increasing level of debt pushed up economic growth rates beyond sustainable levels. Economic growth was increasingly driven by debt-financed consumption (or leveraged investments) and less from production. For decades, developed countries have been consuming at the expense of future generations. Therefore, we can consider a great part of past economic growth in developed countries as artificial or even false. It was simply the product of additional debt and financial engineering and not the result of production, innovativeness, and hard work.

Apart from the disruption caused by the recent financial crisis, the continued and accelerating issuance of additional debt was surprisingly smooth. Three factors contributed to this result. First, and foremost, central banks in developed countries issued an explicit positive inflation guarantee. They targeted (low) positive inflation rates, often between two and three percent, and defended these targets rigorously against any sign of deflation. Even the slightest hint of deflation risk was aggressively and excessively attacked by monetary policies. This inflation guarantee significantly reduced the risk of borrowing or issuing more debt. Debt became a low-risk strategy.

Second, regulatory and tax rules incentivized the use of debt in most developed countries. As interest expenses are tax deductible while interest income is often highly taxed, governments encourage unintentionally an excessive use of debt. It is bizarre that companies, for example, issue additional debt to buy back their own shares (often at high valuations) and receive a tax benefit for doing so. Equally bizarre are the regulatory rules that "incentivize" banks and insurance companies to hold fixed income securities over other asset classes. Regulatory rules also do not require a capital charge for government bonds held by financial institutions, as those bonds are considered risk free.

Third, deficiencies in risk management practices employed by politicians, regulators, financial institutions, companies, and investors also helped maintain temporary stability. They obscured the real dimension of the challenges caused by excessive debt. As a result, top management of many financial institutions was probably not even aware of the enormity of their risk management challenges before the outbreak of the last financial crisis.

As shown in the next chapter, the excessive accumulation of debt and the monetary strategies that have been put in place to accommodate it, in my view, will be the main drivers for a return of inflation to the developed world. What we see today is the initially slow but then accelerating buildup of an enormous pool of inflation risk. Therefore, it is not only the last five years that are responsible for the risk of high inflation, but also the economic and monetary policies put in place over the last three decades. It is very important to understand this distinction.

WHY INFLATION WILL RETURN TO THE DEVELOPED WORLD AND HOW IT MIGHT CAUSE A PERFECT STORM

Two distinctive developments may lead to a return of high inflation to the developed world. Each on its own may cause excessive inflation. However, if these two developments coincide, we may witness a dramatic increase of inflation rates in the developed world. We may call this a perfect inflation storm. For simplicity, I call these developments EMEG Inflation (**E**merging **M**arkets **E**conomic **G**rowth) and LOFIS Inflation

(**L**oss **o**f **F**aith **i**n **S**tability). Chart 1 gives a short overview of the two themes.

Chart 1: The two types of inflation discussed in this book

	EMEG Inflation (Emerging Markets Economic Growth)	LOFIS Inflation (Loss of Faith in Stability)
Main Cause	Continued economic growth in populous emerging market countries	Loss of faith in paper money in developed countries
Drivers	• Increased demand for resources and products originating from strong growth in populous emerging market countries • Global demand exceeds global supply regardless of economic strength in (less populous) developed countries	• Loss of faith in long-term financial stability caused by excessive debt, fiscal deficits, ultra-loose monetary policies • Market participants fear that monetary reality does not match economic reality • People increasingly seek to preserve wealth by preferring real assets over monetary assets

Over the past two decades, we have witnessed a structural break in the world economy that will lead to tectonic shifts going forward. Emerging market countries started to transform themselves into economic powerhouses. To call this process an industrial revolution would be a gross understatement, as the speed of this transformation is about ten times as fast as the period of industrial revolution during the nineteenth and twentieth centuries in Europe. Even more important, the scale of this economic transformation is gigantic. While the industrial revolution encompassed several hundred million people at most, the period of economic leapfrogging impacts billions of people in emerging markets and catapults their lifestyle from poverty and simplicity to that of modern middle-class consumers.

Consequently, the demand for commodities, products, and services originating from emerging markets will increase dramatically over the years to come. Global supply of a wide variety of commodities and products will struggle to keep up with the additional demand from emerging markets, a development that most likely will lead to rising prices and inflation for both developed and emerging market countries. This is EMEG Inflation.

We must not underestimate the impact of EMEG Inflation on the global world and the size and power of the factors driving it. Billions of people in emerging market countries are more or less on the road to becoming typical middle-class families that will build houses, buy cars, furniture, appliances, and other products of which their parents could have only dreamed. They will upgrade their nutrition preferences to consume a diet much richer in animal protein than that of their parents. The latter will lead to higher prices for both meat and feeding stock.

Some readers may dismiss my concerns for EMEG Inflation as exaggerated given the low-growth environment in the developed world and the often cited global "excess production capacity" that presents a buffer against rising demand and its impact on price levels. However, both protection mechanisms against rising prices can disappear quickly. For example, between 2007 and the summer of 2008, inflation rates in many developed countries crossed the five percent threshold. The reason for rapidly accelerating prices was not excessive growth in the developed world. It was the strong economic growth in emerging markets that "exported" inflation to developed countries. EMEG Inflation is therefore an exogenous event that will be hard to contain for developed countries. As consumption levels increase in emerging economies, these countries will become less dependent on exporting their products to the developed world. As a result, global prices are likely to increase.

While EMEG Inflation is a serious threat (as we observed in 2006 and 2007), LOFIS Inflation is much more vicious and dangerous for developed countries. LOFIS Inflation results from a loss of faith in paper money systems. The factors that may lead to LOFIS Inflation include: rising levels of total and government debt, prolonged periods of fiscal deficits, ultra-loose monetary policies, skepticism about the abilities and intentions of politicians and other relevant decision makers, and low economic growth (in absolute and relative terms).[3] As shown, the economic and financial systems in the developed world are not only stretched, but also inherently fragile and unstable. This issue has not been sufficiently addressed, neither before nor after the last financial crisis. In fact, the fragility and instability of our systems may have even increased since then. It seems to be only a matter of time when people will start to raise doubts about the stability of economic, financial, and monetary systems. Eventually, more and more people will seek to preserve their wealth by avoiding domestic monetary instruments and resorting to real assets.

It is hard to imagine that developed countries will be able to address their debt issues without resorting to higher inflation rates (partly induced by excessively loose monetary policies). The real economic growth rates required to turn fiscal deficits into huge surpluses (necessary to begin the reduction of debt levels) will simply be too high to obtain, particularly if we continue in the developed world to fail to implement radical economic and structural reforms that are the necessary foundation to enable higher economic growth rates.

A return of LOFIS Inflation would not be a very unusual event in history. Many people are not aware that the long-term track record for paper money systems is devastatingly poor. Almost all paper money systems

30

eventually cease to exist and in most cases are replaced due to excessive indebtedness and ultra-loose monetary policies. Sometimes currencies died due to excessive LOFIS Inflation, other times governments simply pre-empted the emergence of LOFIS Inflation and introduced a new currency regime.[4]

LOFIS Inflation does not occur overnight. There is no immediate cause-and-effect relationship. Often, there are several years between the implementation of pro-inflationary actions and policies and the emergence of LOFIS Inflation. Once a currency has enjoyed a decent track record over an extended period of time, there is some inertia among market participants to reassess the actual stability of a currency in light of newer (and deteriorating) developments. People simply continue to give credit where no credit is due.

A good, however admittedly extreme, example of LOFIS Inflation is the period of hyperinflation in Germany during the 1920s. Excessive debt, accelerating fiscal deficits, and ultra expansionary monetary policies led to a collapse of the German paper mark currency and made it practically worthless. Case examples of LOFIS Inflation go back thousands of years. Roman Emperor Diocletian was plagued by LOFIS Inflation during the third century. Unfortunately, decision makers in politics and central banks seem to have learned little from past case studies. They continue to commit the same mistakes over and over again.

In fact, the same mistakes made by Emperor Diocletian were repeated by decision makers during the 1970s inflation period and are currently being committed again in Venezuela (e.g., forced price controls).

The introduction of paper money systems has made the risk of LOFIS Inflation significantly greater. It should not surprise us that the vast majority of hyperinflations occurred in the past 110 years. They are a rather modern phenomenon.[5] In fact, metallic currencies, which were common in ancient and medieval times, seem to have a better track record in achieving price stability.[6] Inflation became worse after

31

Gutenberg invented the printing press and governments substituted coins with paper money.[7]

Today's situation in most developed countries fulfills almost all conditions necessary for reigniting LOFIS Inflation. Therefore, if we use our historic experience base, LOFIS Inflation should not come as a surprise. Instead, it would be a normal occurrence given the policies and actions implemented in the past.

THE DEVELOPED WORLD IS NOT BUILT FOR HIGH INFLATION—IT MAY CRASH BECAUSE OF IT

Despite high inflation rates and enormous financial volatility, the 1970s period of high inflation did not lead to a catastrophic meltdown of economic, financial and social stability, and order. The U.S. and other countries went through severe recessions and an extended period of economic hardship was endured. However, order was preserved and after a tough decade the economy recovered. The economic and financial system survived this period of hardship. There was no widespread banking crisis that had people lined up at the doors of their banks.

Unfortunately, if high inflation returned today or in the future, this might be very different. High inflation could tip the developed world not only into a severe economic crisis, but also into a new financial crisis that could easily exceed the damages caused by the last one. In fact, high inflation could unleash a chain reaction of events that could spiral out of control and require a disruptive reset of our financial and monetary system.

The reason for this is simple. The systems that are the foundation of the economy, financial markets, and society in the developed world today were mainly created during a time of low inflation, intended for low inflation. They can neither deal with an event of high inflation nor function well during any type of economic or financial stress. The last financial crisis illustrated this quite frighteningly. We are living in a fragile and unstable world.

One of the key issues that makes today's developed countries so fragile is the enormous imbalance between the financial and the real world. Chart 2 illustrates this.

Chart 2: Relative size of the real economy versus the financial world[8]

Description	Indexed to world GDP (rounded)
Total financial assets (including all equity and debt instruments, loans, BIS derivatives contracts, other financial assets)	Over 1390
"Real" asset base (all tangible and non-tangible nonfinancial assets)	300
Global securitized debt (i.e., all loans, bonds)	143
Global GDP	100
Bank (equity) capital (estimate)	10–15

Chart 2 illustrates several issues alarmingly. First, the size of the financial world is a high multiple of the size of the real economy. It is almost a surreal world that mushrooms independent of the real economy. To put it in blunt words: the monetary reality is detached from economic reality. It is in fact like an "uber-world." Second, banks, the main actors in the monetary reality, hold relatively little capital in relation to the amount of total financial assets, particularly if the complexity of many of these assets is considered. Even relatively small changes in the valuation of these financial assets could wipe out (again) a large chunk of banks' capital bases. And third, volumes of outstanding derivatives have reached enormous levels and keep on growing.

The real size of the financial world is hard to quantify and somewhat obscure. The numbers in Chart 2 are rough estimates to illustrate the proportions between different aggregates. The actual numbers may be even higher. Many types of derivatives are not accounted for in the official BIS statistics. Even if we exclude these derivatives, the remaining number of total notional financial assets is high enough to threaten the stability of the financial system, particularly during a period of high volatility and economic stress.

Admittedly, a big chunk of total financial assets is made up of derivatives contracts. Many people disregard this number. They claim notional amounts do not represent the real risks, particularly as netting procedures reduce the amount of outstanding derivatives significantly.

While this is a fair assumption during stable and low inflation periods, it may not hold true during times of high inflation. The turbulence in financial markets caused by high inflation (and secondary effects such as rising interest rates) may disrupt the derivatives markets severely. Derivatives contracts almost always are tied to nominal (i.e., non-inflation adjusted) aggregates. High inflation rates will impact the nominal value of the underlying assets directly and, as derivatives magnify the nominal price swings of the underlying assets, we can expect huge price swings in the derivatives markets. This increases the counterparty risk of derivatives transactions significantly.

It would be the first time that this gigantic market gets stress-tested for inflation risks. During the 1970s, the last high inflation period in the U.S., the derivatives markets were in their infant stage.[9]

The imbalances between the real world and the financial world are not the only issues to worry about in an inflationary world. There are at least five additional complications that could create massive disruptions in the developed world. I will discuss these complications in Chapter 3.

One of these complications is the lack of expertise among decision makers in the developed world. Few of today's decision makers in politics, central banks, financial institutions, and the business world have ever managed an organization during times of high inflation. As we are coming closer to a massive storm, we realize that the captain commanding our boat never experienced a storm in his life. Not a very comforting outlook.

THE DANGER POINT: THE TRANSITION FROM A PROLONGED PERIOD OF LOW INFLATION TO HIGH INFLATION

In every inflation cycle, you will find several key danger points that present vicious inflation traps. The most critical one is the initial transition from low to high inflation. High inflation dramatically changes the rules for the economy, finance, and business management. Strategies and management paradigms that worked well before the arrival of high inflation might now not only cease to work, but also could cause severe damage. High inflation requires new learning, new thinking, and a completely different strategy. It impacts all functions performed in a company whether finance, procurement, production, inventory management, or human resources.

When inflation last hit the developed world (i.e., the 1970s), few people had such a risk event on their risk management radar screen. They were caught totally by surprise.

Chart 3 illustrates that being surprised back then was the result of negligent risk management. Inflation rates were already moving upward during the late 1960s, fueled mainly by excessive monetary and fiscal interventions in the economy. In fact, the 1973 inflation shock was preceded by at least one smaller inflation shock in 1969 (marked with the number "1" in Chart 3).

Chart 3: Three waves of inflation in the U.S. during the 1960s and 1970s[10]

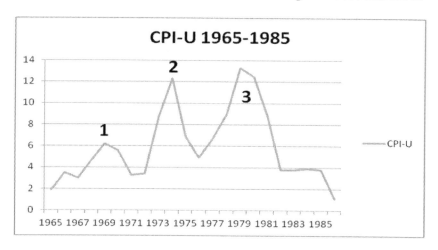

At that time, flawed government and central bank policies invited high inflation back to the U.S. and many other developed countries. More specifically, central banks and governments tried to fine-tune and manipulate economic growth and business cycles. They did so by experimenting with deficit spending policies, economic stimuli, and excessively volatile monetary policies. Federal funds rates, for example, followed a path of wild swings, at times seeking to jump-start a slowing economy and at other times trying to slow down excessive economic growth that pushed up inflation rates.

These experiments occurred at a time when confidence in paper money systems was weakened by recent monetary changes (i.e., the 1971 abolishment of the U.S. dollar's convertibility into gold, the 1973 collapse of Bretton Woods).

The inflation shock of 1973 had severe consequences for the economy, financial markets, and business conditions. After reaching a new all-time high in December 1972, the S+P 500 stock market index lost about fifty percent of its value until September 1974. During the same period, short-term interest rates rose about four percentage points. Fixed income investors suffered significant losses. Companies with financing needs were caught unprepared: equity and bond markets were unavailable or outrageously expensive and banks adopted very restrictive lending policies. Economic growth collapsed and the U.S. economy was in recession in 1974 and 1975. Unemployment rates approached ten percent.

It is worthwhile pointing out that the losses in the stock market (adjusted for inflation) were more severe than those observed during the worst moments of the recent financial crisis that started in 2007. Surprisingly, this shocking event is almost extinct in business memory.

The year 1973 vividly demonstrates that the transition from a time of low or moderate inflation to a period of high inflation is one of the most dangerous points in an inflation cycle. There are other sudden turning points in an inflation cycle, but missing the first one is probably the most severe risk management mistake. Companies and individuals have to do everything possible not to fall into that trap.

WHEN WILL INFLATION ARRIVE?

In risk management, it is relatively easy for experienced people to identify the most significant risks to which an organization or individual is exposed. However, it is close to impossible to predict exactly when these risk events will occur. The same applies to the issue of inflation. It does not take rocket science to identify inflation risk as a severe risk exposure for our society. However, it is nearly impossible to time its occurrence.

You can compare this issue with a dike attempting to hold back significantly more water than it was designed for. And the water levels increase every hour. Even the most sophisticated engineer would not be able to exactly predict when the dike will break. If I were living behind the dike, I would not care about timing this dangerous risk event. My risk management strategy would be simple and effective: move away.

Inflation risk is similar to the above example. The same way the enormous volume of water will become a destructive force once the dike breaks, the unprecedented amount of liquidity will push up prices once people become concerned about future inflation. At the moment, this dangerous level of liquidity has been successfully absorbed by four asset classes: bonds, equity, real estate, and cash. Thus far, the dikes that prevent the liquidity from pouring into the real economy have held up well. However, once the dikes break, this liquidity will stream into the real world and create much harm in the form of inflation.

In fact, inflation risk is much more complicated than any problem in physics or engineering, particularly if we have to deal with LOFIS Inflation. Inflation is always the result of behavioral change. When individuals start to prefer the possession of real assets over the possession of paper money, the velocity of money starts to increase and to accelerate. Human behavior does not obey natural laws, such as those of physics. Human behavior is therefore not exactly predictable regardless of how sophisticated an economic model may be. Human behavior is often irrational and can remain so for extended periods of time. In fact, there is often some inertia that reinforces past behavior (regardless of whether it is rational or not). This inertia can create self-sustaining trends that may camouflage existing economic forces. That is how financial bubbles emerge and why they may last much longer than rational expectation would suggest.

Over the past years, this inertia and following momentum prevented the emergence of LOFIS Inflation. People did not worry about unprecedented debt levels, financial imbalances, or ultra-loose monetary policies. And as long as they do not worry, more money might flow into these four asset classes and push up their valuation to even higher levels. In addition, the demand shock caused by the last financial crisis helped significantly to keep inflation rates low. However, any unsystematic trigger event might end this period of false stability and calmness and unleash inflation.

There is often a significant time gap between the cause and effect of LOFIS Inflation. The German hyperinflation of the 1920s is a good example. For years, Germany managed to get away with its excessive debt issuances, overspending, and ultra-loose monetary policies. As late as 1921, many market participants (wrongly) believed that Germany would turn the corner and recover from its problems. Only two years later, the German currency was practically worthless.

In comparison to LOFIS Inflation, EMEG Inflation is less difficult to predict, as it is directly linked to economic strength in emerging markets. Economic growth rates in emerging markets will determine the arrival of this type of inflation. Economic growth tends to be less erratic than human behavior. And while we are not able to predict exactly future economic growth in emerging markets, we can avoid being surprised by EMEG Inflation by closely monitoring economic growth patterns in those countries. In addition, it may make sense to monitor foreign exchange rates between currencies in the developed world and those in emerging markets, as they might intensify the problem of EMEG Inflation in the developed world. In the long term strong economic growth in emerging markets may weaken developed countries' currencies and by doing so lead to the problem of imported inflation.

In general, a return of high inflation would be a logical consequence given today's economic, fiscal, financial, and monetary situation. Instead of wasting time and resources to predict the exact date of arrival of this risk event, we would be better advised to prepare for it.

EASY STRATEGIES THAT PROTECT AGAINST INFLATION AND TURN INFLATION FROM A RISK INTO AN OPPORTUNITY

There is a significantly asymmetric distribution between winners and losers of high inflation. The few winners are vastly outnumbered by the number of losers and the losses and hardship they endure. This asymmetric distribution is neither accidental nor God-given. It is the result of people following the herd until it is too late. It does not take intellectual brilliance to protect you against the most severe inflation risks. However, you have to start early. As you will learn, relatively simple and easy-to-implement strategies may protect you against the most severe inflation risks. These strategies may also help you to turn inflation risks into an opportunity.

Warren Buffett, the CEO of Berkshire Hathaway, is a good example of this. During the 1970s inflation cycle, a time period that included two severe recessions, a stock market drop of about fifty percent, and extremely volatile interest rates, sometimes reaching levels above twenty percent, Berkshire Hathaway performed impressively.

According to Chart 4, accumulated inflation between 1973 and 1982 reached about 130 percent. Consequently, any investment had to return at least 130 percent (ignoring taxes on capital gains and distributions and transaction costs) to protect the holder against inflation and to preserve the purchasing power of the invested amount. The companies representing the S+P 500 index failed to reach that bar by a wide margin. Most of them destroyed an enormous amount of shareholder value. In other words, adjusted for inflation, your investment in the S+P 500 stock market index was worth much more in 1973 than in 1982. Berkshire Hathaway, in contrast, managed to turn inflation into an exceptional opportunity. Its book value per share increased more than 900 percent during the same period.

Chart 4: Turning inflation risks into an attractive opportunity: Warren Buffett shows that it is possible[11]

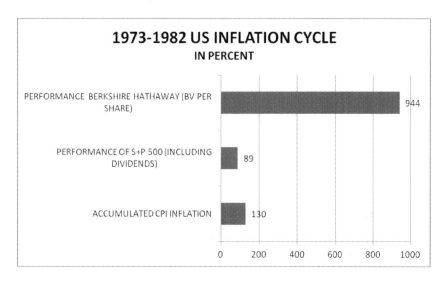

Warren Buffett's outperformance during the 1970s period of high inflation was not accidental or a random event. His publications about inflation prove that his understanding of inflation issues was simply way ahead of anyone else's. For example, a 1976 article[12] on inflation lets us imagine how detailed Buffett's understanding of inflation issues was at that time. He was one of the few people who understood how the new economics in times of high inflation work and he prepared for it earlier than most other CEOs and investors did.

Warren Buffett did not employ an army of rocket scientists to develop his successful strategies. Nor did he have specific and costly computer programs that guided him. Instead, his strategies seemed to have been derived from critical thinking, fact-based analysis, and anticipative risk management. There is no reason why others could not learn from this superb performance and replicate certain strategies and tactics to address future inflation risks.

Many companies learned from their early mistakes in managing inflation risks. While the S+P 500 index lost about fifty percent of its value during the first inflation shock of 1973, companies did much better during the second inflation shock, which occurred in 1977–1982 and exceeded the severity of the first inflation shock of 1973–1974. As a result, the S+P 500 index actually gained seventy-six percent during the second inflation shock. While this is a modest gain compared to the high inflation rates of that time, it was, relative to the 1973–1974 stock performance, a much better outcome. It proved that companies learned their lessons and adapted much better to this risk event.

It is fascinating to see that relatively simple strategies put in place at the right time could have protected both companies and individuals during past periods of extreme inflation. For example, any German who would have exchanged his savings for a combination of precious metals, stable foreign currencies (i.e., U.S. dollar), and real assets (i.e., agricultural fields, a little garden, tradable goods) at a time when fiscal deficits, government debt, and money printing were sending clear inflation warning signs, would have turned inflation into a real opportunity during the time of the German hyperinflation. Similar strategies would have worked as well during most other inflation cycles, including the 1970s inflation crisis in the U.S. or the more recent emergence of high inflation in Venezuela.[13]

Part III of this book aims at helping you to start developing appropriate inflation strategies. I explain that inflation strategies must be holistic in order to capture all risk exposures, dynamic to adjust to a rapidly changing environment, and tailor-made to your specific situation (e.g., risk appetite, risk absorption capacity, risk management skills). I also explain the "typical" first and second order effects that come with inflation and how interconnectivity within and across economic and financial systems may set off shock waves and unintended consequences that are likely to lead to massive disruptions. I discuss ideas on how to prepare strategically for these issues.

A successful inflation strategy must be dynamic. This sounds like commonplace and generic consulting advice, but in reality this will be one of the key factors determining your success. You must see inflation as a sequence of phases that builds a cycle (see Chart 5). Each phase requires a fundamentally different strategy than the previous one. In fact, almost every aspect of a company's value chain needs to be readjusted when the inflation cycle moves from one phase to the next. A successful strategy in phase 1 will almost certainly fail in phase 2.

Chart 5: Understanding the inflation cycle and its phases

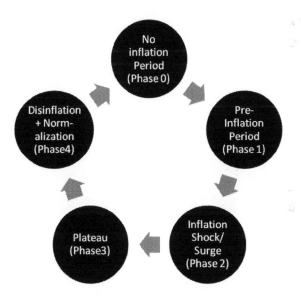

The actual inflation problem begins in phase 1. Let us call this phase the pre-inflation period. Many people misperceive phase 1 as a period of economic strength and prosperity. Between 1970 and 1972, the U.S. stock market reached new highs and the economy grew strong during phase 1 of the new inflation cycle. A euphoric mood was spreading among companies and investors. People failed to recognize that unsustainable fiscal, monetary, or economic policies are the main causes of temporary economic and financial prosperity.

In phase 2 (i.e., the inflation shock) the problem unfolds abruptly and fast. Inflation rates start to accelerate and the majority of people tend to get caught unprepared. This is why I like to call this phase an inflation shock, even though it should not be considered a shock, as this risk event should have been anticipated by a company's risk management efforts. During phase 2, business and economic conditions change dramatically: banks tighten credit policies (even for "good" customers), interest rates increase rapidly, and the economy is likely to suffer a recession.

Eventually, inflation rates start to level off and reach a plateau (i.e., phase 3). At this time, companies have to make sure that they do not fall into another dangerous inflation trap. Companies must adjust their strategies radically to prepare for the beginning of phase 4, a period of disinflation (i.e., falling inflation rates). During this period of disinflation or normalization, economic conditions change dramatically and require swift and decisive strategic adjustments. For example, while short-term variable rate debt financing would have brought a company to the emergency room during phase 2, it will now be the preferred financing strategy as companies want to profit from rapidly falling interest rates.

At any phase of an inflation cycle, a company can fail to survive. The German industrialist Hugo Stinnes (1870–1924) is a good example of this. Stinnes and many other industrialists created fortunes and industrial empires by radically exploiting "the new rules of economics" dictated by rapidly rising inflation rates. The strategy was simple: as inflation rates accelerated, Stinnes and other industrialists used debt extensively to buy real assets such as companies, businesses, and infrastructure investments. Stinnes knew that as long as credit is available and inflation continues to increase, this strategy was not likely to fail. The assets rapidly increased in nominal (and often real) value, while the value of debt was rapidly diminished by inflation.

Shortly before his death, Stinnes recognized that the times were changing. The German inflation cycle was approaching phase 4. The turbo-charged debt-based acquisition strategy would get the Stinnes empire into big trouble. In fact, Germany went through a radical financial reset as its old currency (the German paper mark) was replaced by the new Rentenmark in 1924. Inflation disappeared almost immediately. Stinnes recognized that the old inflation strategy must be stopped and replaced by a strategy that made the industrial empire less dependent on debt. Unfortunately, after his death in 1924, his successors failed to understand the warnings and continued with the old strategy. Very quickly the Stinnes empire suffered tremendous economic, financial, and business problems and was later broken up by its creditor banks. The introduction of a new stable currency was accompanied by restrictive monetary policies, a typical occurrence after times of high inflation. Germany was determined to prevent at any costs another rise of inflation rates. As a result, the economy slowed down and banks restricted the supply of new credit to customers.

To help companies and individuals manage an inflation cycle, this book presents a new framework that can be used as a compass to guide them. The framework is called the "Four Phases Inflation Management" model (FPIM model). The FPIM model focuses on the four most critical phases of an inflation cycle (i.e., phases 1 to 4 in Chart 5). It forces adoption of a dynamic approach to inflation management.

Chapter 9 describes the FPIM model in great detail, while Chapter 10 illustrates it in action. A retrospective case study shows how you could have managed the 1970s inflation cycle quite easily by using the FPIM model as a compass. The model urges you to ask the most important questions to survive a period of high inflation: What phase of the inflation cycle are we in? When will the next phase start? How does my strategy have to be adjusted to work during the next phase of the cycle? What are my most pressing risk exposures? What are the most attractive opportunities for me?

Companies should embrace a return of high inflation as both a severe risk and an attractive opportunity. Most likely, high inflation will be a very disruptive event that changes the competitive landscape in any industry. For companies that are well prepared to deal with these changes, high inflation may present a once-in-a-lifetime opportunity to leapfrog into a better competitive position. It may enable companies to outperform their competitors that are strategically unprepared for rising inflation rates. Therefore, the disruptiveness of high inflation may create significant opportunities for those prepared to deal with it.

The strategies discussed in Part III have been developed predominantly for companies. Individuals can use the same tools and processes to develop personal inflation strategies. Chapter 14 explains how to approach the risks and opportunities of inflation in your personal life. As you will see, this requires a much wider perspective than just focusing on your investment strategy.

HOW HIGH INFLATION MAY DRAMATICALLY CHANGE THE ECONOMIC ORDER OF THE WORLD

This book is written from the perspective of developed countries. This does not mean that emerging and developing countries will not be at risk for high inflation. They are. It is quite possible that they are in better positions to deal with high inflation. In fact, it is possible that the return of high inflation will be a catalyst for an inversion of the relative economic significance of emerging market countries versus developed countries. In other words, emerging market countries might be the real winners of the next inflation cycle, at least in relative terms.

First of all, emerging markets seem to be much less exposed to the problem of LOFIS Inflation (i.e., loss of faith in paper money). In these markets, debt levels are relatively low, economic growth is robust, education systems have surpassed those of the developed world in many aspects, and demographics are favorable. Second, many emerging market countries have struggled with high inflation in the recent past. This experience will be valuable during the next inflation cycle. They are definitely ahead on the learning curve regarding inflation management skills. Last, many emerging market countries have carefully analyzed the mistakes of developed countries in terms of creating excessively complex and fragile systems. They most likely will not repeat our mistakes.

For the developed world, I foresee a disruptive and volatile future. The economic and financial misery might be of significant proportion. We must make sure that the economic and financial pains caused by high inflation do not lead to social instability as in the past.

When the next inflation cycle is behind us, we must make sure that we do not repeat the same mistakes by building our economic future on the shaky foundation of debt, fiscal deficits, leverage, and inflation. This, however, requires understanding that mild deflation in normal times is not necessarily a bad thing. Deflation is only destructive in the context of an economy built on excessive debt, leverage, and fiscal imprudence.

THE INFLATION PARADOX: WHY YOU NEED TO PREPARE NOW

There are three important messages. First, inflation is a serious threat for the unprepared. Second, simple strategies could have protected companies and individuals against these severe risks in the past. They may work as well during the next inflation cycle. Third, sophisticated market participants can turn inflation risks into opportunities.

The caveat for the last two is that you must act early. At a certain point of the inflation cycle, risk mitigation strategies will not be available or they will be too costly. At that time, you will have to face a massive storm unprotected. This is the inflation paradox. You must prepare for a storm when most people, including recognized experts, may tell you not to worry.

At the moment, a wide range of inflation strategies is available to companies and individuals who take inflation risks seriously. Therefore, my recommendation is simple: prepare for the worst and hope for the best. Do not base risk management strategies on hope and gamble that everything will be fine. The price for being wrong is extremely high when it comes to inflation risks.

PART II: UNDERSTANDING THE CONTEXT, THE PROBLEM, THE THREATS, AND THE OPPORTUNITIES

CHAPTER 2: THE THREAT OF A PERFECT INFLATION STORM— WHY HIGH INFLATION MAY RETURN TO THE DEVELOPED WORLD

In the past, many experts dismissed fears about high inflation in the developed world. These experts have grown increasingly confident in their belief that high inflation is not a risk event worth worrying about. Some of them even ridicule people who warn of high inflation, which should alarm you.

The reality is that inflation often arrives significantly delayed following the policies that caused it. This delay can take years.

In this chapter, I seek to explain why the danger of high inflation is real by expanding on two distinct developments that each on its own could lead to significant inflation problems in the developed world: EMEG Inflation and LOFIS Inflation (as explained in Chapter 1). If both types of inflation coincide, inflation rates in the developed world may spiral out of control and create significant damage to the economy, financial markets, and society. Such a situation would be a perfect inflation storm with potentially catastrophic consequences.

TWO DISTINCT DEVELOPMENTS LEADING TO HIGH INFLATION

We are currently witnessing a tectonic shift in the world economy. Emerging markets are undergoing a process of turbo-charged industrialization and economic transformation. Billions of people are leaving a rather agricultural way of living and "upgrading" to modern society. Never before have we witnessed a situation of economic transformation that impacted such a large group of people. It is truly a unique event.

This transformational change is occurring simultaneously in many parts of the world, including Asia, South America, and, increasingly, parts of Africa. This process, which started a couple of decades ago, will have a tremendous impact on the global demand for commodities, the global consumption of products and services, and the overall global balance of demand and supply for all products and services. Very soon, the number of modern consumers will grow from under one billion to several billion. The resulting economic growth is incompatible with low inflation rates in the developed world. Competition for commodities, products, and services among developed and emerging countries will increase and this will push up prices everywhere in the world. In this context, it will be less relevant whether the developed world will return to the strong economic growth rates it enjoyed in the past. The strong rising demand in emerging markets will be sufficient to offset lower growth in developed countries. Consequently, prices will go up globally regardless of the strength of economic growth in developed countries. This is EMEG Inflation.

The second factor threatening stable prices in developed countries is quite different from EMEG Inflation. In fact, it is more troublesome and dangerous. It is inflation that will result from an increasing loss of faith in paper money systems in the developed world.

Over the past decades, developed countries have adopted economic, fiscal, and monetary policies that, in the long-term, are unsustainable and therefore irresponsible. As a result, the developed world is exposed to at least three unsustainable situations: record levels of total debt, an imbalance between the size of the financial world and the real economy, and an addiction to excessively loose monetary policies.

Eventually, as these situations become unsustainable, market participants will begin to question the stability and reliability of paper money systems in the developed world. The result will be a preference for keeping wealth either in the form of real assets or in more stable foreign currencies. This change of behavior will increase the velocity (i.e., turnover) of money. Domestic paper money increasingly becomes a hot potato that must be passed on as quickly as possible. This change in behavior will lead to accelerating inflation. This is LOFIS Inflation.

Each of these individual occurrences could lead to substantial inflationary pressure and painful disruptions of economic, financial, and social stability. If, however, they emerge simultaneously, the result would be truly devastating and catastrophic, particularly for the developed world. The developed world would then be challenged by rising inflation caused by strong growth in emerging markets and loss of faith in paper money. We could call this a perfect inflation storm, a constellation that to my knowledge has never occurred before in our history. Chart 6 summarizes the two forms of inflation.

Chart 6: A Perfect Inflation Storm: simultaneous emergence of EMEG Inflation and LOFIS Inflation

Demand Driven Inflation (EMEG Inflation)
- Fast track industrial revolution in emerging markets
- World economic growth above inflation-neutral threshold
- Driven by population-rich emerging markets becomng global consumers

Loss of Faith Driven Inflation (LOFIS Inflation)
- Market participants in developed countries lose faith in paper money
- Mainly driven by fiscal deficits, government debt, and expansionary monetary policies in developed countries

UNDERSTANDING THE RISK OF EMEG INFLATION IN THE DEVELOPED WORLD

EMEG Inflation is the result of changes in the demand-supply balance. Demand-driven inflation emerges when, due to strong economic growth, the demand for products and services outpaces available supply and capacities. In other words, relative scarcity of commodities, resources, products, and services leads to rising prices.

In the classic view of economics, this type of inflation was considered relatively harmless as governments and central banks possessed adequate tools to deal with the problem. More specifically, economic and monetary measures to cool down economic growth have proven effective to deal with demand-driven inflation. Today, the situation is more complicated and dangerous for developed countries. EMEG Inflation originates outside of the control spectrum of developed countries. Therefore, monetary measures (e.g., higher interest rates) may prove ineffective in combating the problem of EMEG Inflation. In the worst case, such measures may lead to a combination of lower economic growth and even higher inflation. Restrictive monetary policies would lower economic growth in developed countries and this in turn would weaken exchange rates. As a result, imports from emerging markets to the developed world would become more expensive (i.e., the problem of imported inflation).

The risk of EMEG Inflation in the developed world was present in the early 2000s. The impressive economic growth in emerging markets led to increasing prices for commodities, food, and other products, as discussed later in this chapter.

Growth in emerging markets is structurally different from growth in developed countries because it is commodity and resource intensive. Growth in emerging market countries occurs mostly as a result of producing, assembling, or constructing real products and is less linked to services or administrative functions. It has both direct and indirect impacts on developed markets. The direct impact refers to higher prices for commodities and resources used in production processes. The indirect impact refers to derivative effects of higher input costs and higher demand. For example, an upgrade in living conditions (a result of strong economic growth in emerging markets) might lead to a higher demand for protein-rich food (i.e., meat products), which in turn will push up costs of feeding stock, such as grain prices.

We can learn about this issue by looking at the development of the auto industry. Twenty years ago, the demand for cars in China did not impact global inflation rates in a noticeable way. Chinese new car sales during early 1990 numbered about one million. Today, China has become the biggest sales market for new cars in the world. In 2014, almost twenty million new cars were sold in China.[14] It is absolutely feasible to expect this number to grow to thirty million new car sales in the short term and fifty million new car sales over the next twenty years. The inflation impact of such a development will be immense, incorporating not only the commodities and resources needed for building these cars sold in China (i.e., direct impact on inflation), but also the additional need for production machinery, facilities, and dwellings for factory workers in both car production companies and their suppliers. Given that economic growth in emerging markets concerns mainly the production of hard products and not the production of soft products (such as services or software), the inflation impact of such growth will be much bigger than many people anticipate today.[15]

Another factor contributing to EMEG Inflation can be seen in the increasing preference for food derived from animal proteins (e.g., meat) in emerging markets. This change in nutrition preferences will lead to a substantially higher demand for meat products in the future. This change will also impact the costs of feeding stock (e.g., grain prices) and all transport related costs to get meat products to emerging markets.

EMEG Inflation originating from strong economic growth in emerging markets is not a remote threat for our future. We already witnessed an outbreak of EMEG Inflation prior to the outbreak of the recent financial crisis. The sharp rise of inflation rates in developed countries in 2007 and early 2008 was mainly fueled by EMEG Inflation. Many people have forgotten that inflation rates in 2007 and 2008 reached alarming levels: top monthly year-on-year comparisons peaked at 5.3 percent in the U.S. and 4.8 percent in the U.K.[16] This inflation was the result of impressive economic growth in emerging markets that pushed world economic growth to levels close to or above four percent between 2004 and 2007. You should note that during this time period, economic growth in developed countries was not excessive. Inflation was imported to the developed world. It did not originate here.

The outbreak of the financial crisis interrupted the strong inflation momentum, which was essential for central banks in the developed world to be able to implement dramatically expansionary monetary policies. As global demand dropped, inflation rates decreased substantially, turning an inflation scare into a deflation scare. Chart 7 illustrates the rise and fall of CPI inflation in the U.S. before and after the outbreak of the financial crisis.

Chart 7: U.S. Inflation (CPI-U) between 2006 and 2010—an example of EMEG Inflation[17]

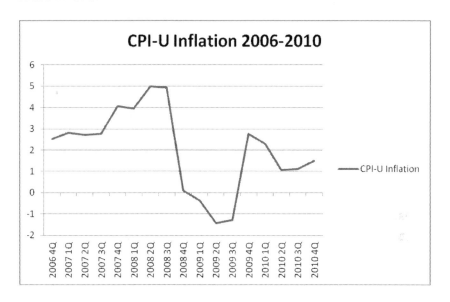

While the positive inflation trend was interrupted in 2008, it was not eliminated. As soon as economic growth in emerging markets returns to its normal growth trajectory, we should expect inflation rates to trend upwards again and EMEG Inflation to re-emerge. In fact, growth rates even lower than those of 2007 may be sufficient to ignite EMEG Inflation. This is due to base effects. GDP levels are much higher today and lower growth rates produce additional demand similar to what was observed in 2007.

If we look back at the relationship of world economic growth to inflation, we come across an interesting observation. It seems that prolonged world economic growth at a magnitude of about three and one-half to four percent cannot be absorbed by developed countries without resulting in high inflation.

For example, the two inflation shocks of the 1970s were preceded by global economic growth reaching levels of close to four percent (or more) as Chart 8 illustrates.

Chart 8: The connection of high inflation and strong global economic growth[18]

The 1970s Period of High Inflation First Inflation Shock			The 1970s Period of High Inflation Second Inflation Shock		
Year	Global Economic Growth	CPI-U Inflation	Year	Global Economic Growth	CPI-U Inflation
1971	4.0 %	3.3	1976	5.1 %	4.9
1972	5.6 %	3.4	1977	4.0 %	6.7
1973	6.6 %	8.7	1978	4.3 %	9.0
1974	1.8 %	12.3	1979	4.0 %	13.3

The same pattern is found when analyzing the rise of U.S. inflation in the late 1980s. In this case, world economic growth rates between 3.3 percent and 4.6 percent experienced in the period from 1984 to 1989 were sufficient to push U.S. inflation rates eventually to a level of 6.1 percent in 1990 (see Chart 9).

Chart 9: Short return of high inflation in the 1980s[19]

The 1970s Period of High Inflation First Inflation Shock		
Year	Global Economic Growth	CPI-U Inflation
1984	4.6 %	3.9
1985	3.8 %	3.8
1986	3.3 %	1.1
1987	3.5 %	4.4
1988	4.6 %	4.4
1989	3.7 %	4.6
1990	2.7 %	6.1

We can state that all recent periods of significant U.S. inflation were preceded by periods of strong economic world growth. While more research is needed to better understand the changing weights of domestic and international inflation drivers, we can formulate a hypothesis that inflation in the developed world has become more globally driven. The root cause of inflation in developed countries may originate in emerging markets as they grow; the economic and monetary policies of developed countries will not control the inflation they are experiencing. Even worse, it may well be the case that emerging markets will experience less inflation pressure than the developed world. This is the case when developed countries' currencies depreciate versus those from emerging market countries enjoying strong productivity growth. In such a situation, emerging markets may have less interest to engage in anti-inflationary policies as they will suffer less than developed countries.

Given that global economic growth is forecasted by some experts to reach levels of three and one-half to four percent in the near future, we should take this as a warning of the return of EMEG Inflation. Regardless of short-term developments and speculations, we should assume that eventually EMEG Inflation will become a very serious problem for developed countries. Emerging markets will continue to grow—only massive social unrest may stop this natural development path. This growth will lead to a continuous upgrade of consumption and spending patterns of billions of people. Therefore, it is not a question of whether EMEG Inflation will occur, but only a question of when.

LOFIS INFLATION: LOSING FAITH IN PAPER MONEY SYSTEMS

We tend to take the stability and reliability of paper money systems for granted. The overwhelming majority of people in developed countries expect not only that all businesses will accept their paper money, but also that it will buy relatively the same quantity of goods. Even in the light of record levels of debt, enormous fiscal deficits, and ultra-loose monetary policies, our confidence in paper money has not been shaken in a significant way.

This is surprising if we look at the history of money in general and paper money in particular. Most paper money systems did not survive in the long term. A large number failed and had to be replaced with new paper money systems. Even the two major paper money systems that survived for more than 200 years, the U.S. dollar and the British pound, do not show impressive stability. Both have been impacted by enormous inflation over past decades. The purchasing power of both currencies is today only a fraction of what it was in the past.

Paper money systems are based on confidence. As long as people have confidence in a paper money system, it tends to work well. As soon as this confidence starts to erode, inflation will accelerate. It is irrelevant if the confidence people have in a paper money system is justified. This has two important implications. First, a paper money system can continue to work well even though the actual economic, fiscal, and monetary conditions have significantly deteriorated. Second, a paper money system can deteriorate even though the economic, fiscal, and monetary conditions have not changed in a significant way. The first issue is due to unjustified confidence (and is often the reason why inflation reacts with a time delay to deteriorating economic conditions); the second issue is a result of unjustified loss of faith.

Given the ongoing deterioration of economic, fiscal, and monetary conditions, the first issue, unjustified confidence in today's paper money systems in developed markets, concerns me. I am afraid that eventually market participants will realize the dimension of today's problems and imbalances and will doubt the stability of paper money systems. The deteriorating confidence in paper money will lead to an increasing velocity of money as people prefer to store their wealth in real assets and foreign currency assets. Such behavior will undoubtedly lead to accelerating inflation, which is LOFIS Inflation.

There are many examples of LOFIS Inflation in history. One of the most famous is the hyperinflation in Germany during the 1920s. Only a few cases of LOFIS Inflation spiral out of control, though. Very often, governments and central banks manage to regain control over inflation as they rebuild confidence in the system. However, people should not forget that the damage from LOFIS Inflation is permanent. Price levels never go back to the levels prior to the LOFIS Inflation crisis. A period of drastic deflation is required to make good on the loss of purchasing power inflicted by a period of LOFIS Inflation. In other words, savers and retirees must face up to the bitter truth that the loss of purchasing power suffered due to high inflation is permanent.

LOFIS Inflation should not surprise us. The policies and situations that ultimately lead to LOFIS Inflation have been remarkably similar. Unfortunately, if we look at a checklist of ingredients of LOFIS Inflation, we realize that most are in place today. Chart 10 illustrates this alarming issue.

Chart 10: Checklist of required ingredients for LOFIS Inflation

Required input factor for LOFIS Inflation	Present today?
Over-indebtedness of government	**Yes**
Prolonged periods of significant fiscal deficits	**Yes**
Expansionary monetary policies by central banks	**Yes**
Substantial amount of liquidity in the system	**Yes**
Perception of ineffective politicians and governments	**Yes**
Increasing negative perception of a country's future prospects (i.e., rising pessimism)	**Yes**
Weakening of exchange rate	**Depends on country**

As mentioned, there is often a significant delay in the cause-effect relationship that leads to LOFIS Inflation. Unjustified confidence in a paper money system does occur and may last longer than most people would anticipate. Often it triggers a reassessment of the stability of a paper money system and ends the inertia caused by unjustified confidence. Then, LOFIS Inflation can spread rapidly.

In those situations, governments and central banks must act swiftly and decisively to regain credibility and stop LOFIS Inflation. Unfortunately, they might do the opposite, as upcoming elections and other factors motivate decision makers to give in to populist demands. For example, U.S. decision makers failed to address the root causes that led to inflation shocks in 1969 and 1973–1974. Instead, they gave in to populist demands and introduced (partial) price controls, reduced interest rates, and created large fiscal stimuli. They addressed nonmonetary causes for a weak economy with monetary and fiscal policies. Unsurprisingly, inflation returned in 1977 in a more dramatic and vicious way. At that time, it almost spiraled out of control.

Germany in the 1920s was less successful. When inflation spun out of control in 1922, government and central banks were helpless in fighting to save the German mark. In the end, the German mark was practically worthless. In November 1923, one U.S. dollar could be exchanged for 4.2 trillion German paper marks. [20] The German paper mark had practically died. Investors in German paper mark-denominated securities and savings accounts lost practically everything. We should remember that the decay of the German currency and its eventual death occurred within less than six years.

I do not anticipate a period of hyperinflation in the developed world at this time, though it is possible if current policies are not rectified in time and additional mistakes are committed by decision makers in governments and central banks. Nevertheless, an inflation period similar to the one experienced during the 1970s in the U.S. (when inflation rates reached the low teens), could lead to catastrophic damages to the economy, financial markets, and society. We do not need a hyperinflation to get into a very severe and dramatic situation.

When faith in a paper money system fades away, companies and individuals will treat paper money increasingly like a hot potato. They will try to pass it on in exchange for real assets (or more stable foreign currencies) as soon as possible. Companies, for example, will change their cash management strategies dramatically. They would rather build up inventories than hold cash. And they might delay sales to anticipate higher prices due to inflation. They might even withhold business transactions, if the proceeds cannot be transformed into an inflation secured asset. All these strategies will increase inflationary pressure: Inflation will feed inflation.

Individuals will behave similarly. For example, during the height of the German hyperinflation, wives came to factories at lunch time to get their husbands' paychecks. They then rushed to stores to get real assets for the checks. Anecdotal evidence suggests that similar things are happening in Venezuela at the moment. People there avoid possessing paper money and instead opt for hard assets of any type.

While velocity of money is still very low, companies and investors are happy to keep the equivalent of many trillions of U.S. dollars in cash or liquid assets (i.e., savings accounts, treasury bills, government bonds). They are not concerned about an increasing velocity of money that would result in significantly higher inflation rates. However, this assessment of the economic and financial situation may change and then there will be little time or opportunity to make the right moves.

It is important to stress that LOFIS Inflation can occur despite significant economic weakness. Surprisingly, economists were not aware of this possibility until the 1970s inflation cycle presented a situation of simultaneously low economic growth and high inflation. This phenomenon, later to be known as "stagflation," caught many economists by surprise.

Today, Venezuela is a good example of LOFIS Inflation. The country experiences persistent double digit inflation rates that in 2014 crossed the bar of fifty percent. High inflation coincides with a weak economy, high unemployment, and low capacity utilization. Trust in the local currency has steadily decreased despite the government's and central bank's efforts to restore it through currency and financial reforms, political changes, and new policies.

The chances for LOFIS Inflation have significantly increased since central banks have adopted ultra-loose monetary policies after the outbreak of the financial crisis in 2007 and governments have engaged in voluminous stimuli programs that further increased excessive debt levels. However, we should not think that the risk of LOFIS Inflation emerged only with these recent steps and policies. Even before the outbreak of the financial crisis, there was substantial LOFIS Inflation risk in the system.

First, there is an increasing imbalance between the size of the financial world and the size of the real economy. The monetary reality is completely detached from the economic reality. The size differential makes it increasingly improbable that the real economy would be able to bail out the financial sector again as it did in 2007 and the following years. Instead, the next financial crisis could take down both the financial world and the real economy.

Second, even before the financial crisis, total debt levels in absolute and relative terms were unsustainable. Unfortunately, total debt levels have further deteriorated. Any deleveraging in the private sector has been more than offset by additional debt issued by government entities.

Third, the complexity and the fragility of the financial system in the developed world has been an alarming problem for a long time. It works well in times of low stress and low volatility. However, it becomes uncontrollable and unmanageable when stressed by high volatility events. It is inexcusable that in the time since the recent financial crisis, more has not been done to simplify and separate the financial system and its subsystems to make it more robust and stress-resistant. It now might be more complex and fragile than at any time before.

In my view, LOFIS Inflation is almost unavoidable. The only question will be: How bad will it become and will we be able to stop it once it has arrived? The debt problem seems to be so out of control that only higher inflation rates may succeed in controlling it. Central banks seem to encourage LOFIS Inflation, as they engage in ultra-loose monetary policies and flood the market with liquidity. They overestimate how well they will be able to contain inflation once it starts to increase. As in the late 1960s and 1970s, it should not surprise us if inflation surpasses target rates set by central bankers in the developed world.

IS HIGH INFLATION UNAVOIDABLE?

I am frequently asked whether high inflation is an unavoidable outcome for the developed world given current fiscal, financial, economic, and monetary challenges. In my view it is. Central banks have chosen this policy and make no effort to conceal it. They publicly state that they want to raise inflation rates. The current situation is comparable to when Julius Caesar crossed the Rubicon; he knew that a war would result. He reportedly remarked, *"alea iacta est"* (The die is cast); that is, we have passed the point of no return.[21]

Central banks and many economists seem to hope that they can re-inflate the economy and that higher (but controlled) inflation rates will help address current imbalances and excessive debt levels.

I do not argue that at the acute stages of the financial crisis, some sort of liquidity injection, fiscal stimuli, and lower interest rates were necessary to avoid a total collapse of the economy and financial markets. However, we continued with an increasing intensity to address nonmonetary problems with monetary policies. This increases the risk for excessive LOFIS Inflation in the developed world significantly. What should have happened are radical structural reforms to increase productivity, to improve education systems, to reduce the size of governments, and to cut government spending. A blueprint for such reforms has been presented by Germany. Early in the 2000s, Germany introduced a radical reform of government, education systems, health care, labor and business laws, and its regulatory system to make the country more competitive. It was a courageous, bold move initiated by its chancellor, Gerhard Schroeder. Although he lost the next election, he brought Germany back on an economic growth path. The so-called Agenda 2010 was a reform package that was painful for many Germans. However, Germany's success today and its impressive performance even during the most recent financial crisis were significantly impacted by these structural reforms.

It will be increasingly difficult for any developed country to change course and pursue a path similar to the one Germany took years ago. Therefore, we should accept that higher inflation rates will most likely come our way and that we need to adopt new strategies.

There are limited alternatives to this path. It is by now almost impossible to generate economic growth sufficient to enable developed countries to grow out of their current debt and fiscal problems. As structural reforms have not been implemented, it is hard to identify drivers of growth that could accelerate current economic growth rates to substantially higher levels that would enable governments to achieve budget surpluses to start paying down their debt. Even if we succeeded in reaching this economic growth miracle, such an outcome would most likely produce higher inflation rates (e.g., demand-driven inflation).

There are two additional options that governments and central banks could employ to address the current economic, fiscal, and monetary malaise. They could surprise the markets with an overall debt restructuring program or engage in a currency reset that helps eliminate excessive debt levels.

Both strategies are radical, abrupt, disruptive, and, therefore, highly dangerous. We know from our understanding of complex systems that it is very difficult to intervene in such systems without causing unintended consequences. The more radical an intervention, the higher the danger that the situation spirals out of control, malfunctions, and becomes unmanageable.

The reality is that central banks will most likely continue the way they chose years ago. Total debt levels will become unmanageable as soon as interest rates start to rise closer to normal levels. Therefore, they will continue with ultra-loose policies until inflation has kicked in and started to eat away a good chunk of the debt mountain. Then they will withdraw their ultra-loose policies. This will be the danger zone, as we do not know how successful they will be. If we are lucky, we will see a temporary period of high inflation that will be extremely painful for savers and retirees. We will experience sharp recession as we did during the 1970s, but the sky will clear up as it did after 1982. If we are unlucky, the situation will spiral out of control and there will be even higher inflation rates than during the 1970s. In both cases, we will be at risk of a major financial crisis. Unfortunately, this will be the price we will have to pay for past excessiveness and irresponsibility.

CHAPTER 3: THE DEVELOPED WORLD IS NOT PREPARED FOR HIGH INFLATION—ITS CONSEQUENCES WILL BE SEVERE AND DANGEROUS

The previous chapter outlined how the developed world is exposed to significant inflation risks. I described how EMEG Inflation and LOFIS Inflation in particular may create substantial harm to our economy, financial markets, and society. Many people underestimate the danger of inflation. They think that high inflation is only about some prices rising a bit. They miss the crucial issue that high inflation sets off second and third order effects that deteriorate our economy and stress our financial markets. When we look at these issues in detail, we develop quite shocking insights: Never before in history has the developed world been so vulnerable and unprepared to face inflation risks. Most of our economic, financial, and social systems have been developed for low inflation. If they are stressed with high inflation, they most likely will become unmanageable and uncontrollable. Among others, there are five complications unique to the modern developed world that could amplify the damaging effects of high inflation to extreme levels. These five unique complications must be understood in detail and monitored closely to avoid nasty surprises.

We have to understand that the developed world has become an extremely fragile and complex system. As the financial crisis painfully illustrated, modern systems in the developed world were and still are ill-equipped to deal with any form of stress or volatility. High inflation, however, is one of these stress events to which the modern world is extremely vulnerable. We not only fail to understand the modern financial world, we are also unable to manage it or control it once stress events have occurred. A simple risk event like a reversal of house prices in the U.S. (after a decade of unrestrained price increases) could set off a financial crisis. This demonstrates the inability of regulators, politicians, and top managers to control the modern financial world. The complexity, connectivity, and fragility of the modern financial world set off a wildfire of uncontrolled chain reactions and unintended consequences that took everyone by surprise.

A return of high inflation will put enormous stress on economic, financial, and social systems in the developed world, perhaps triggering even bigger shockwaves for the economy and financial markets than the last financial crisis. This is due to five unique complications the world is exposed to. Also, keep in mind that the last financial crisis was eventually contained by measures that are unavailable during high inflation: ultra-loose monetary policies such as "unlimited" liquidity, artificially low interest rates, and central bank intervention in fixed income markets. There will not be any easy way out during the next financial crisis.

THE FIVE UNIQUE COMPLICATIONS YOU MUST CLOSELY MONITOR

This chapter describes in detail how five unique complications will destabilize the modern developed world if high inflation returns. Chart 11 illustrates these issues. These complications, which might impact the macroeconomy as well as your company (or family), need to be placed on a company's risk management radar screen and require timely monitoring.

Obviously, there are additional factors that could derail the fragile systems on which the developed world is built. However, once you understand the concept, you are likely to draw the right conclusions on how erratic the environment can become once high inflation (or other stress events) occurs. The five unique complications are not mutually exclusive but heavily intertwined. In other words, the resulting damages might be intensified by reflexive feedback loops among the five complications.

Chart 11: Five unique complications of the modern world that could amplify the damage caused by high inflation

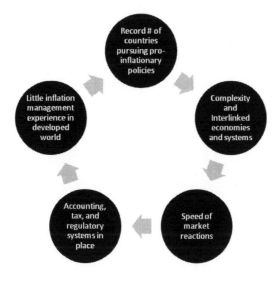

Complication No. 1: A record number of developed countries simultaneously implement pro-inflation policies

For the first time in economic history, nearly the whole developed world simultaneously implements aggressive pro-growth policies consisting of fiscal stimuli, deficits, and ultra-loose monetary policies. We have never experienced such a constellation before. Many developed countries seek to weaken their currencies to lift inflation rates and to promote their exports of products and services.[22] Historic evidence suggests that such strategies are highly dangerous. The scale of these pro-growth policies and the lack of real structural reforms to improve a country's competitiveness create future challenges. Almost all developed countries address structural nonmonetary economic problems with solely monetary policies.

Once high inflation returns to the developed world, companies and investors will face a difficult challenge: In what currency can they safely park and protect their excess cash, liquidity, and wealth? It does not seem that any developed country is particularly interested in strengthening its currency, which helps fend off inflation.

The scale of the problem becomes quite apparent when we look back in history. For example, during the 1920s, high inflation was a problem in Germany, but not a global threat for other developed countries. Thus, investors could find many stable currencies in which to invest. In the 1970s period of high inflation, U.K. and U.S. investors could convert their liquid funds into German Deutschmarks or other currencies that had track records of fighting inflation. At this time the Deutschmark roughly doubled in value compared to the U.S. dollar. Again, safe currency alternatives were available for investors in high inflation countries.

It is unclear whether such safe havens now exist or whether they are able to absorb gigantic volumes of international excess liquidity and accumulated wealth in times of rising inflation fears. If investors do not find currency safe havens, a very dangerous course of action is likely to emerge. Instead of converting their liquidity into a foreign currency, they may buy hard assets. This behavior, however, will further fuel inflation and start a negative feedback loop that makes the problem increasingly unmanageable. Stable currencies lack the capacity to absorb excess funds for inflation protection in the future.

In a worst-case scenario, these funds would flow into real assets (including inventories of any sort, nonperishable food goods, used cars, commodities). We have seen such developments in countries suffering from inflation that have taken government action to limit access to foreign currencies for companies and individuals. For example, this occurred in Germany during the 1920s hyperinflation and more recently in Argentina and Venezuela.

It is possible that some emerging markets will enjoy the status of safe haven currency in the future and will absorb some of the excess liquidity from developed countries looking for inflation protection. This is not a completely unreasonable development, as many emerging markets have low debt levels, restrictive central banks, and commitment to keep inflation low. Based on their recent experience, emerging markets decision makers know that high inflation destabilizes political and social order and therefore do everything in their power to contain this problem. In fact, such a constellation could well lead to a substantial strengthening of emerging markets' currencies, and this in return would lead to more inflation in developed countries as the cost of imports rises (imported inflation).[23]

Complication No. 2: Explosive growth of complexity of economic, financial, and social systems in developed countries

Excessive complexity is found not only in financial markets, but is present everywhere in modern society. Products are more complex today than at any point in the past. Regulations that govern design and elements of products, processes, and services have become a "complexity monster" as well. One economist recently mentioned that in the U.S. alone businesses are confronted with over 3000 regulations.[24]

As a result, companies and individuals must operate in very complex systems in which costs are driven up as well as risks. The relationship between complexity and related costs and risks is not linear. It is exponential, making unnecessary complexity dangerous and destructive of value.

At times, complex systems and solutions are necessary due to the issues they are seeking to address. However, in most cases, complexity is unnecessary and the result of poor balancing between additional functionality of a system and its value generation. The costs and risks of unneeded complexity in systems and processes may remain invisible to most people as long as no stress events or volatility occurs. For example, cars have morphed from being robust to highly complex, as they are loaded up with electronic systems that provide additional functionality (e.g., internet access; DVD players; electric seats, windows, and mirrors; computers) that is uncritical to the primary purpose of the product: to drive from A to B. The additional complexity comes at a significant cost and poses additional risks (e.g., malfunctioning). Maintenance costs are significantly higher than during the times of robust and simple cars. Also, reliability of modern cars has decreased significantly in my view.

Our modern society in general and our financial systems in particular have developed similarly to the example of modern cars. Banks have transformed from simple savings, lending, and payment providers into highly complex entities performing a wide spectrum of financial engineering, trading and arbitraging. Even experts fail to understand and control them. Regulations that govern financial institutions have failed to make banks safer and are likely to continue not to do so. In most developed countries, systems and processes are excessively complex, hard to understand, and, in many instances, goal defeating. This has become worse since the last financial crisis.

Formerly simple activities have become unnecessarily more complex, and as a result are more burdensome, time-intensive, costly, and risky. The real danger of overly complex systems is that we are unable to control them once stress events have occurred. In fact, the recent financial crisis has shown us that we easily become victims and not beneficiaries of our complex systems. In today's developed world, we lack the ability to react quickly and decisively to contain a possible risk event. This problem is growing as complexity continues to increase. The tragedy is that much of the complexity found in developed countries does not create any value. It is simply a cost, a distraction, and a significant risk factor. As this may sound a bit theoretical, let me give you a real-world example.

For centuries, banking was easy to understand, mostly involving deposit taking and lending activities. Compare how a simple transaction was dealt with before the 1970s and how it is dealt with today. Consider the following example: European Bank A makes a fixed rate loan to ABC Manufacturing for five years at a four percent interest rate.

Before the 1970s, this transaction would have been a standard piece of business easily dealt with in Bank A's accounting systems.

Banks today have to deal with domestic and international governmental and regulatory agencies, rating agencies, and greedy and impatient investors. Therefore, this simple transaction can result in a complex web of business activities and derivative transactions, multiplying the overall deal volume by a factor of five or more. Let me explain how a modern investment or commercial bank might deal with this loan.[25]

Situation: European Bank A lends ABC Manufacturing US$100 million over five years at a fixed rate of four percent. A series of additional transactions is likely to follow. Bank A might not like to be exposed to such a high amount from a single entity (i.e., credit risk). It therefore buys from U.S. Bank B a credit default swap to hedge against the risk of a default of ABC Manufacturing. In addition, Bank A might swap the currency risk with Bank C. Finally, banks typically don't like long-term fixed rate loans, as rising funding costs may create substantial interest rate risk. It therefore engages in an additional derivative transaction with Bank D in the form of an interest rate swap. While Bank A has protected itself against certain market risks (i.e., foreign exchange, credit default, interest rate), it has accumulated three additional counterparty risks to other banks (i.e., Bank B, Bank C, and Bank D). There are several ways Bank A can eliminate all or some of these risks. For example, it could buy a credit derivative from insurance company AA to insure against one default of the three bank counterparty risks, assuming it is unlikely that more than one of the three banks defaults during the term of the derivatives (this is called a "first to default basket swap"—note that Bank A now also has a counterparty risk to insurance company AA). In short, in modern banking, simple transactions may be the starting point of complicated derivatives that *create additional and often more complex risks that lead to complex connectivity risks.*

This example demonstrates how developed countries create potentially unmanageable complexity risks, offering several important lessons. First, the volume of the underlying business transaction that is the starting point for the creation of a series of complex transactions represents only a fraction of the overall amount at stake. In other words, a simple loan default can easily lead to losses that are three or more times higher than the original principal amount (in notional terms). Second, it is nearly impossible for one bank manager to understand fully the web of transactions linked to the original loan or the overall connectivity among all banks. And third, if we aggregate all transactions in the financial world, we see a mountain of complex transactions with questionable economic value and enormous risk potential.[26]

The volume of all outstanding derivative transactions globally is at least ten times the amount of world GDP. In fact, this is most likely an understatement if we include all forms of derivatives including bilateral agreements that are not captured by exchanges or settlement agencies. In other words, the real economy (i.e., the production of products and services) is a fraction of the value of all financial assets hidden in the financial world. Valuation of these derivatives is not easy and in some cases we can only estimate their value. If we experience an economic or financial stress event (such as the return of high inflation), the volume of these derivatives could produce enormous losses. Even worse, given the complex connectivity in the derivatives markets, losses can quickly spread due to complex counterparty risks. For example, if Bank A has insured a potential loss through a derivative with Bank B and later Bank B cannot fulfill its obligations from this derivative contract, Bank A might be in trouble even though it hedged its risk exposure. The connectivity risk in derivatives markets is extremely complex and might be discovered too late.

It is worrisome that almost all accounting systems developed to deal with these financial assets were created in times of low inflation. High inflation (and second order effects such as higher interest rates) is likely to impact valuations of many derivatives dramatically. I have my doubts whether all financial institutions are well prepared to deal with these complex issues and their potential implications.

Extreme complexity is present not only in the financial world. Our legal system is equally complex. When U.S. President Reagan and Federal Reserve Chairman Volcker successfully ended the period of high inflation in the U.S. during the early 1980s, they employed decisive, bold, and fast decision making. They did not have to worry about a wave of lawsuits. Today's situation is different. During the recent financial crisis, we encountered countless instances of legal issues or complexity that slowed down bold decision making or prevented it. We are still witnessing countless legal proceedings that are based on cases that originated during the last financial crisis or before.

I believe that our risk management capabilities to deal effectively with high inflation are severely reduced by excessive complexity in developed countries' economic, financial, and social systems. As a consequence, containing inflation will be much more difficult than many people believe.

Complication No. 3: Market reactions in the developed world occur at lightning speed and often pre-empt actions by authorities

Business and financial transactions occur at lightning speed. Billions of dollars can move in and out of currencies, equities, and bonds within seconds. During the financial crisis, these fast moving high-volume transactions contributed to the destabilization of financial markets. A rumor was enough for currencies to move erratically or the valuation of bank stocks to collapse within minutes. As volatility fed volatility, financial markets were destabilized and the negative effects quickly spilled over to the real economy.

The actual problem was that transactions occurred so quickly and in such large volumes that they deprived politicians or regulators of any chance to restore calm and normalcy. Uncontrollable chain reactions destabilized the financial system. The situation was comparable to a nuclear power plant facing a meltdown.

Even rumors can initiate high-volume financial transactions within seconds. For regulators and decision makers in politics, financial institutions, and businesses, such a situation is extremely hard to contain.

Dealing with crisis situations in complex systems requires circuit breakers in order to gain time to critically evaluate the situation or the problem at hand and develop and implement appropriate strategies. In today's high-speed markets, decision makers do not have enough time for careful analysis and therefore they implement crucial policies based on incomplete analysis or gut feelings. Obviously, this increases the probability of poor decisions that can further fuel a panic.

During the 1970s inflation period, decision makers had time for reflection and devising effective strategies. Derivatives markets were in their infant stage, and stock market and foreign exchange market movements occurred at a substantially lower speed than today. For example, even though the S+P 500 index lost about half of its value in reaction to the first inflation shock in 1973, this loss was spread over twenty-one months. If inflation rates comparable to those from the 1970s occurred today, the resulting damage to the economy and financial markets would not only be bigger, it would also occur much faster. It is likely that because of the higher speed of financial transactions, market participants would react in a more erratic and undisciplined way than in the 1970s.

It is not an exaggeration to compare the speed in today's world with that of the 1970s to a leopard and a turtle. Some hedge funds trade on the premise of being a fraction of a second faster than other market participants (so-called high-speed trading). Communication technology makes content available to billions of people in real time. If a central banker gives a speech in Japan, you can be sure that it is available in English within seconds globally.

It is extremely difficult for politicians and central bankers to operate successfully in such a high-speed world. This is particularly the case when it comes to situations in which stress events raise the chances for overreactions and uncontrollable chain reactions. The job to control high inflation in 1980 would have been much more difficult for Volcker and Reagan in today's environment in which a wrong interpretation of an interview can set off massive waves of financial volatility.

Complication No. 4: Today's business and financial infrastructure systems are not built to withstand inflation

Most of today's business infrastructure systems (e.g., accounting, regulatory, tax, legal, financial) have been developed over the past three decades and are based on the assumption of permanently low or, at a maximum, moderate inflation rates. For example, regulatory systems in banking and insurance are forcing companies to adopt strategies that clearly will backfire during times of high inflation, making them vulnerable. Banks and insurance companies are highly incentivized to hold government bonds over almost any other form of financial asset. Banks and insurance companies are, consequently, among the biggest holders of long-term government debt, an asset that is very likely to suffer valuation losses in times of rising inflation rates.

Today's accounting systems insufficiently differ between nominal and real aggregates and do not address the issue of monetary depreciation. There are many issues hidden in depreciation schedules, tax loss carried forward structures, or goodwill investments in times of high inflation. For some, these will be substantial windfall profits and for others they will be dangerous windfall losses.

Long-term financial planning tends to ignore or underestimate the effects of future high inflation. Financing structures may turn out to be incompatible with high inflation or legacy pension plan liabilities may explode due to a clause in the fine print that offers pension holders generous inflation protection.

There is a problem not only with macro systems, such as the overall accounting system and their incompatibility with high inflation. Many of the countless micro systems in financial institutions and companies will prove inadequate to deal effectively with inflation, and this contributes to additional volatility and risk. Planning, pricing, and calculation systems and processes must be more flexible in dealing with frequent and substantial price changes of all input factors and final products. Equally, banks' financial systems must deal with much higher price volatility than in normal times. Interest rate risk management becomes much more complicated than before. Insurance companies active in long-tail business, in which a contract covers a client over multiple years, face particular difficulties. If an insurance company fails to account for higher future claims costs (due to inflation), the insurer can suffer horrific losses. Equally, if a life assurer fails to anticipate interest rate movements due to inflation, guarantees granted by a policy (annuities or endowment portions of the policy) might cause substantial losses.

I am doubtful that infrastructure systems of companies, financial institutions, or governments in the developed world can deal with these challenges successfully. Nor do I believe that they will be able to upgrade these systems in time to meet the new requirements. As a result, we will see poor decision making, decreasing companies' ability to deal with inflation. On a macro level, these problems will add to the overall volatility issues that result from an increase in inflation rates.

Complication No. 5: The majority of today's decision makers in politics, business, and finance have little experience in dealing with inflation

The majority of today's decision makers in the developed world do not have any relevant experience in inflation management. They are simply too young to have experienced the 1970s period in active professional management positions. Managing a company during times of high inflation requires a completely unique skill set and experience base. Not having such skills and experiences is likely to lead to many strategic and operational mistakes causing reduction of shareholder value. We witnessed this during the first two years of the 1970s inflation period when most business leaders were caught not only unprepared by the sudden rise in inflation but also did not know how to respond to high inflation once it was there.

Emerging markets managers are likely to have significant competitive advantage over their peers in developed markets. They have learned to manage inflation in the more recent past and therefore accumulated relevant and valuable experience. This could give emerging markets companies a significant competitive advantage over their peers in developed markets.

WHAT IS THE WORST-CASE SCENARIO?

Inflation has always been disruptive to the economy and society. It will not be different this time. While it certainly may help over-indebted governments and entities in the short-term, it will bring enormous disruptions for the overall economy and financial markets.

The five unique complications, as do other imbalances and distortions in the economy and financial markets, make the next inflation period particularly dangerous. It is possible that inflation will spin out of control in one or more developed countries and lead to disruptions as seen during the Weimar Republic in Germany. It all will depend on decision makers' ability and willingness to move up the learning curve and acquire crucial skills once inflation has arrived. There is a potential underestimation of the impact of the many distortions, imbalances, and overly leveraged situations in the developed world. Chart 12 illustrates some of these dangerous situations.

Chart 12: Dangerous distortions, imbalances, and overly leveraged situations

Segment	Issue
Bond Market	• Overall size in comparison to real economy • Distortion of valuation (i.e., record low interest rates) • Liquidity issues once interest rates start to rise
Derivatives Market	• Prices linked to nominal aggregates (exposure to inflation risk) • Size (absolute and relative to GDP) • Transparency • Connectivity risks • Quality of documentation of derivatives
Interest Rate	• Artificially low interest rates might swing back swiftly • Stability of interest rate swap market • Adverse yield curve shifts
Banking Sector	• Exposure to interest rate risk • Counterparty and connectivity risk (derivatives, loans) • Liquidity risks and capital adequacy issues
Asset Markets	• Valuation distorted by artificially low interest rate risk • Leverage (e.g., debt financed investments)

While I hope that when the time comes decision makers in politics, regulatory bodies, and central banks will rectify the situations for which they are at least partly responsible, I do not necessarily rely on this. Decision makers were often too slow in the past to fight inflation or were forced by public pressure and elections to give in to populist demands that made the problems worse. We saw this preceding the second inflation shock during the second half of the 1970s.

Due to the five unique complications that are present today, any mistake by decision makers to fight inflation will quickly have more painful consequences than in the past. Given the enormous complexity of today's financial markets and their size compared to the real economy, we cannot simply expect that everything will turn out to be fine. In a worst-case scenario, we will experience an even more dangerous financial crisis than the last one. The need for governments not only to bail out the banking sector again, but to reset the overall financial system is possible. Obviously, the holder of any monetary asset would be exposed to enormous risks in such a situation. On the other side, a reset may provide an attractive opportunity to kick-start the economy with a new paradigm that is solidly anchored in the principles of robustness, simplicity, and sustainable economic growth. Financial engineering will have no place in such an environment; in contrast, industrial engineering and manufacturing will experience a renaissance.

CHAPTER 4: HUMAN FAILURE TO ANTICIPATE BIG RISK CATASTROPHES—THE TYPICAL CONDITIONS THAT PRECEDE MAJOR RISK EVENTS

When I told people that I was writing a book about the impact of high inflation on our economy and society, the reactions were unenthusiastic. Few people thought there was a need for such a book. Most people believed that worrying about high inflation was as justified as worrying about a shortage of sand in a desert. They based their views on comments and assessments from governments, central banks, and financial institutions who *"uni sono"* claim that people should not worry about inflation. If at all, people should worry about the opposite: deflation.

Unfortunately, experts have terrible track records for anticipating major risk events or catastrophes. Prior to any major risk event, the majority of experts did not anticipate the specific danger. We have seen this pattern in the economy, financial markets, and in other aspects of life. The 1929 Great Depression was as much a surprise to experts as was the burst of the new economy bubble (2001), the outbreak of the recent financial crisis (2007), and the nuclear accident in Fukushima in Japan (2011). In short, despite all the investments in risk management, we are still poor at anticipating major crises and catastrophes, even if there are clear warning signs. This is true in all aspects of life, but it is particularly true for inflation risks. Very few inflation spikes were correctly anticipated by the majority of experts or by the general public.

There is actually a systematic pattern to the genesis of major risk events and I recommend that everyone become familiar with these patterns. Understanding them is a crucial step in anticipating major risk events in time (such as inflation risk events). Therefore, let me explain this important topic before we return to the discussion of inflation risks and opportunities. Do not expect that opinion leaders and so-called experts will do this job for you—they have done poorly in the past in anticipating major risk events and are likely to do so in the future. You are responsible for yourself.

The three conditions that often precede disastrous risk events

Twenty years of advising on strategy and risk management topics taught me a simple, but very important lesson. Three conditions often precede a major risk management disaster. First, there has not been a specific risk event for an extended period of time. Typically, decision makers in governments and businesses (wrongly) interpret the absence of severe risk events as the result of good risk management practice. They therefore (wrongly) assume that they are in control of all major risks. For example, the absence of a major nuclear power accident since Chernobyl (1986) led to unrestrained and unjustified confidence in the safety of nuclear power and the manageability of the associated risks. Decision makers felt they fully understood and controlled this technology and therefore could contain the risks associated with it. The accident in Fukushima shattered this belief and led to a remarkable U-turn in how governments assess the risks of nuclear power energy.[27]

The second condition is related to the first one: The majority of people and businesses do not anticipate a particular risk event. Therefore, if this risk event occurs, it will be a surprise for which they are unprepared. Unpreparedness in the context of a severe risk event leads to erratic and irrational behavior and decision making, which often increases the damage caused by a risk event.

The third condition is met when respected authorities, perceived experts, or opinion leaders express strong optimism about the prospects for the future and dismiss risk fears as unjustified. For example, even shortly before the outbreak of the financial crisis, many top bank managers and analysts expressed their confidence in a bright and exciting future for the banking sector and the economy. Such remarks are a strong indication of overconfidence and inadequate attention to risk management issues.

Typically, they initiate a wave of enthusiasm among stakeholders and society. At a time when people should review their risk management readiness, such remarks from authorities encourage people to do the opposite and take even more risks. We saw this happening during the new economy boom when overly confident market outlooks by investment analysts set off new waves of massive stock purchases of internet companies at unsustainable valuation levels.

Chart 13: Understanding the warning signs for risk management disasters: Three conditions to watch for

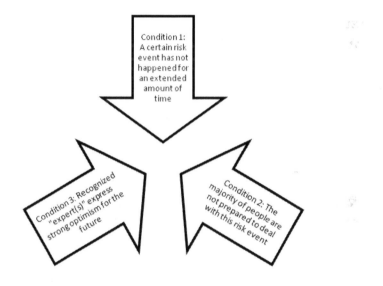

The recent financial crisis is a good illustration of the concept in more detail. For a prolonged period of time, we did not experience a significant banking, real estate, financial, or credit crisis (condition 1: prolonged absence of a risk event). The absence of such risk events raised our belief in the stability of our financial system, its decision makers' competence, and their risk management abilities to an unjustifiably high level. Few people anticipated a major financial crisis. More specifically, few prepared for the risk of a reversal of U.S. residential home prices and its impact on the banking system (condition 2: majority of people are not prepared for a particular risk event). Instead, many bank CEOs and investment analysts further fueled the bubble by expressing confidence in the U.S. housing market and related financial securities (e.g., CLOs, mortgage bonds) and the health and attractiveness of the banking sector in general (condition 3: recognized expert[s] express strong optimism for the future).

Eventually, it was the level of collective unpreparedness combined with the arrogant and unjustified confidence in the financial system's invulnerability that made the 2007 financial crisis such a terrible event. For the sophisticated risk manager, the financial crisis should not have come as a surprise. In fact, one should have expected such a crisis to happen at some point in time. The financial crisis was the logical result of excesses in many areas of the economy, the financial markets, and society.[28]

The past financial crisis is only one of many crises or severe risk events that were created or significantly amplified by the presence of the three conditions described. Chart 14 shows a selection of other severe risk events that followed the same pattern. In each case, the astute observer should have recognized the warning signs that were clearly visible and should have prepared accordingly.

Chart 14: Presence of three risk disaster conditions in the past and in the future

Risk event	Condition1: Absence of a specific risk event	Condition 2: Collective unpreparedness	Condition 3: Authorities dismiss risks
Great Depression (1929)	Yes	Yes	Yes
Impact of Hurricane Katrina (2005)	Yes	Yes	Yes
Nuclear accident in Fukushima (2011)	Yes	Yes	Yes
New economy bubble (2001–2002)	Yes	Yes	Yes
Inflation spike (1973–1974)	Yes	Yes	Yes
High inflation in the future	Yes	Yes	Yes

It is important to note that risk events rarely turn disastrous if these three conditions are not present. In general, risk management activities tend to be sufficient and effective if a population has been hit by a major risk event (condition 1), collectively anticipated such an event (condition 2), or respected authorities warned loudly and clearly of the presence of a major risk threat (condition 3). For example, many people believed that on the first day of the year 2000, computers around the world would crash and create unprecedented chaos. Old computer programs recognized a year only as a two digit number. Experts were afraid that many computers could falsely read the year 2000 as the year 1900. As a consequence of this potential risk, governments, regulators, businesses, and technology companies engaged in an unprecedented information technology effort that scrutinized every critical piece of software (ranging from medical systems to logistics and bank systems) to identify and mitigate possible IT risks. The transition to the year 2000 went smoothly and no significant risk events emerged. Collective preparedness and authorities taking this specific risk threat seriously helped turn a potentially high-risk event into a nonevent. This was a superb case study for best practice risk management.

Chart 15: The impact of preparedness on risk events

Possible risk event	Condition1: Absence of a specific risk event	Condition 2: Collective unpreparedness	Condition 3: Authorities dismiss risks
Year 2000 computer meltdown	No (new risk threat)	No	No
	Result: No risk event occurred		
Chaos due to introduction of new currency (Euro) in Europe (2002)	No (new risk threat)	No	No
	Result: No risk event occurred		

We should expect that human society will learn from past risk management mistakes and will therefore closely watch for the presence of these three conditions. Unfortunately, this is not the case. Human society proves to be remarkably stubborn in refusing to learn from past risk management mistakes. This explains why we find so many similar risk management disasters in history—we simply fail to learn from past mistakes. This is particularly true when it comes to the world of business and economic developments.

The three conditions for major risk management disasters are present when it comes to inflation risks. These conditions are not only met, they are flashing bright red warning lights. The absence of excessive inflation in the developed world for more than thirty years gives us (unjustified) confidence that our systems and approaches are working well at controlling and containing inflation (condition 1). As a consequence, society fails to prepare adequately for such a possible risk event (collective unpreparedness, condition 2). This is true for decision makers in politics, central banks, financial institutions, and businesses, as well as for individuals, a large number of whom publicly refute the existence of excessive inflation risks (condition 3). All warning signs are blinking red, but few people have taken notice.

Excessive inflation is a phenomenon that rarely comes as a surprise to the astute observer. There are great similarities in the conditions that led to excessive inflation in historic case examples: excessive (government) debt, extended periods of fiscal irresponsibility, ultra-loose monetary policies (often as a consequence of the first two conditions), and high levels of excess funds and liquidity in the financial system. Whether it was excessive inflation during the reign of Roman Emperor Diocletian or during Germany's period of hyperinflation in the 1920s, the underlying factors that ultimately led to high inflation tend to be very similar. We must fear that once again we may choose to ignore the lessons learned from history and that many companies and individuals will again suffer the painful consequences of being caught unprepared for high inflation.

CHAPTER 5: THE CURRENT SITUATION IS NOT UNPRE-CEDENTED AND THE LIKELY OUTCOME SHOULD NOT SURPRISE US

Many decision makers and experts consider the current economic and financial situation in the developed world as unprecedented. They claim that today's "new situation" requires new solutions to lead us back to our economic growth trail before the outbreak of the last financial crisis. As they see it, any solution implemented by governments, central banks, and regulatory bodies should be seen as an experiment. There is no guarantee of success for any of the extreme measures that have been implemented over the past years.

In this chapter, I dispute the claim that the current situation is unprecedented. If we decompose the structural elements that are the foundation of our current economic and financial malaise, we quickly realize that we are facing more or less the same problems that we have faced so many times before in history. More specifically, we fell into the common trap of overspending and over-indebtedness and, as before, we are now trying to address these problems with ultra-loose monetary policies and more government spending (i.e., fiscal deficits). Judging from similar historical precedents, we should not be surprised to get the same result of high inflation in the future as previous generations experienced by following this troublesome path.

Tragically, we believe that the current situation is unprecedented and fail to see the real issue for concern. As described in Chapter 3, the developed world faces a number of unique complications that could turn inflation risks from a serious into a severe or even catastrophic risk event. It is the set of unique complications that is unprecedented, not the structural issues of overspending and over-indebtedness. Failing to understand this difference may expose us to very serious risks.

NOTHING IS UNPRECEDENTED

Let me explain this important topic in more detail. Decomposing the current economic malaise into its core elements, we find these issues:

- Governments in most developed countries have been overspending since the early 1980s (i.e., the end of the last inflation cycle). Absolute and relative indebtedness (i.e., debt to GDP ratio) has been climbing continuously over the past decades.
- In most developed countries, private households followed the trend set by governments by indulging a constantly increasing appetite for debt.
- Consequently, total debt to GDP ratios have risen in absolute and relative terms and are for many parts of the developed world above 300 percent.
- A benign interest rate environment (i.e., interest rates had been falling for about thirty years) facilitated the buildup of debt and its maintenance.
- Slow economic growth makes it increasingly difficult to reduce the debt mountain. Current debt levels would be unsustainable if interest rates were close to the long-term average.
- Central banks stepped in and engaged in ultra-loose monetary policies to drive down interest rates to record low levels (to help indebted entities). They also provided a gigantic liquidity program to the banking sector and the economy.

We find many similar situations in economic history. In fact, the combination of overspending and over-indebtedness of governments and private households is common, as is the response of central banks (or governments) to resort to ultra-loose monetary policies (and more spending) to address the associated problems.

Roman Emperor Diocletian fell into the same trap. His overspending led to substantial inflation that plagued his administration for a prolonged

95

period. Diocletian committed the same mistakes that were later repeated by many politicians trying to fight inflation. He introduced strict price controls for many goods, wrongly believing that governments could order inflation to stop. Price controls backfired and made the situation worse. Goods were withdrawn from the official market and black markets developed. The mistake of introducing price controls to fight inflation is quite common. We have seen this unsuccessful policy during the 1970s period of inflation in the U.S. and more recently in countries such as Venezuela.

Diocletian also used expansionary monetary policies. For example, he initiated measures to debase the currency and to produce more money to pay government expenses. As paper money was not used at the time, Diocletian changed the mix of metals used to make coins, decreasing the amount of precious metal used for certain coins. As expected, his tricks were spotted by the general population and people became even more suspicious of the Roman currency. Exaggerated levels of LOFIS Inflation were the inevitable result of these monetary experiments.

Judging from history, high inflation seems to be a normal occurrence that happens regularly in most countries. As mentioned, the long-term stability of any non-gold standard currency has been very poor. In most cases, the devaluation of paper money or any other form of non-gold standard currency is the result of phases of overspending by governments or private households and an increase of debt leverage. As these issues occur regularly, inflation has been a frequent visitor in economic history. It may come with a time lag, but it is likely to come when central banks retreat to ultra-loose policies to remedy the effects of the "misbehavior" of governments, companies, or private households. Unfortunately, the combination of ultra-loose monetary policies and further fiscal deficits are still seen as valid strategies to address the economic issues caused by overspending and over-indebtedness.

Superficially, one could wrongly believe that such measures are harmless. Decision makers continue to resort to controlling levels of higher inflation without raising taxes or cutting entitlement payments. However, high inflation often comes at a high price. As an economic and social phenomenon, it is, in fact, uncontrollable. The idea of being able to choose a moderately higher inflation rate and to lock it in for some time is naive. Once inflation has been set into action, it often spirals out of control and quickly destabilizes social and political order. As people see the purchasing power of their hard earned savings dwindling away due to rising inflation, they react with anger, distrust, and disappointment. It is then easy for extremist political parties to gain support and build momentum to derail the political status quo.

This occurred in the 1920s period of hyperinflation that destabilized Germany and, at a minimum, helped prepare for the rise of the Nazi party and its ideology that ended in a terrible catastrophe. Hyperinflation played a big role in derailing the young democracy in Germany.

It is naive to believe that the current situation is unprecedented. The situation today is no different from past phases of overspending and over-indebtedness. If history is any reliable guide, the message is clear: Any outcome of the current strategy of fiscal deficits and ultra-loose monetary spending that does not involve significantly higher rates of inflation would be a surprise.

WHAT IS REALLY UNPRECEDENTED

While the structural elements of today's economic malaise in the developed world are not unprecedented, there are at least two unique complications. First, the imbalance between the sizes of the financial world and the real economic world has never been as extreme. The monetary world is detached from the economic reality. It seems that the real economy is too small to bail out the financial world one more time if things get out of control. The leverage employed by market participants and governments in the form of debt and derivatives is too vast compared to the real size of the economy in the developed world.

Second, the number of countries that simultaneously follow inflationary policies is unprecedented. The developed world shares the same potentially disastrous strategies of overspending and ultra-loose monetary policies. It will be hard to find any currency safe harbor once high inflation re-emerges in the developed world. This might encourage market participants to drop paper money and seek shelter in real assets. Such behavior would set off a deadly inflation spiral.

These two complications are not on the risk management agenda of most politicians, central bankers, and top managers. They expect this time will be different and that they will be able to control inflation at the levels they target. From a historic perspective, there is limited hope that this will have a positive end.

AN IRONY OF HISTORY

Most of the countries involved in World War I struggled with economic weakness and high inflation.[29] High inflation was the result of a shortage of non-war goods as most production capacity was used to manufacture military equipment and goods needed for soldiers. Most countries were also heavily indebted due to war expenses. In short, most involved countries faced tough economic problems after the war.

There were basically two strategies available to tackle these economic problems. Surprisingly, they are similar to the basic strategies being discussed today to address the economic problems in the developed world. The first strategy was pro-growth. In short, governments continued to issue more debt, engaged in even higher fiscal deficits, and invested in infrastructure, economic stimuli, and entitlements. Obviously, this strategy must be supported by an expansionary monetary policy. The second strategy, in contrast, focused on re-establishing fiscal and financial health to the country, commonly referred to as the austerity strategy. Proponents of this strategy demanded that governments cut expenses and seek balanced budgets. In addition, restrictive monetary policies were thought to help end the inflation problem.

Germany then was a strong proponent of the first strategy. After the war, government spending continued to be at levels high above government revenues. The money was spent on infrastructure enhancements and entitlements. Domestic bond issuances helped finance the shortfall and drove up government debt levels to very high levels. Keep in mind that Germany was a low debt country before the war started. The strategy of deficit spending was supported by an ultra-loose monetary policy. Not surprisingly, Germany experienced a short economic recovery during the period 1920–1921. This recovery was artificial and unsustainable; it was driven by unsustainable monetary policies instead of structural improvements of the economy. About two years later, Germany collapsed under the weight of hyperinflation. Its currency became practically worthless. While the government eliminated its domestic debt, the vast majority of savers, retirees, and charitable foundations had to pay the price. Social destabilization and low confidence in the new political system (i.e., the Weimar Republic) were the logical consequences.

The United States was very concerned about unsustainable spending, as its debt-to-GDP ratio sharply rose to levels not seen since the Civil War (even though the U.S. debt-to-GDP ratio compared to other countries was relatively low).[30] The U.S. therefore followed a strategy contrary to that pursued by Germany, that of strict austerity. As we know today, the U.S. chose the right path. After a short, but admittedly tough, recession, the U.S. regained its economic strength and enjoyed years of strong growth during the 1920s, the roaring twenties.

It is ironic that today the two economic power houses have switched places. Germany today prefers the strategy of austerity and structural economic reforms, even at the price of a few years of economic pain. On the other side, the U.S. (and most other developed countries) follows policies similar to those pursued by Germany after World War I. It seeks to improve economic conditions by adding more debt and more government deficits to the economy. It also seeks to accommodate these policies with ultra-loose monetary policies. Some developed countries, such as Japan, make no effort to conceal their interest in forcing inflation rates up. It is very hard to imagine how those policies would actually work, particularly if they are not accompanied by real structural reforms that target the performance potential of an economy. The only way these policies can help is by forcing up inflation rates eventually. However, as we know from history, inflation is a process almost impossible to contain. Therefore, I label these strategies high-risk policies.

It is quite possible that years from now economics and history students will question why we refused to learn from history. It seems so obvious from historic analogies that policies put in place today could quite likely cause destabilizing rates of inflation in the future. Professors might have a hard time explaining today's economic and financial myopia to their future students.

LONG-TERM PROSPERITY IS MORE IMPORTANT THAN FALSE SHORT-TERM BOOMS

When we look at the effectiveness of economic, fiscal, and monetary strategies, we increasingly shorten our perspective. The developed world is impatient and most people prefer fast results to long-term stability and sustainable value creation. We ignore the long-term consequences and implications of our short-term actions and then we wonder why things do not improve.

After World War I, the U.S. was right to focus on long-term prosperity, even though it meant accepting a short recession. The U.S. went through a short but harsh period of recession and two years of deflation. Prices fell in 1921 by 10.8 percent and in 1922 by 2.3 percent.[31] However, economic recovery started in 1922. Deflation did not prove to be the monstrous danger to the economy perceived today by many experts.

Granted, the U.S. was then not a highly indebted country. It was fiscally responsible and prudent in comparison to many European counterparts.

Although Germany eventually collapsed due to its irresponsible strategy of overspending, over-indebtedness, and excessive money printing, it enjoyed a short period of economic boom. In fact, this boom attracted many foreign investors who were blindsided and failed to see the true reasons for this false boom. Germany was on an unsustainable path of destructive deficit making and monetary destabilization, as charts 16 and 17 illustrate.

Even though some of the deficits were used for productive investments in its infrastructure and to build new canals, ports, and electricity plants,[32] a big part of its spending was consumed by enlarged entitlement programs, administration costs, and unproductive spending.

Chart 16: German fiscal deficits[33]

Year	Fiscal deficit (in percent of income)
1914	- 18 percent (nominal)
1915	- 15 percent (nominal)
1916	- 26 percent (nominal)
1917	- 51 percent (nominal)
1918	- 44 percent (nominal)
1919	- 234 percent (based on Goldmark)
1920	- 194 percent (based on Goldmark)
1921	- 127 percent (based on Goldmark)
1922	- 165 percent (based on Goldmark)

Not surprisingly, the excessive stimuli introduced by the German government and ultra-loose monetary policies introduced by the German Reichsbank led to a short economic boom (February 1920 to May 1921). During this short period, the German mark strongly appreciated and internal prices in Germany somewhat stabilized (although not food prices).

Financial markets completely misjudged the validity and sustainability of this economic boom. The value of the mark against the U.S. dollar improved almost forty percent between February 1920 and May 1921.[34] Domestic and foreign investors' confidence in a German recovery motivated them to invest in the German mark and German fixed income securities. Such gross forms of misjudgment are surprising, as many macro variables clearly showed that the economic boom was false. The scale of fiscal deficits should have been a clear warning sign as to the health of the German economy. Equally, the fact that money in circulation increased about fifty percent and debt levels almost doubled should have warned investors to stay away from the German currency.[35] The information appearing in Chart 17 gave no reason for optimism regarding the German economy or its currency.

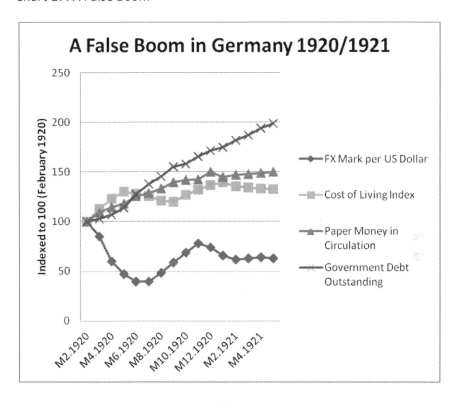

Many investors discovered too late what happened. They were too enthusiastic about a potential German turnaround and they wrongly believed that the pro-growth strategy was finally starting to work. They failed to think critically and to question the real drivers of the German stabilization of the early 1920s and their sustainability.

As the underlying structural issues remained unaddressed, the excessiveness regarding fiscal and monetary stimuli demanded its price: the German mark finally collapsed in November 1923, about two years after all the enthusiasm about Germany's potential recovery. It was a total disaster for anybody invested in the mark or in German debt. In 1913, one U.S. dollar could buy about four marks; ten years later, you needed 4.2 trillion marks for one U.S. dollar (if anyone accepted marks at all).[37]

Between 1913 and 1923, Germany's economy and social situation suffered a dramatic deterioration. In 1913, Germans full of confidence and optimism regarding their future would never have thought that such a fast decline was possible.

It is too easy for us to look back at German decision makers in politics and central banks and accuse them of naivety or foolishness. They were highly educated people and I do not doubt that a lot of thinking went into their eventually disastrous financial and economic decision making. But they got it totally wrong. They not only underestimated the dangers of inflation and their inability to contain it, they also failed to understand the economics of inflation and that strategies that worked well before would become dangerously destructive in a high inflation environment. Maybe they were more surprised about the implications of high inflation than the fact that inflation emerged.

The lesson we learned from the occurrences after World War I is clear. We must not judge the effectiveness of fiscal, economic, and monetary policies by looking at short-term results. In the short term, the results in Germany in the early 1920s were probably better than those seen in the U.S. The U.S. strategy of pursuing long-term growth by accepting short-term pain caused by austerity measures and economic reforms succeeded in the mid- to long-term. It is imperative that we understand that our situation and the policies we engage in are not unprecedented.

PLEA TO TODAY'S AUTHORITIES: LEARN FROM HISTORY

We can only hope that all decision makers in politics and central banks in the developed world who are in favor of more debt, higher fiscal deficits, and expansionary monetary policies have done in-depth analysis and research to prevent a repetition of Germany's destructive experiences of the 1920s. We should not worry about hyperinflation. Even moderate levels of inflation could destabilize financial markets due to the unique complications described in Chapter 3. Focus on short-term improvements at the expense of long-term stability and sustainability could have disastrous consequences for inflation management.

Germany was a healthy and stable country in 1913. The fact that Germany collapsed economically only ten years later and ended up in chaos with a brutal dictatorship should get us thinking. Maybe today's authorities and their highly educated associates have done a rigorous analysis of their policies and their likely outcomes. Maybe these analyses show some angles and insights of which I am not aware. I hope that this is the case because otherwise we are on a road filled with dangerous and unpredictable risks that will threaten not only our economy, but also the stability of society.

CHAPTER 6: WHEN WILL HIGH INFLATION ARRIVE? WHY HASN'T IT ARRIVED YET?

To the surprise of many people, published inflation rates in developed countries have remained remarkably low over the past years despite ultra-loose monetary policies having been implemented. After rising to levels of five percent during the summer of 2008, reported inflation rates have fallen significantly and have remained at low levels. This is in contrast to many emerging and developing countries, which still face substantial inflation issues (e.g., Venezuela, Argentina, Russia, and India).

In light of most recent inflation data, many experts in developed countries declare the fear of high inflation as unjustified. Many of these experts believe that we should worry more about deflation than inflation. Therefore, they demand that central banks continue their ultra-loose policies.

It is not only too early to declare victory over inflation risks, it is also quite dangerous to do so. Inflation risks are not eliminated. They are present and need to be understood and addressed. The current economic and financial situation is quite complex and one can easily become confused when trying to make sense of current developments, including reported inflation data. There are several seemingly inconsistent developments going on in the developed world. As stated, despite ultra-loose monetary policies and record absolute and relative debt levels, reported inflation rates are extremely low in most developed countries. Yields of government bonds suggest extremely low credit risk, despite record debt levels. Low- and middle-class families complain about rising household costs despite low inflation numbers reported by governments. How does this fit together?

In this chapter, the current and future inflation situation in developed countries is presented. More specifically, the following key issues that need to be understood when assessing inflation risks are discussed:

- Inflation was already dangerously high in 2007–2008. It was then temporarily contained by a powerful deflationary force (i.e., the outbreak of the financial crisis).
- There are three additional deflationary forces at work that hold back inflation rates. However, these forces are losing strength and might wane soon.
- High inflation is already present in many aspects of life. Financial assets (e.g., bonds, stocks), real estate, health care, and education are some examples.
- Most CPI calculation methodologies do not capture the full extent of price increases we are exposed to. They exclude important issues such as secondary costs (e.g., future repairs, disposal costs), shorter product life spans, and deterioration of product quality (requiring more service, more frequent replacements).
- The greatest concerns are EMEG Inflation and LOFIS Inflation. The conditions under which they develop are discussed. As LOFIS Inflation is the result of a behavioral change, I explain how this change might occur and why it is possible to anticipate LOFIS Inflation, but impossible to time its arrival accurately.

UNDERSTANDING THE CONTEXT: WHY DID INFLATION RATES COLLAPSE AFTER REACHING A PEAK IN 2008?

In 2007 and early 2008, inflation rates rose sharply in many developed countries, reaching levels of about five percent during the summer of 2008. In emerging market countries, inflation rates climbed to double digit levels. Since then, inflation rates have collapsed to such low levels that more and more people are concerned about deflation threats. Inflation fears have subsided, even though current policies should make us more nervous about future inflation.

Many people wrongly interpret today's low inflation rates as proof that the extreme fiscal and monetary measures in the developed world work well. In their view, the fears about higher inflation are unjustified.

The reality is quite different. If we decompose the current inflation situation and the forces that shape it, there is little reason to celebrate a victory over inflation. The threat is more pronounced than at any point in the past. Current inflation rates might not reveal this threat since they are significantly influenced by four strong deflationary forces, which might subside in the near future (see Chart 18). These deflationary forces struggle with inflationary forces resulting from ultra-loose monetary policies and high debt leverage. Future inflation rates will be determined to a great extent by the balance of these forces. We may witness a situation in which inflationary forces may offset the effect of deflationary forces. This is when EMEG Inflation or LOFIS Inflation will occur. In other words, we may see soon a situation in which global economic growth returns to the long-term trajectory (particularly in emerging markets) and the influence of deflationary forces (as shown in Chart 18) start to disappear. Therefore, we should prepare now for a substantial rise of inflation rates in developed countries.

Let us first take a closer look at the deflationary forces that currently hold back price increases in developed countries. Chart 18 summarizes the four most important of these.

Chart 18: The four most powerful deflationary forces

Deflationary Force	Description	Assessment
Force 1	Financial crisis of 2008: collapsing global demand	Strong deflationary force in the past, now waning
Force 2	Outsourcing of production and administrative activities	Strong deflationary force in the past, now waning
Force 3	Demographic trends: aging society impacts demand for products and services	In general, deflationary force
Force 4	Technology	Deflationary force for CPI calculations, but not necessarily for real inflation

The first and probably most important deflationary force was the outbreak of the financial crisis in 2008, which led to a collapse of global economic demand. Since then, economic recovery has been very slow (despite fiscal and monetary interventions).

This unleashed a powerful deflationary force that abruptly ended the rise of EMEG Inflation around the globe. At that point, EMEG Inflation had already reached levels of about five percent in many developed countries. In the U.S., CPI inflation peaked at levels above five percent in the summer of 2008 (see Chart 19).

The rise of global inflation in 2008 was mainly a result of strongly booming emerging markets. This economic boom created a higher demand for commodities and other products. This additional demand led to rising inflation rates. Even though GDP growth in the U.S. was not excessively high between 2006 and 2008, the enormous demand from emerging markets overcompensated for the domestic weakness. More specifically, a strong increase in EMEG Inflation originated from outside the developed world. It would have been difficult for developed countries to rein in this rise of EMEG Inflation if we had not experienced a financial crisis that—at least temporarily—cooled down overheating economic growth in emerging markets.

Chart 19: EMEG Inflation spike in 2008 due to booming emerging markets[38]

Year	CPI-U (USA)	U.S. GDP growth (real, in percent)	World GDP growth (real, in percent)
2003	1.9	2.5	2.7
2004	3.3	3.6	4.0
2005	3.4	3.1	3.5
2006	2.5	2.7	4.1
2007	4.1	2.1	4.0
July 2008	5.6		
2008	0.1	-0.3	1.4
2009	2.7	-2.8	-2.2
2010	1.5	2.5	4.0
2011	3.0	1.6	2.8
2012	1.7	2.3	2.2

The inflation spike of 2008 teaches us an important lesson. A country can experience EMEG Inflation even though its domestic economy is far from overheating (note low GDP growth rates for the U.S. in 2007).

It is not sufficient to monitor domestic economic conditions only when watching out for possible inflation threats. We must also follow international and global economic trends to avoid being caught unprepared by EMEG Inflation. Global GDP figures may be a good start. Prolonged periods of strong global growth at levels of about four percent seem to be sufficient to initiate rising price levels caused by EMEG Inflation (see Chart 19).

The financial crisis has provided some breathing space when it comes to EMEG Inflation. It removed the conditions for EMEG Inflation, at least temporarily. The risk of EMEG Inflation initiated by emerging markets is likely to reoccur. As the world economy in general and emerging markets in particular seem slow to recover from the abrupt collapse of global demand, we must still prepare for a renewed occurrence of EMEG Inflation risks. Due to higher GDP base effects, even lower levels of global GDP growth may be sufficient to kick off a new wave of EMEG Inflation.

Therefore, the financial crisis has been a powerful deflationary force over the past several years. Its deflationary momentum, however, is clearly waning as economies are recovering from a severe demand shock.

The second deflationary force results from outsourcing expensive production and administrative jobs from developed countries to emerging and developing countries. For decades, this process has had a deflationary effect on developed countries as part of the cost savings was passed on to consumers.

The threat of outsourcing kept domestic wage growth in developed countries at low levels. In many developed countries, wages have grown significantly less than inflation rates for a prolonged period. However, wages and salaries have risen strongly in emerging countries over the past decade. It becomes more difficult to find new outsourcing locations that offer significant cost savings. In some instances, we have seen companies reverting outsourced production and administrative jobs back to developed countries. The strength of this deflationary power has clearly peaked and is likely to wane in the future, even more so if emerging markets' currencies start to appreciate due to strong economic growth.

Demographic changes are responsible for the third deflationary force in developed markets. Aging populations show a different pattern of spending. In general, these shifts in spending patterns constitute a deflationary force. Retired people in general do not make major investments in housing, renovations, cars, or consumer electronics. They live in established households and they may need to downsize rather than expand. Aging populations are likely to spend less money than they did previously.

There may be some notable exceptions. Expenditures for health care or travel increase as a population ages. As these spending categories influence CPI calculations, there is a counterbalancing inflationary force that may grow stronger. We should expect the overall deflationary force of aging populations to remain strong.

The fourth deflationary force is technological innovation and the general use of technology. Technology presents a strong deflationary force as its use in production and administration processes increases. Technology seems to decrease the costs for many activities. Companies tend to pass along some of these cost savings to consumers in lower prices. Technology also enables better transparency of prices which helps keep prices down.

It is unclear if technology will continue to be a significant deflationary force. There are several aspects of technology that might be inflationary. For example, healthcare costs have increased in part due to the use of expensive medical equipment. Secondary costs from the use of technology need to be understood before we can make any assessments about future deflationary or inflationary effects. These secondary costs include maintenance, replacement, and longevity issues. The use of technology might also have negative side effects. The sometimes addiction-like use of smart-phones or tablet computers during work hours for non-work activities may be costly for employers as it decreases employee productivity. Therefore, technology may not be a significant deflationary force in the future. In fact, it may even turn into an inflationary force if patterns observed in the recent past (e.g., higher maintenance costs, shorter product life spans, lower quality) become more widespread. For example, modern cars loaded with complex technology often require more frequent and more expensive maintenance work and repairs.

These four deflationary forces are at least partly responsible for the containment of inflation rates in the recent past. They help explain why the 2007–2008 inflation buildup came to a standstill. The strength of these deflationary forces may weaken and be offset by other inflationary forces.

INFLATION IS ALREADY HERE

Published inflation data from most developed countries suggest very low inflation rates for the time being. However, this data do not capture all aspects of inflation. There are at least five significant issues that are not sufficiently addressed in most official CPI calculation methodologies, as Chart 20 illustrates.

Calculating inflation rates is extremely difficult and government agencies do a great job in meticulously gathering data to calculate CPI and other inflation indices. This is done transparently but has limitations. It is necessary to understand the limitations of inflation data early enough to take protective action.

There is little dispute that high inflation is present in many aspects of today's life. For example, healthcare costs have been increasing much faster than reported aggregate CPI data in many countries. This has become a serious inflation threat for many people. Another example of fast rising expense categories is education costs, which have risen greatly. The quality of education seems to have deteriorated in many developed countries. For example, a study by the Program for International Student Assessment (PISA)[39] suggests that high school students in developed countries are falling behind their peers in some high-growth emerging markets. Not only do people have to pay more for education in many developed countries, they seem to get an inferior product compared to that of many emerging market countries that top the list of the latest PISA studies.

The issues of official government-reported inflation rates are now considered. Please note that methodologies differ between countries. Therefore, the relevance of the issues listed in Chart 20 may vary within the group of developed countries.

Chart 20: The five most pressing issues regarding official CPI data in developed countries

Issue when interpreting official inflation data	
1	Exclusion of financial assets
2	Adjustments made to raw data
3	Exclusion of quality deterioration, maintenance cost issues, and decreasing product longevity
4	Exclusion of secondary costs
5	Changing methodologies

The first issue concerns the exclusion of some relevant products and assets. Many inflation methodologies do not include the price development of financial assets such as bonds and equities. Most people acquire these assets (or a derivative of them) for their personal retirement plan. Strongly rising bond and equity prices require higher retirement savings, making employee retirement more expensive. This type of inflation is not sufficiently reflected in inflation statistics, even though it negatively affects many.

The second issue regarding CPI inflation data has to do with the complicated adjustment processes that transform raw input data for a wide range of products and services into an aggregated CPI figure. CPI calculations often ignore the actual price paid by a consumer. Statisticians adjust the actual purchase price paid to reflect a wide range of product enhancement issues (such as quality, performance, upgrades).

For example, if you pay $1000 for a new laptop computer in a store, this does not mean that CPI calculations use the same $1000. Most likely, this figure is reduced to reflect quality improvements (e.g., faster processor, larger memory). These adjustments seem to be reasonable and necessary to ensure data compatibility over time (to compare apples with apples), but they are not without some major problems. First, countries with significant consumption of technology products (or other products that are subject to similar adjustments) tend to report lower inflation rates due to these adjustments. [40] Second, the alleged quality improvements of products causing CPI adjustments are often not material or are just catching up with new standards. In many cases, the consumer does not have the option to buy a new laptop that offers the old specifications to take advantage of deflationary developments in technology. New standards do not allow him to operate such a product anymore. Therefore, he is forced to pay the higher cash price for the product even though CPI figures would suggest he paid less. Industries continue to set new standards for performance and technical specifications at a fast rate. Using a ten-year old computer today seems to have become challenging if not impossible for most common applications due to compatibility, connectivity issues (e.g., interfaces to printers or digital cameras), or other issues (processor speed required for antivirus programs or standard software, availability of spare parts). The higher performance or quality standard is therefore a mandatory requirement to maintain the present standard for computer equipment. For consumers the message is clear: the cost savings or deflationary trends in many products will never materialize in terms of actual cash savings. [41]

A better way to look at the real inflation rate of items, such as consumer electronics, is to analyze the total household spending on them. In other words, how much does it cost to keep an average standard in terms of performance and capabilities of all products and services typically used in today's households? The total spending per year would incorporate all costs associated with a specific category including purchase price (spread over years of usage), repairs, subscriptions (e.g., mobile phone and data services), maintenance, insurance, taxes, and other related costs. In many cases, the total spending required to maintain an average standard rose much more than official inflation data suggest. Analysis of the cost development of consumer electronics will reveal that actual cost developments often do not match the specific inflation rates for this category within CPI calculations.[42]

One of the key reasons for this development is the decrease of product longevity, quality, and robustness. Today's televisions and refrigerators do not have the same twenty-to-thirty-year use expectancy of those from a few decades ago.

The issue of shortened life expectancy and lower quality and robustness of many consumer products is the third sufficiency issue of CPI calculations in Chart 20. This issue regarding CPI data is a major factor leading to a substantial understatement of actual consumer price inflation and will gain relevance as both product quality[43] and longevity decrease. Gone are the times when you bought a piece of equipment and expected it to serve you reliably twenty or more years, which is also an environmental issue as discarded consumer products are piling up. In fact, the additional disposal costs for such products eventually end up in higher tax rates or fees charged to producers or consumers.

A wide range of products suffer from two serious shortcomings. First, their life expectancy seems to have significantly shortened. Modern products may offer more gimmicks and functionality, but they lack longevity and reliability. Your refrigerator may connect to your smart phone and have fancy touchpad screens, but no sales person would promise you that it will work reliably twenty years or longer without needing costly repairs. Inflation rates should adjust for these issues.

Second, repair costs of today's products seem to be significantly higher than a generation ago. Given the high rate of electronic parts embedded in today's consumer products, they need to be assessed and repaired by a specialist using expensive equipment. As the robustness of many products has decreased significantly, they require more frequent repairs and maintenance.

These concerns constitute an important inflation issue that is neglected in most CPI calculation methodologies. If we adjust purchase prices for more frequent replacements, higher repair costs, and less reliability, we will detect a substantial inflation issue that is not sufficiently recognized. Even if a refrigerator is cheaper than fifteen years ago adjusted for inflation, most consumers will end up paying for more frequent and more expensive repairs and for shorter replacement intervals.

For many products, deteriorated quality and longevity require the purchase of expensive extended warranty policies, which typically add an additional (and often substantial) cost to the purchase. Note that extended warranty policies tend to be limited to the initial five years of use. Policies that cover the following years are hard to find (which gives you an indication of the planned longevity of modern goods). This additional warranty cost is also often ignored by inflation statistics.

While CPI calculations may recognize repair costs, they fail to capture the extent of the issue.[44] Official statistics may base repair costs on past and outdated product quality assumptions derived from products of the past.

Therefore, CPI calculations may miss an important inflation driver as they fail to capture total costs spread over the lifetime of a product. It is likely that we substantially underestimate the longevity of today's products in current CPI calculations. I have witnessed a significant decrease of life span and quality based on a wide variety of products ranging from cars to kitchen utensils. Transferring this negative experience into a statistically sound data base to adjust inflation data is challenging, but needs to be done to obtain more reliable inflation data. For the time being, product longevity and quality assessments in official inflation data will lag behind more recent trends and developments and will therefore likely understate inflation.

There is little data available on this important topic. The shortened life span of many consumer products is an increasing problem that impacts actual inflation rates and also the environment.[45] You can do your own survey to test my hypothesis of shorter life spans and lower reliability of consumer products. For example, you may list all products or services you have bought over the past five years that have already now experienced a material issue (e.g., defect, usage interruption). Compare this list with one that you would have prepared a generation ago (you may ask your parents, relatives, or friends for help). In my case, this analysis had shocking results.[46]

There is an additional CPI issue related to product quality that is worth investigating. If we compare 1960s food prices with those of today, CPI data seem to be relatively accurate. Basic food price development is in line with reported CPI figures. However, the picture changes dramatically when we add a quality dimension. For example, if we compare 1960s' organic food prices with today's, it seems that CPI data fail to account accurately for the difference.

In many developed countries in the 1960s, food was often similar to what we consider organic today. In Germany it was easy and affordable to buy untreated natural food. Farmers offered their produce at local markets at affordable prices. Industrialized agriculture was practically nonexistent.

Today, untreated natural products cost significantly more than average products. Do inflation calculations accurately reflect those quality differences? Today, organic and natural foods have become very expensive. For many, this option has become unaffordable.

With regard to food inflation, the issue extends to processed food. We can describe the underlying inflation issue as follows: prices per calorie probably rose in line with officially reported CPI data. For some forms of heavily processed food, costs per calorie may have even decreased. Prices for high-quality food, however, most likely have increased at a substantially higher rate than official CPI data suggest.

The fourth issue of CPI data is related to the previous one. CPI or PPI data do not capture secondary costs that are associated with the production or use of a product. CPI data on energy costs do not contain secondary costs for environmental destruction or future storage (or cleanup) costs for nuclear components, for example. CPI data on food costs do not capture secondary healthcare expenses that arise from consuming unhealthy food products. Secondary costs appear in higher health insurance costs, government and municipality fees, and taxes.

The fifth issue regarding CPI data refers to the often changing methodologies for calculating CPI data. Some people claim that these methodologies and adjustments have led unintentionally to lower inflation rates. There are countless articles on how the introduction of a new currency (i.e., the Euro) has led to substantial price increases for many products that were not reflected in actual CPI prices. I do not intend to go deeper into this complicated issue, but there may be some merit to these claims.

The main point of this section is to demonstrate that even though widespread inflation comparable to that of the 1970s has not yet arrived, current inflation rates may be substantially higher than CPI data suggest. If CPI calculations are adjusted for the issues in Chart 20, the result would be significantly higher inflation rates. This would explain, in part, why many lower- and middle-class families struggle financially despite low inflation rates reported by governments. In relation to median income levels, inflation may already now be excessive.

WHEN WILL BROAD-BASED INFLATION ARRIVE IN THE DEVELOPED WORLD?

The next wave of higher and broad-based inflation is likely to be caused by either EMEG Inflation or LOFIS Inflation (or both). The issues described previously may be trivial when inflation rates rise on a broad basis. At that time, reported CPI figures will clearly suggest an inflation problem regardless of calculation problems. EMEG Inflation will be caused by strong economic growth in emerging markets. As billions of people in emerging markets upgrade their standards of living and consumption patterns, they will push up the demand for products, commodities, and services. This in turn will lead to a global rise in inflation rates. This will occur when global growth rates come close to about four percent or if growth rates in emerging markets recover to those prior to the financial crisis.[47] The recent financial crisis has led to a demand shock, and it may take a few more years to return to such growth scenarios. EMEG Inflation should not come as a surprise as economic indicators are likely to warn us in time.[48]

The situation is much more complex and difficult for LOFIS Inflation. As LOFIS Inflation is a much more dangerous issue, it is discussed in more detail. LOFIS Inflation will be the result of a process that will weaken the faith in paper money systems in developed countries. This process will increasingly motivate market participants to exchange cash or monetary wealth for real assets of any sort or for more stable foreign currencies. A cocktail of serious issues will be responsible for the decreasing faith in fiat money. These issues include over-indebtedness of developed countries, prolonged periods of fiscal deficits and other imbalances, decreasing trust in authorities' ability to end economic malaise, and ultra-loose monetary policies.

An emergence of LOFIS Inflation should not surprise us given historic precedents. The same mistakes of decision makers prior to previous outbreaks of LOFIS Inflation are being committed. The real question is not whether LOFIS Inflation will emerge, but when, where, and how bad it will be. This depends on authorities' decisions once inflation rates start to rise and trust in paper money starts to crumble. It is possible that after a period of significant pain, volatility, and wealth redistribution (i.e., from savers to debtors) caused by LOFIS Inflation, the right decisions will allow the developed world to return to price stability or at least moderate inflation levels. The decisions needed to return to normalcy will be painful and unpopular. Decision makers will need courage and must accept unpopularity in the short term. If they fail to do so, inflation can spiral out of control as in Venezuela or during the Weimar Republic in Germany. It takes the courage of decision makers such as Reagan and Volcker to defeat rising inflation.

While LOFIS Inflation is likely to come, it is extremely difficult to predict when it will arrive. LOFIS Inflation is the result of a change in thinking patterns and behavior of market participants. Given current circumstances and historic examples, it is likely that faith in paper money will decrease and then, as a result, LOFIS Inflation will arrive (i.e., real assets valued over paper money). However, we are unable to determine exactly when this shift will occur.

As long as the majority of market participants do not question the stability of paper money, inflation rates may stay low despite the debt problem or extremely ultra-loose monetary policies. Excess liquidity is likely to drive up the valuation of financial assets (such as stocks, bonds, or other silo assets such as real estate) without impacting CPI figures.[49] The money flow into these specific assets is unlikely to spread to real assets that count for CPI calculation purposes. The wealth effect of rising prices of financial assets will boost confidence among people and this will create an unjustified sense of safety. This can go on for some time, until a trigger event that will initiate a reassessment of the economic, fiscal, and monetary situation. At that point, such a reassessment will likely lead to behavioral changes that may lead to a rapid emergence of LOFIS Inflation. As a result, prices of all products will rise abruptly in an accelerating manner. Price rises will cover a wide spectrum of products and services and will not be limited to only a handful of asset classes or cost categories.

We know from risk management that inertia can prevent such a reassessment for a prolonged period of time. Even if situations are clearly fragile and unsustainable, market participants may continue to hold on to their old views. In such situations, financial bubbles will get even bigger before they ultimately burst. This is the reason why the internet bubble could grow to such incredible dimensions in the early 2000s before its eventual burst or why the housing bubble reached such an excessive level before it finally burst. Human behavior seems to be increasingly momentum driven. Maybe the ability and willingness to conduct critical thinking is lost. We become seduced by our own inertia that motivates us to follow past trends blindly and abstain from critically questioning the stability and sustainability of current situations.

There is an important conclusion to be drawn regarding the limitation of risk management. While we can anticipate most risk events, we are unable to predict exactly the timing of their occurrence. Any risk event that is at least partly the result of a change in human thinking and behavior will not obey natural laws as we know them from physics or chemistry. The very same human behavior can continue for a prolonged period of time even though every objective analysis would deem it irrational. This is particularly true for risk events such as inflation, which are the direct result of human decision making and behavior. While high inflation rarely (if ever) occurs out of the blue, it is hard to predict the timing of the emergence of human behavior that leads to rising inflation rates (i.e., the dumping of paper money in favor of real assets). Chart 21 illustrates this important topic.

Chart 21: Anticipation and predictability of human behavior-induced risk events

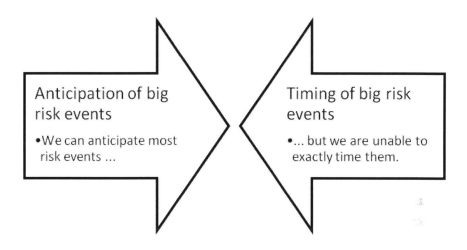

Anticipation of big risk events

•We can anticipate most risk events ...

Timing of big risk events

•... but we are unable to exactly time them.

LOFIS Inflation is typically the result of a multistep process, as Chart 22 illustrates. Often, there is a need for a trigger event to force reassessment of inflation risk. In the past, similar trigger events have caused dangerous chain reactions as people reassessed their inflation risk exposure and changed the allocation of their assets and wealth.

Such reassessments of a financial or economic situation are often arbitrary and unplanned. For years, southern European countries had accumulated huge debt in both absolute and relative terms; however, investors did not seem to care. They continued to view and price European sovereign debt from different countries as a relatively homogeneous good. This practice changed only when a trigger event happened. The trigger event was a series of articles that focused on the potential unsustainability of Greece's indebtedness and economic situation and the rising probability of Greek default. Abruptly, the riskiness of all European governments was reassessed and repriced.[50] It is likely that the arrival of LOFIS Inflation will follow a similar pattern.

Chart 22: Transmission mechanism leading to LOFIS Inflation

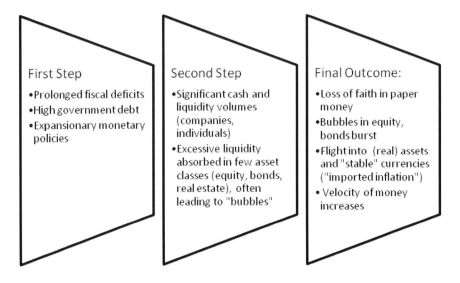

First Step
- Prolonged fiscal deficits
- High government debt
- Expansionary monetary policies

Second Step
- Significant cash and liquidity volumes (companies, individuals)
- Excessive liquidity absorbed in few asset classes (equity, bonds, real estate), often leading to "bubbles"

Final Outcome:
- Loss of faith in paper money
- Bubbles in equity, bonds burst
- Flight into (real) assets and "stable" currencies ("imported inflation")
- Velocity of money increases

Economies with long records of stability tend to benefit from their past achievements longer than a rational analysis would justify. There is a perception lag that prevents people from changing their view on an economic situation to reflect most recent developments and actual data. As a consequence, some countries engage in inappropriate behavior and policies for an extended period of time. In the case of inflation, a long record of stability may cover up policy mistakes and bad decisions for a prolonged time. Having a long record of stability may therefore delay the advent of LOFIS Inflation substantially. Reality will eventually prevail and reassessments of paper money systems may then lead to dramatic economic shifts and turbulence.

Germany during the late 1910s and early 1920s is a good example. There was a significant delay between Germany's irresponsible economic, fiscal, and monetary decisions and the actual arrival of hyperinflation. Even though Germany experienced elevated levels of inflation for an extended period of time, those inflation levels were relatively low given the excessive policies the government and central bank had implemented and the debt situation the country faced. Germany initially profited from its past record of fiscal and economic stability. It took several years until LOFIS Inflation finally picked up speed in Germany. This ended with a period of hyperinflation and eventually the total collapse of the German currency.

There is no doubt that central banks in the developed world pursue ultra-expansionary policies. Most of the money created has not yet flowed into the real economy. It has driven up prices of financial assets and real estate. These asset classes function as silos that prevent these funds from reaching the real economy. Market participants and individuals still have confidence in the stability of paper money. The enormous amounts of money held in cash or fixed income securities otherwise would have been moved to real assets and inflation-protected currencies.

As the money that is currently absorbed by bond, equity, or real estate markets, or held as cash, will then look for new protection from inflation, it will enter the real economy and push up inflation. Unfortunately, we cannot predict exactly when this will happen. It could be an isolated commodity price shock, or a comment from a famous investor or some other event that will trigger such a fundamental behavioral change.

Investors are caught in a dilemma. As long as the majority of people remain unconcerned regarding inflation risks, the party in bond or equity markets will continue. Leaving the party too early may lead to significant opportunity costs. Staying too long at the party, however, may expose investors to significant repricing risks and financial losses. This dilemma is what makes LOFIS Inflation management so challenging.

This dilemma, however, should not serve as an excuse for continuing uncritical cyclical behavior. It is not the task of sophisticated risk management to time the market, but to anticipate potential risk events and prepare for them. Trying to time the market creates unnecessary risks. It is inexcusable to get caught unprepared for risk events that appear on our radar screens. Do not spend too much time trying to predict when EMEG Inflation or LOFIS Inflation will arrive. Instead, make sure that whenever high inflation arrives, sufficient preparations are in place.

CHAPTER 7: FINANCIAL INSTITUTIONS AND HIGH INFLATION—A DISASTER WAITING TO HAPPEN?

During the last high inflation period in the developed world in the 1970s, financial institutions struggled tremendously to deal with the consequences of high inflation. Both banks and insurance companies were caught unprepared in 1973 when inflation rates surged unexpectedly. Within a period of about twenty-one months, U.S. banks lost almost half of their market value, while insurance companies' share prices declined by almost sixty percent.[51] In fact, the insurance sector was among the hardest hit during the inflation surge in 1973 and 1974.

In this chapter, there are two important points. First, history suggests that financial institutions struggle enormously to deal with rising inflation rates. In the absence of sophisticated preparation, rising inflation rates may severely damage the stability and profitability of many financial institutions. Second, today's situation makes rising inflation even more dangerous for financial and economic stability. Extreme interconnectivity among financial institutions, an enormous use of complex financial derivatives, and the sheer size of the financial industry and its assets relative to the real world economy, pose unprecedented risks to the stability of the financial industry and the financial system. It is important for financial institutions to devote significant resources to understanding the impact of high inflation on their business models and economics. Nonfinancial institutions are well advised to have a detailed plan available should the financial sector get disrupted by high inflation. Assuming the financial system will work well under the stress of high inflation is dangerous and naïve. High inflation and its derivative effects, such as rising and volatile interest rates or deteriorating credit quality, could cause a new crisis for the financial sector that would surpass the last financial crisis.

During the 1970s inflation cycle, shareholders in banks and insurance companies went on a rollercoaster ride as their investments became highly volatile. Both banks and insurance companies were hit hard by the first inflation shock in 1973. During the second inflation shock (1977–1982), banks and insurance companies were better prepared. Share price performance for banks and insurance companies was positive in nominal terms (+37 percent and +76 percent, respectively). Over the complete inflation cycle, however, both sectors failed to create real shareholder value as share price appreciation lagged inflation rates substantially.[52]

The biggest problem for financial institutions was caused by the initial surge of inflation in 1973. This first inflation shock took financial institutions by surprise. Management failed to understand that rising inflation and its derivative effects, such as rising interest rates, yield curve shifts, and general financial volatility, required sophisticated strategies that preempt market shifts and changing industry economics. Failing to implement those required risk management strategies left financial institutions dangerously exposed to severe risks.

Insurance companies suffered greatly as they were exposed to two severe risks. First, their investment portfolios, which administer clients' funds prior to claims payments, suffered severe losses as their investment strategies failed to anticipate inflation. Second, insurance companies' prior underwriting and pricing decisions failed to factor in future higher inflation rates.

Initial inflation shocks can be very severe for financial institutions, particularly if they are caught unprepared. A substantial amount of shareholder value can be destroyed permanently. High inflation today is a more dangerous challenge to financial institutions than at any time in the past.

NEW AND UNCHARTED WATERS: WHY A NEW FINANCIAL CRISIS IS IN THE MAKING

Managing financial institutions successfully through past inflation cycles was a demanding task. For today's managers, this task will be exponentially more demanding than during past inflation cycles. Fundamental changes in financial markets over the past decades present unique challenges to top management. Four developments significantly increase the vulnerability of financial institutions to inflation shocks:

- A gigantically large (and more complex) derivatives market
- A network of interconnectivity among domestic and international financial institutions due to mutual derivative transactions and other business interactions
- An unsustainable divergence between the volume of financial assets and the size of the real economy, which will make bailouts of troubled financial institutions more challenging
- A growing dependence on (artificially) low interest rates and certain yield curve shapes.

These four developments have created a situation that could lead to a new financial crisis bigger than the last one.

Chart 23 explains some of the issues and their proportions.

Chart 23: Understanding the dangerous proportions between the real world and the financial world[53]

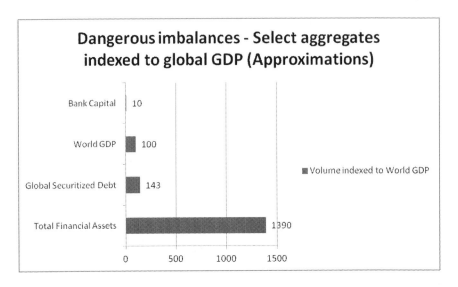

Chart 23 illustrates several problems that could turn into major issues if inflation rates rise. First, the size of the financial industry measured by the amount of financial assets on banks' balance sheets has grown over the past decades much faster than the real economy. As higher inflation leads to severe volatility in the value of these financial assets, the potential losses relative to the real economy are greater today than during the 1970s inflation cycle. It will be increasingly difficult for the real economy to recapitalize the financial system if something goes wrong. We know from past experience that initial inflation shocks can severely impact the asset classes to which financial institutions are exposed. As capital levels of many banks are relatively low in comparison to the nominal size of the assets they hold, there is only a small buffer of capital available to absorb valuation swings of these assets. The problem is that regulatory capital rules often fail to capture the real risks to which banks are exposed. As a consequence, it is quite possible that banks considered undercapitalized are actually overcapitalized in relation to their real risk exposure and that other banks that are considered appropriately capitalized are actually undercapitalized given their real risk exposure. Due to risk management complexity, it is hard for regulators to set required capital levels that sufficiently address the actual risk exposure of a financial institution.

The second issue that could lead to severe disruptions has to do with the size of the global derivatives market. Even without rising inflation, the derivatives market is a potential source of future instability. Warren Buffett is reported to have compared it to weapons of mass destruction.[54]

Derivatives are bets by two or more parties on the future value of one or several assets or benchmarks. The price of a derivative contract is derived from the value and volatility of the underlying asset. It is difficult to find reliable data on the total size of the derivatives markets. The Bank for International Settlements (BIS) reports the notional size of OTC traded derivatives to be above US$710 trillion in 2013,[55] almost ten times the global GDP.[56] The notional amount of all derivatives is likely to be significantly greater than the numbers reported by the BIS. The reason is that many derivatives (e.g., insurance derivatives, derivative structures built into other common financial and nonfinancial products) are not included in BIS statistics. Built-in derivatives structures are common in many products even though they are often not recognized as such. For example, any form of warranty on a consumer product is in a strict sense a form of derivative. It promises a payment conditional to a certain (risk) event. If this warranty promises a replacement regardless of age of the product, this warranty also includes an inflation derivative exposing the grantor of the warranty to inflation risks.

During the financial crisis of 2008, insurance companies found that products such as variable annuities often consisted of many complex built-in derivatives structures, exposing them to unanticipated risks and losses.

It is important to understand that derivatives expose the owner of such a contract to a wide range of risks. One of the most critical is counterparty risk, which refers to the ability of the counterparty to make good on potential obligations. In times of financial stress, some counterparties might struggle to honor their contractual responsibilities. In such cases, protection bought through derivatives may turn out to be worthless. Dangerous chain reactions might occur, impacting many interconnected financial institutions.

The key issue with derivatives in times of high inflation is that their value is usually linked to <u>nominal</u> aggregates. There is no adjustment for inflation. Therefore, high nominal price swings in the value of an asset will lead to even bigger price swings for the derivative linked to this asset. Most people are not aware of this issue, as high inflation has never occurred in an economy that had large derivatives markets.

Many experts seek to diffuse concerns about the risks of derivatives by pointing out that there is a difference between the notional amount of outstanding derivatives and their actual value. Additionally, these experts claim that netting procedures, which refer to the offsetting effect of two opposite contracts held by the same owner, reduce the overall notional amount of outstanding derivatives. While both points are valid during normal market conditions, the situation is fundamentally different in times of high inflation. In today's low inflation and low interest rates environment, the value of the BIS recognized derivatives is a fraction of their total notional amount. The advent of high inflation is likely to change this relationship significantly. As high inflation rates push up the nominal value of many underlying assets to levels unanticipated by the market, derivatives will magnify these nominal price movements. As a result, some derivative counterparties may have obligations that exceed significantly their initial expectations. This could create a major credit issue for the financial system. Netting procedures may not anticipate the ability of a counterparty to make good on its obligations.[57]

The derivatives markets may not withstand the challenges of high inflation without severe disruptions. For example, the global interest rate swap market may experience severe disruptions, if interest rate volatility is similar to that of the 1970s, as Chart 24 illustrates.

Chart 24: Interest rate volatility during the 1970s—could today's financial institutions absorb a similar volatility?[58]

Year	U.S. short-term interest rates (3 month treasury bills—secondary market)
June 1972	3.9 %
September 1974	8.1 %
December 1976	4.4 %
March 1980	15.2 %

The interest rate derivatives market is one of the biggest derivatives markets. Over the past decades, there has not been interest rate volatility comparable to that observed in the 1970s and early 1980s. Central banks helped create a low volatility interest rate environment that ensured falling rates for an extended period.

During the 1970s, the derivatives market was almost nonexistent. It did not have the potential to create major harm even though inflation rates moved up and down wildly, as did interest rates. Today the situation is completely different. Many banks and insurance companies actively use interest rate swaps as important risk management tools. They depend on a functioning orderly market for these instruments. As interest rates steadily decreased over the past thirty years, there was little stress on the derivatives market. This calm may soon be over if inflation rates force interest rates to reverse their course.

Most financial institutions claim immunity against the risk of rising interest rates, probably with the use of derivatives. This claim is hard to believe. Someone must hold the other side of the interest rate trade and it may be held by financial institutions. This position will become quite painful once interest rates start to normalize. Some financial institutions may not be as fully hedged as they claim. There may be numerous financial institutions that take the other side of the interest rate positions (i.e., bet on continued low interest rates and sell large-scale protection against rising interest rates to other financial institutions or corporate entities). Those financial institutions may suffer massive losses.

Given the immense connectivity among global financial institutions, financial losses and instability may spread quickly. Even rumors about a possible default due to an assumed derivative exposure could create massive problems for the sector. In contrast to the last financial crisis, it will not be possible to calm the markets with ultra-loose monetary policies. The reason is simple: Loose monetary policies would fuel additional inflation leading to a further destabilization of the sector. Central banks may be forced to adopt more restrictive policies, even in light of financial and economic instability.

Severe financial crises often occur when ultra-loose monetary policies have been reversed and interest rates are forced to move upwards. They are the result of excessively loose monetary policies, but they tend to erupt when expansive monetary policies are being replaced by more restrictive ones. Therefore, we will face an acid test of the financial system and its markets once inflation rates trend upwards and interest rates follow this trend.

INFLATION RISKS FOR BANKS: PREPARE FOR A BIG STORM

All banks have one issue in common. The basic structure of the core banking business is inherently unstable and fragile. In essence, banks receive (mostly short-term) money from depositors and savers and lend it (typically at longer terms) to individuals and businesses. This simple business model comes with a long list of risks. Interest rates might change and affect lending and deposit activities in an adverse manner. A recession may lead to credit defaults. Depositors may withdraw their money faster than anticipated, leaving banks to struggle for liquidity and funding as their lending agreements tend to be long term and cannot be reversed on short notice.

Today's banks engage in a multitude of businesses that involve lending, trading, asset management, investment banking, risk management, and other activities. Therefore, banks are exposed to large and complex pools of risks. The last financial crisis gave us a taste of what can go wrong when the banking environment is rocked by stress and volatility. Only extreme ultra-loose monetary policies and decisive government action avoided a massive meltdown of the financial sector.

As a result of these policies, banks profited from falling interest rates and steepening yield curves. Investing excess liquidity in government bonds or other low-risk fixed income securities provides banks with such an attractive margin that they may not be motivated to expand consumer and business lending. Using deposits or cheap central bank funds to invest in fixed income securities may be sufficient for banks to generate good returns. This simple strategy helped banks after the financial crisis to rebuild their capital levels.[59]

The problem is that such a strategy is not sustainable as it depends on conditions that are exceptional and may not continue in the future. Getting banks to become addicted to these abnormal conditions is like spreading the seeds for the next financial crisis. A superficial look at banks may not reflect this enormous danger. The reality, however, is that banks not only neglect their original business systems (e.g., customer lending), but also expose themselves to substantial interest rate and funding risks. Once interest rates turn, such a strategy can backfire immensely.

The return of higher inflation will enforce such a reversal of interest rates. This may expose a bank to a multitude of issues as almost all business activities of a bank will face inflation headwinds. In general, banks' business models are not compatible with the challenges presented by rising inflation rates (see Chart 25). This is even more the case with modern world banking operations, their excessive use of derivatives, and their exposure to complexity and connectivity risks.

Chart 25: Banks' vulnerability to rising inflation (selection of issues)

Area	Description of Inflation issues and risks
Funding	<ul><li>Funding for existing and new lending business will become more expensive and less available</li><li>Inter-banking market and other funding markets may become unreliable as funding sources</li></ul>
Lending	<ul><li>Recessionary developments will drive up credit defaults</li><li>Mispricing of risk as banks underestimate future inflation and interest rates</li></ul>
Trading	<ul><li>Fixed income securities held by banks may result in huge trading losses (e.g., government bonds)</li></ul>
Business	<ul><li>Rising costs of employees and infrastructure (when business margins decrease at the same time)</li><li>New business volume may decrease significantly (leaving the bank stuck with an expensive infrastructure)</li></ul>
Capital	<ul><li>Capital shortage likely due to credit and trading losses</li><li>Higher nominal value of loans (reflecting inflation) require increased capital base</li><li>Decreasing credit ratings of counterparties raises capital needs</li></ul>
Systemic risk	<ul><li>Connectivity among banks may lead to chain reactions through the sector if a bank gets into trouble</li><li>Even sound banks may become weakened by rumors or general market nervousness</li></ul>
Derivative and structured products exposure	<ul><li>Extreme volatility in financial markets may result in losses of derivatives and structured products</li></ul>
Interest rate risk	<ul><li>Rising interest rates and shifting yield curve may make core businesses unprofitable</li></ul>

As the selection of issues in Chart 25 illustrates, banks are exposed to a large number of inflation challenges. Many of these can be mitigated or at least partly addressed if the bank's management anticipates them and develops and implements appropriate strategies.

Sophisticated banks may have done so already. Because of the immense connectivity among all domestic and international banks, it is important that all banks prepare. If, for example, second-tier banks remain dangerously exposed to inflation risks, their problems may easily spread. During the last financial crisis, even the most sophisticated banks were affected by exposure to weaker peers (e.g., via trading credit lines or derivatives transactions). This has not been significantly addressed by regulators. Banks remain heavily interconnected. Therefore, the next crisis will not hinge on being too big to fail, but being too connected to fail.

INFLATION RISKS FOR INSURANCE COMPANIES: BE AWARE OF INITIAL INFLATION SHOCK

The complexity of insurance companies makes it difficult to assess their vulnerability to inflation. Superficial analysis tends to underestimate their exposure to inflation risks. Evidence suggests that insurance companies are highly exposed to risks caused by an extended period of low inflation followed by an abrupt and severe inflation shock.

Property and casualty insurance (P+C) is distinguished from life insurance. Both businesses are highly exposed to inflation risk, but quite differently. The focus of this book is on P+C insurance, as life insurance companies require analysis of geographic differences in product design, regulations, and accounting procedures.

Insurance companies consist of two main business activities: insurance and investments. The insurance function provides customers with coverage against predefined risks (e.g., fire, flood, theft). The investment

138

business invests the policyholders' funds until claims are made. This period in which claims funds are available for investments can last several years. Therefore, successful investment management plays a crucial role in the profitability of an insurance company.

Insurers face the highest inflation risks at the beginning of a new inflation cycle. They tend to get hit with major losses when inflation rates initially surge after a prolonged period of low or moderate inflation. A sudden rise of inflation rates can create substantial damage to the stability of an insurance company because rising inflation affects both business activities (i.e., insurance and investments).

The core insurance activity suffers from claims payments higher than estimated due to inflation effects. The key problem is that insurance companies estimate future inflation rates as they make future claims more expensive. If inflation rates abruptly and unexpectedly rise, future claims payments will rise. Insurance companies may not have anticipated this sudden rise in inflation rates and will experience higher claims payments than estimated. The longer the coverage period of an insurance policy, the bigger the insurance company's inflation problem. Businesses that have coverage periods of five or more years (so-called long-tail businesses) are typically the bigger inflation traps for insurance companies.

The investment activities of an insurance company are also negatively impacted by a rise of inflation. Almost all asset classes in which insurers invest are likely to experience losses due to rising inflation rates. This is particularly the case for long-term bonds and stocks, as witnessed in 1973–1974. Recessions and higher interest rates can also negatively impact commercial real estate investments.

Losses from core insurance business and investment activities could threaten the survival of an insurance company. In 1974, many insurance companies in the U.S. struggled, facing unexpected high claims payments and significant losses in their investments. There are other areas of an insurance company's business model that are exposed to inflation risks. Chart 26 summarizes a selection of these risk issues.

Chart 26: Selection of inflation risks for insurance companies

Area	Insurance risks when inflation rates start to rise sharply
Investments	• Major losses of equity investments • Major losses of fixed income investments, particularly long maturity investments • Regulatory rules and adverse business conditions may enforce liquidation of investments at distressed levels leading to material losses
Underwriting of insurance risk	• Mispricing of policies leads to substantial losses, particularly for multiyear policies (i.e., long-tail business) • Inadequate reserves to meet current/future claims • Administrative costs of administering claims and policies substantially higher than anticipated
Financial management	• Losses from different sources lead to inadequate capital position and require capital increases at a difficult time • Administrative expenses (e.g., salaries) increase faster than expected putting pressure on profit margins
Government and regulatory rules	• Governments may enforce price control measures on policies • Regulatory rules may incentivize or even require the implementation of actions that increase inflation risks (e.g., requirement to invest in fixed income investments)
Risk management	• Credit risk of reinsurers can become a serious issue • Risk management models cannot handle inflation specific challenges • Complexity of many products (e.g., built-in guarantees) may amplify problems
New business volume and product design	• Customers cancel nonessential policies due to financial pressure • New businesses volume is substantially lower than planned as customers are forced to avoid nonessential spending • Inflation adjustments built into past products sold

Insurance companies have to deal with severe cost pressure as underwriting and claims management are labor intensive. If new business volume decreases, as it typically does during times of economic stress, insurance companies have to deal with an expensive business infrastructure that often cannot be downscaled fast enough. In fact, costs for business infrastructure tend to behave like fixed costs increasing an insurer's vulnerability to inflation.

There are additional issues to worry about. Reinsurers who take on peak risks of primary insurance companies may be severely weakened by the impact of high inflation, particularly if they cannot diversify their inflation risk. As substantial amounts of risks are typically shifted from primary insurers to reinsurers, this is a serious issue. If a reinsurer defaults or its credit rating is severely weakened, a primary insurer needs to restructure its reinsurance program at a very unfortunate time. This is both risky and expensive.

The most critical time for an insurance company is in the transition from a prolonged period of low inflation to a period of fast rising inflation. This inflation shock presents an extremely challenging task to the insurance sector.

Once higher inflation rates are established, insurance companies can actually profit from them. This sounds counterintuitive and is a complex issue. While the initial inflation shock may be quite painful, prolonged periods of high inflation may present interesting opportunities to insurers. A close look at the 1970s inflation cycle reveals insights. While the market value of listed insurance companies fell almost sixty percent during the first inflation shock (1973–1974), it increased by about seventy-six percent during the second inflation shock (1977–1982).[60]

To a certain extent, this relatively strong performance was due to learning effects. Insurance companies learned to turn inflation into an opportunity (or at least less of a threat). Top management avoided many of the mistakes committed during the initial inflation shock of 1973–

1974. Top management captured some positive developments that come with longer periods of high inflation. For example, the price sensitivity of customers tends to decrease. During periods of low inflation, customers react immediately to any form of price increases and are willing to switch insurers. It is then difficult to enforce any price increases. After several years of high inflation, customers get used to rising prices and insurers may then more easily raise their policy prices, sometimes even beyond the requirements of inflation. This generates additional profit for an insurance company. Insurers may also profit from higher interest rates as they can invest policyholder funds at higher yields. Insurers may also change product design and policy features to decrease their exposure to inflation. All these issues may help an insurance company be more profitable at later stages of an inflation cycle.

To protect against inflation risks, insurance companies have to implement timely effective risk management strategies. This might be difficult as the sector tends to behave cyclically, which may lead insurance companies to increase their inflation risks before inflation rates rise. This fatal development happened in the U.S. in 1973–1974.

Life insurance companies [61] face three specific challenges. First, customers might cancel their contracts and demand early repayments, which can result in substantial prepayment risks. Then, the insurance company might be forced to liquidate parts of its investment portfolios (typically long-term bonds) at a time when market prices for fixed income securities are lowest. Second, many legacy products (in some cases, even newer products) have a complex product structure that offers numerous options, features, and guarantees to the customer. Many of those features may expose a life insurance company to enormous inflation and interest rate risks. Third, life insurance companies may be short of sufficient capital to support their business due to investment losses and other adverse developments caused by high inflation. They may be forced to strengthen their capital base at a time when equity (or other) markets will not commit additional capital in general, certainly not to the complex life insurance sector.

What makes it even more difficult for them is the complexity of their underlying business relative to the P+C business. They must devote significant resources to gain a detailed understanding of how inflation impacts their company and the industry, including second and third order effects and connectivity issues. They must detect all inflation traps or they may be in for a nasty surprise once inflation rates start to rise.

A weakened insurance sector is a big liability to the overall economy. The insurance sector is enormously important for economic prosperity. Insurance companies are important providers of capital to the economy (due to their huge investment portfolios). They are also facilitators for all kinds of investment transactions. House purchases financed by mortgages may fall through if the buyer is not able to obtain affordable homeowner insurance. Small- and medium-sized businesses are likely to postpone business investments or scale back business activities if they cannot insure against typical business risks. In such situations, they may be required to maintain a higher capital buffer for unforeseen risks. Insurance companies provide an important and affordable risk management function for the consumer. Insuring consumers against unpredictable perils and risks is an important function that can lead to higher consumer spending rates. A consumer who has transferred or hedged the most important risks may not feel the need to save huge amounts of money for unpredictable risk events. People in emerging markets tend to have higher savings rates partly due to the absence of common insurance products (e.g., home and health insurance). Therefore, it is of utmost importance that insurance companies not experience the difficulties of the inflation shock of 1973–1974.

CHAPTER 8: LESSONS TO BE LEARNED FROM HISTORY

Over the course of history, we have seen many periods of high inflation. While there are specific circumstances in each period that we need to understand, we can nevertheless detect some general recurring patterns. History offers a rich and priceless collection of very important lessons when it comes to dealing with high inflation. You find many examples of smart companies or individuals turning inflation into a great opportunity and making a fortune. You also find others who are caught unprepared in dealing with a sudden rise of inflation and are brutally punished by the consequences of their inaction. Even more irritating are the companies and individuals repeating exactly the same mistakes committed by others during past inflation cycles. Many of us miss the enormous opportunity of learning from historic precedents.

Therefore, studying past inflation cycles is an essential activity to prepare you for this dangerous risk event. A few lessons from history should encourage you to widen your experience base for handling inflation. Handling high inflation successfully requires two things: an understanding of past inflation cycles (i.e., experience) and the application of critical, logical thinking. Experience can be derived from studying past inflation cycles yourself or learning from experts who possess this knowledge. It helps you to recognize patterns, anticipate good and bad moves by regulators, politicians, markets, and competitors, and it enables you to react faster and be better informed than your competitors.

Critical thinking is necessary to deal with variations from history that occur in any inflation cycle. While many patterns tend to repeat themselves, human behavior and specific circumstances may change. You need critical and logical thinking to anticipate these variations and to adjust your actions and strategies to the respective situations.

LESSON 1: DO NOT WAIT FOR EXPERTS TO RING THE ALARM BELL FOR HIGH INFLATION

The longer a country has been exposed to low inflation, the higher the chances that its people are not prepared to deal with rising inflation rates. They simply do not have inflation risks on their radar screen. This is true not only for many companies and individuals, but also for acknowledged experts. Most experts and opinion leaders in politics, business, and finance simply fail to anticipate inflation risks.

Social processes such as groupthink and the urge to reduce cognitive dissonance are probably the reason why so many of us fail to anticipate structural changes in our environment, be it inflation or other risks. You may read articles published prior to the outbreak of the last financial crisis in 2007. You will be shocked by the number of experts who not only failed to anticipate the looming crisis, but also predicted benign and prosperous times to continue. Study any major risk event in history and you will find similar results. Be it the stock market crash of October 1987 or the Great Depression that started in 1929, the majority of experts failed to anticipate major risk events.

One of the biggest mistakes is to delay your risk management preparations until the experts' consensus on inflation risks changes. By then, it may be too late to avoid significant losses. Many inflation mitigation strategies will be unavailable or excessively expensive once inflation risks are predicted. As a consequence, you might get stuck with significant risk exposures in your business, financing, and investment activities.

To mitigate your inflation exposure, you must implement strategies early. Secure a first mover advantage before inflation risks materialize. Warren Buffett executed such a strategy perfectly during the 1970s inflation period. As a result, he liquidated investments before they fell, raised liquidity levels, and raised new debt before it became excessively expensive. It took time until Buffett's strategy paid off, but he was prepared when most others were not. He ignored the consensus of experts that did not foresee any inflation or other risks prior to one of the most challenging economic and financial periods in modern U.S. history.[62]

LESSON 2: INFLATION CYCLES DO NOT FOLLOW A STRAIGHT LINE

Inflation cycles do not run in a mechanistic or predictable order as they do not obey laws of physics. They are the result of human decision making and actions, which can be both rational and irrational. As the majority is likely to fail to anticipate rising inflation rates, do not expect enlightenment once inflation has arrived and misjudgment is evident. Companies and people will then act irrationally and unpredictably, dealing emotionally with a situation that (at least initially) exceeds their comprehension and management capabilities. A period characterized by high volatility and irrational market outcomes results. In those situations, people often abandon their own capacity for critical thinking and seek strength and comfort in groups. They are likely to follow new leaders regardless of how qualified they are.

If one can decode those social and psychological phenomena and escape the perils of groupthink and unqualified leaders, exceptional opportunities may arise. For example, during 1973–1974, stocks fell by about fifty percent and price earnings ratios fell to exceptionally low levels. The same experts who advised buying stocks when they were expensive, then advised not to buy stocks when they were extremely cheap.

During times of high inflation, behavior becomes irrational. The people who see conditions overly positively prior to a major risk event will see things overly negatively once the risk event has materialized. In addition, being hit by a major risk event unprepared may lead to irrational and volatile decision making. These two behavioral patterns will lead to a rollercoaster ride during an inflation cycle. It will be anything but a straight line.

There is no immediate cause and effect during times of high inflation. The delay between cause and effect can take several years due to our inability to deal with the new situation in a rational, unemotional way.

 As history shows us, at the beginning of World War I, the German government pursued fiscal and monetary strategies that were not sustainable. Under normal circumstances those strategies should have led to a fast debasement of the German currency and a swift upward movement of inflation rates. Surprisingly, it was not until 1922 that the vast majority of people realized that the German paper mark had no future. Only then, exchange rates and inflation rates spiraled out of control, as Chart 27 shows.[63]

Chart 27: Exchange rate U.S. dollar/German mark 1914–1923 reflecting explosion of inflation[64]

Year	One U.S. dollar gets you ... German marks
1914	4.5
1915	5.16
1916	5.72
1917	5.67
1918	8.28
1919	46.77
1920	73
1921	191.93
1922	7589.27
1923	4,200,000,000,000

Note: All figures for month of December

Even more astonishing was the euphoria about German economic policies and conditions between 1920 and 1921 that led to a temporary strengthening of the German mark by about forty percent.[65] There were no hard facts that suggested German policies were going to lead to a happy ending (see also Chart 17). For the most part, foreign investors poured money into Germany, hoping for a normalization of inflation rates and a strengthening of the German economy. This occurred only two years before the German currency became practically worthless, a dramatic misjudgment by domestic and international investors and experts.

LESSON 3: ONCE A TRIGGER POINT HAS BEEN REACHED, INFLATION MAY ACCELERATE DRAMATICALLY

The delay before inflation's arrival may cause a dangerous complacency and unjustified euphoria among market participants and businesses. The consensus will be that the perceived risks of these ultra-loose policies were overstated by the critics and that these policies by central banks were necessary. Experts who take the opposite view will be singled out and heavily criticized.

Such thinking is dangerous because people will delay weatherproofing companies and household finances against inflation risks. When real inflation signs emerge, it will be too late for affordable protection.

Once an inflation trigger point arrives, the rise of inflation can accelerate dramatically. Employees and unions will demand higher wages and better benefits packages, companies will raise prices for their goods and expand inventory levels, and investors will dump many of the monetary assets they previously preferred to protect their wealth with real assets.

Inflation rates shoot up quickly, worsening the complete business environment. Chart 28 illustrates the dramatic scale and speed of inflation shocks in the U.S. and the U.K. during the 1970s.

Chart 28: Sharp increases of inflation rates after reaching a trigger point[66]

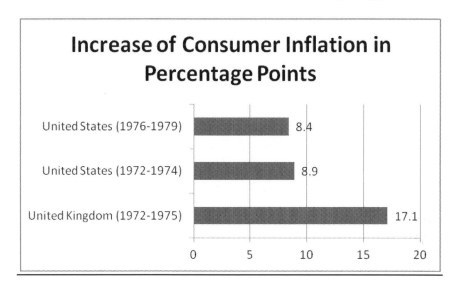

Keep in mind that rising inflation will impact the complete value chain of business. Procurement, production, human resources, and financial management—no activity can escape inflation risks. Companies unprepared to deal with these challenges in time will be exposed to a severe deterioration of business conditions that endangers profitability and survival. During the inflation periods mentioned in Chart 28, a large number of different sized companies did not survive on their own. They were bailed out, taken over, or dissolved.

LESSON 4: DO NOT EXPECT THAT DECISION MAKERS HAVE LEARNED FROM HISTORY—EXPECT REPETITION OF THE SAME MISTAKES FROM THE PAST

It is naive to assume that decision makers will make rational decisions based on the lessons learned from previous inflation cycles. Decision makers in governments, central banks, and businesses are likely to repeat the same mistakes of the past 2000 years of inflation history. This is due to three different forces: an overly short-term focus on policy actions, a lack of historic experience, and a tendency to give in to populist demands. As a result, policymakers will prefer short-term relief over long-term cures and stability.

In many inflation cycles, governments resort to excessive and ineffective measures such as price controls. Typically, decision makers focus on products and issues that have a high priority for their constituents and the general population. These include rent, consumer goods, food products, and fees (e.g., train and bus tickets). Government-mandated price controls have a poor track record in history. Roman Emperor Diocletian had to realize that price controls would not solve inflation problems during the third century. His measure of using draconian price controls actually worsened the situation.

Price controls tend to make matters worse as companies exposed to higher input costs either withhold or reduce production, or sell the majority of their products to foreign countries, increasing the domestic shortage. In such situations, governments follow up by mistakenly introducing foreign exchange controls, banning exports, or implementing complex business control and permit systems.

As an economy is a very complex system, such one-sided government intervention often leads to a significant deterioration of the economic situation and social stability. Second order effects and connectivity issues lead to outcomes that are not in the interest of the stability of the country.

Former Federal Reserve Chairman Greenspan describes in detail how government officials unsuccessfully introduced price controls during the 1970s inflation cycle in the U.S.[67] They should have known better, but they introduced such measures anyway and failed terribly.

Familiarize yourself with the common mistakes committed by governments, central banks, companies, and market participants. It is fair to assume that many of these mistakes will be repeated.

LESSON 5: FORGET WHAT YOU LEARNED IN BUSINESS SCHOOL—HIGH INFLATION CHANGES EVERYTHING

High inflation puts management into a different environment in which traditional rules and tactics no longer work. For example, strategies for financial management, inventory management, procurement, and cash management must be adjusted (often reversed) to cope successfully with high inflation. Many conventional management paradigms that are generally accepted in developed countries may be harmful in a high inflation environment. We learned in business school about the need to keep inventories low (to reduce the need for excess capital in a business). The paradigm of "just-in-time" inventory management is commonly accepted in production facilities (i.e., reduction of inventory leads to lower storage and financing costs).

During times of inflation, you likely do the exact opposite. You raise your inventory levels as they appreciate with inflation. In fact, you may conduct your cash management through inventory management. It is not uncommon for companies in high inflation countries like Venezuela to transfer excess cash into inventories. This is done for two reasons. First, the after-tax return on inventory is most likely higher than that on short-term bank deposits. Second, high inflation often disrupts delivery channels. You cannot rely on the timely availability of certain materials or products for your inventory. In periods of high inflation, delivery contracts typically are broken if agreed-upon penalties are not high enough. Suppliers often find themselves in a situation in which demand from new customers willing to pay excessively high prices emerges at very short notice. In such instances, suppliers may prefer to fill the order of the highest bidder and delay a previous order, even if this results in a penalty.

Numerous additional examples show that business school lessons might be obsolete during times of high inflation. For example, high debt leverage can prove extremely beneficial if structured appropriately (i.e., long-term, fixed coupon, no strings attached). Cash may be better invested in real (tradable) assets even if these assets are not related to a company's business. Some of the wild diversification efforts seen during the 1970s might have been a desperate attempt by top management to save their cash and capital from the eroding effects of high inflation or to leverage debt, as inflation enables the repayment of the principal with devalued currencies. In contrast to common management paradigms, investing cash (or debt) in unrelated businesses may make sense as long as these businesses are stable and provide protection against inflation.

LESSON 6: THINK OF INFLATION HOLISTICALLY AND UNDERSTAND HOW IT IMPACTS SYSTEMS INSTEAD OF FOCUSING ON ISOLATED ACTIVITIES

High inflation dramatically changes how economic, financial, and social systems operate and behave. The more complex a system, the more dramatic its reactions to rising inflation.

The developed world has a substantial level of complexity and interdependency in its economic, financial, and social systems. It is important to understand how these systems are likely to react in a high inflation environment. Top managers must understand how high inflation impacts the systems to which their businesses and all other relevant systems are exposed. This requires a holistic management approach. Missing some risk factors or connectivity issues or ignoring second and third order effects may have grave consequences for a business. Managers must ask the following questions: What then? What if? What does it mean to me? Relentlessly asking these questions may help detect issues that need to be addressed to weatherproof a business against inflation risks.

As inflation evolves, it will bring new challenges and opportunities. Managers need a dynamic approach to inflation management to adapt to constantly changing challenges.

LESSON 7: ADD UNDERSTANDING INFLATION TO YOUR LIST OF CRITICAL SKILLS

Managers often get away with a trial and error approach or by muddling through complex situations. While these experimental or learn-as-you-go approaches work fine in many situations, they can lead to serious issues during times of high inflation. High inflation does not forgive mistakes and management mistakes will be punished brutally.

It is crucial to learn the workings of inflation before it emerges. You need to understand in detail how high inflation may impact the economy, your industry, and your company. You need to understand the potential exposure of your company to inflation risks *before* inflation becomes a problem. You need to understand the potential strategic responses available to you and to craft implementation strategies at an appropriate time. Certain financial and nonfinancial hedging strategies may disappear once inflation rates have crossed a certain level. Then the majority of people will be unwilling to sell inflation hedges to you.

Not having in-house inflation management experience is therefore a serious omission. Hire or contract experienced consultants to help you build the skill set in-house. You must ensure that you can access at any time those inflation management skills prior to the rise of inflation rates.

LESSON 8: INFLATION MAY PRESENT AN ATTRACTIVE OPPORTUNITY IF YOU UNDERSTAND IT WELL

When you approach inflation, you must look at it from two perspectives. First, you must understand the perils, risks, and challenges that come with it. You must identify the threats that it poses to your business. This is the most important task. Most people will fail at this. History suggests that periods of inflation produce very few winners and large numbers of losers.

Those who have familiarized themselves with the mechanics and workings of inflation may not want to stop there. They will seek to turn inflation into an opportunity. This might actually be easier than you think, particularly if your competitors fail to take appropriate action regarding inflation risks.

During normal economic times, it may be difficult for a company to challenge or disrupt the competitive landscape or market structure in an industry. Industrial leaders typically possess strong competitive advantages based on products, history, reputation, or locks on customer franchises or market segments. Without the presence of a disruptive risk event, it may be difficult for a company to attack the market leaders in an industry. Often, these disruptive events are related to innovations, technological progress, or abrupt change in the risk management landscape. Inflation can be such a disruptive event that provides many companies with the only chance to successfully challenge established market structures and leapfrog to a much improved competitive position. In fact, high inflation can be seen by sophisticated players as an attractive opportunity for a competitive repositioning. For example, inflation was one of the main events that enabled Hugo Stinnes to leapfrog from a business newcomer to one of the most influential and richest industrialists in Germany during the early 1920s. Inflation may also have enabled Berkshire Hathaway to build a sizeable and strong position in the U.S. insurance business during the 1970s inflation cycle.[68]

Business history is full of enlightening examples of companies shaking up established industry structures, investors obtaining great fortunes, and ordinary individuals taking advantage of market disruptions caused by inflation.

There is an inherent attractiveness in most significant risk events. The biggest risk events often disguise the biggest opportunities. Sophisticated players, those who understand the new rules of the game and know how to use them to their advantage, can turn inflation from a risk into an opportunity. Many people overlook this and limit themselves to purely defensive steps when dealing with inflation. They indeed protect themselves against inflation risks, but they miss a chance to jump ahead and achieve significant competitive advantages.

PART III: WHAT YOU CAN DO—DEVELOPING STRATEGIES TO DEAL WITH HIGH INFLATION

CHAPTER 9: THE TOOL—THE FOUR PHASES INFLATION MANAGEMENT MODEL (FPIM MODEL)[69]

A big mistake people make is to believe that inflation is a one-dimensional, static problem. They believe that a single static strategy will protect against inflation risks, similar to a single immunization shot protecting against the ever-changing flu virus. Such static thinking is dangerous and may lead to severe losses during an inflation cycle.

In my experience, it has been helpful to think about high inflation as a cycle or sequence of different phases. Each phase has its own unique set of challenges and opportunities and therefore needs its own tailor-made strategy. When the inflation cycle moves from one phase to another, your strategy must anticipate this move. Otherwise, you may not be able to deal with the new challenges and opportunities that arise.

During any phase of the inflation cycle, you may be severely punished if you fail to anticipate the necessary strategic requirements. This result occurs regardless of whether you did an excellent job of anticipating previous phases of an inflation cycle. As mentioned earlier, inflation is not forgiving; at any stage of an inflation cycle, your company may fail if you do not anticipate the challenges and risks in your environment. An inflation cycle will not give you time to rest. You and your company will be constantly challenged.

Chart 29 shows the phases of a complete inflation cycle. At first glance, you may think that this concept is too simple for an advanced company or advanced investor. However, you must understand that any change of inflation rates can have brutal consequences if you are not properly prepared. In fact, both rising and falling inflation rates can be equally damaging for unprepared companies.

A successful strategy, therefore, adjusts all relevant activities of a company's value chain to the respective issues posed by each phase of an inflation cycle. This includes financing, accounting, inventory management, procurement, marketing, and production. Each activity of a company's value chain can be subject to severe inflation traps that management must understand and address. Chart 29 depicts an inflation cycle as a five phase system including a phase of no inflation (phase zero). Later in this book, when we talk about developing strategies to cope with inflation, we will drop phase zero and focus exclusively on the four remaining phases. For completeness, however, Chart 29 shows the five phases that modern economies undergo over the course of time. It is important to remind ourselves that even the phase of no significant inflation is a normal and recurring period in the overall cycle of rising and falling inflation rates.

Chart 29: The five generic phases of an inflation cycle

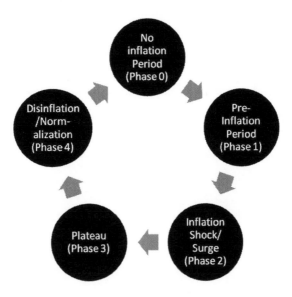

Any inflation cycle starts with phase 0, the period of no visible inflation issues. At that point, few people have inflation risks on their radar screen. Many politicians, central bankers, and managers tend to believe that this phase is infinite and that inflation issues are a thing of the past. This misperception is one of the reasons why inflation will eventually return. Authorities underestimate inflation risks and engage in strategies that will eventually awaken inflation in the future. In paper money systems inflation is never defeated for good. Instead, it is only dormant and will reappear much faster and more viciously than most people can imagine.

The longer an economy or country has been pampered with low inflation rates, the more likely it is that high inflation will eventually (re)appear. For example, the long period of low inflation after World War II might have seduced central bankers in the U.S. (and other countries) to overuse monetary instruments in an attempt to smooth out business cycles and avoid (sometimes healthy) recessions. Practice great caution if pro-inflationary policies are used excessively by central bankers and politicians, particularly after a prolonged period of low inflation rates.

Once a new inflation cycle starts, businesses will not be able to relax for long. Management will be constantly busy and challenged to prepare for the respective phases of an inflation cycle. This includes the period of rising inflation rates (phase 2), the period when inflation rates plateau (phase 3), and eventually the period of falling inflation rates (phase 4). Each phase demands its own strategic responses to protect a company from a rapidly changing business environment. At any phase of an inflation cycle, a company may suffer seriously if it misses crucial turning points in an inflation cycle. The key factor of success is to anticipate these turning points and to implement proper strategic responses at the right time.

A classic example of the challenges of inflation management is the impressive rise and subsequent steep fall of the Stinnes empire during the 1920s hyperinflation cycle in Germany. Hugo Stinnes was one of the most successful German industrialists and entrepreneurs during the 1910s and 1920s. He had an exceptional economic mind and a superb understanding of the mechanics of inflation. Stinnes mastered the first phases of the German hyperinflation cycle extremely well (phases 1–3).

He built an industrial empire by basically leveraging debt to acquire a large number of companies and industrial stakes. He repaid his debt later with hugely depreciated money. He knew that using debt was a good inflation hedge, and he was often referred to as the "king of inflation."

Stinnes wisely anticipated the end of the German hyperinflation period and shortly before his death instructed his family to radically reverse his current strategy. He knew that accumulating debt was now a dangerous strategy no longer to be reduced by high inflation. After his death in 1924, his successors ignored his warnings and continued the strategy of debt-based expansion. Soon the Stinnes empire was caught unprepared to deal with the new situation of low economic growth, a new but stable currency, and low inflation. Creditor banks took control and broke up the Stinnes empire.[70]

Many companies and individuals commit similar mistakes when dealing with an inflation cycle. Anyone unprepared to deal with the respective risks and opportunities of each phase of an inflation cycle is likely to be caught unprepared at some time. To avoid this dangerous risk, I have developed a tool that helps keep focus on the crucial four phases of an inflation cycle. This simple tool may be adapted to one's needs and preferences. In some cases, it may make sense to divide one phase into two or more sub-phases to enable a more fine-tuned and surgical response to the challenges of an inflation cycle. For the purpose of this book, let us stick to the four core phases and call the tool the "Four Phases Inflation Management model," or FPIM model (see Chart 30).

Pre-Inflation Period (Phase 1)	Inflation Shock/Surge (Phase 2)	Plateau (Phase 3)	Disinflation/ Normalization (Phase 4)
• Clear signs that inflation threat is rising • However, most decision makers ignore or dispute inflation threat • Last chance to weatherproof companies for inflation	• Rapid increase of inflation rates beyond market expectation • Recession likely to happen • Increased volatility of financial markets (interest rates, FX, stocks)	• Inflation rates have peaked, but remain at high levels • Companies must start to reverse all inflation strategies or risk serious damage when inflation decreases	• Normally as a result of central bank action, inflation rates decrease (sharply) • Interest rates fall sharply • Many inflation strategies that worked well in phase 1 may prove fatal during this phase if not revised

163

The tool starts in phase 1 of an inflation cycle when authorities implement decisions that will later lead to an acceleration of inflation. Preceding phase 1 is often a long period of low and stable inflation and therefore many people miss detecting these changes in the business environment that will later expose them to significant inflation risks. As I mentioned before, it is important in today's world of fiat paper money systems to view inflation as a recurrent problem, not a singular occurrence of the past. Economies based on fiat money systems should view periods of high inflation as normal occurrences and not as exceptions.

As it may be sometimes difficult for managers to detect early warning signs for an economy moving from phase 0 to phase 1, Chart 30 presents a selection of potential warning signs. It is important to note that the warning signs for EMEG Inflation may be quite different than those for LOFIS Inflation.

Chart 31: Typical phase 1 developments

Typical developments in phase1	Possibly leading to …	
	EMEG Inflation	LOFIS Inflation
Excessively loose monetary policies	+	++
A central bank that is hyperactive and deeply involved in the economy	+	++
Artificially low interest rates (due to central bank policies)	+	++
Prolonged period of government fiscal deficits	+	++
High absolute and relative levels of government debt	+	++
High levels of (unused) cash in the economy		++
Inflation is not an immediate concern of market participants		+
High debt leverage in the economy (companies, households)		++
Emerging asset bubbles (due to excess liquidity and low interest rates)	+	+
Rising skepticism and doubts regarding politicians and central bankers		++
Limited slack in the economy (unused capacity utilization)	++	
Bargaining power for higher wages is increasing	++	
Signs that demand for commodities, products, and services is starting to outpace supply	++	

It is not uncommon to mistake phase 1 for a time of prosperity and progress. Some developments might actually suggest that the economic situation is improving and risks are diminishing. For example, during the initial phase 1 of the 1970s inflation cycle, U.S. stock markets reached an all-time high (December 1972) and the economy was perceived as being strong. The overall sentiment was characterized by confidence and euphoria about the future. Most companies and individuals failed to see the economic reality in 1972. In 1973, phase 2 of the new inflation cycle started, and it exposed many companies and people to the harsh reality of an inflation-induced recession. Stock markets subsequently lost about half of their value over a twenty-one month period. Needless to say, most companies and people were caught totally unprepared and had to struggle to overcome the enormous challenges presented by a sudden rise of inflation rates.

During phase 2 of an inflation cycle, managers and individuals learn the hard way that the economy and financial markets are more fragile and weak than they previously thought. Unexpectedly, they find themselves in a severe economic storm. That is why we see so many erratic and seemingly irrational decisions during phase 2 of an inflation cycle. Many managers then realize that keeping capital and cash levels low is wrong. They also realize that relying on cheaper short-term variable financing puts them in a difficult spot when interest rates start to rise. Phase 2 is also the time when managers learn the hard way how important long-term procurement contracts for commodities and production materials are in a world of rising prices. With the arrival of phase 2, many established business and management paradigms have to be revised.

Phase 2, however, is not only doom. It presents exceptionally attractive opportunities for those prepared for this situation. At the end of phase 2, investors can purchase stocks and other investment assets at extremely low prices. Companies that did their homework and prepared for the challenges of phase 2 may substantially improve their competitive position, increase market share, or even acquire struggling, undercapitalized competitors at low valuations. The number of companies and individuals who profit from phase 2 of an inflation cycle tends to be low. This is not because it is difficult to exploit the opportunities presented by phase 2, but simply because most people do not do their homework and are not prepared to deal with the risks and opportunities of this phase.

Rising inflation in phase 2 impacts the complete value chain of a company and requires timely strategic and operational readjustments to avoid a dramatic deterioration of profitability. While financing strategies are at the core of safe survival during times of high inflation, they are not the only area of concern. Procurement, pricing, and inventory management issues are also of high importance. The sophisticated CEO may profit from earlier preparation and by understanding how and exactly where high inflation will impact business. Successful CEOs will use the inflation action plan that they diligently prepared before inflation rates started to rise.

In phase 3, inflation remains elevated, but inflation growth rates reach a plateau. It is now crucial to closely monitor central bankers and politicians, who have to make tough decisions that are vastly unpopular (i.e., continue with restrictive monetary policies, stick to conservative fiscal budgets and cut deficits, and commit to structural reforms to kick-start the economy). It takes enormous courage for politicians and central bankers to be determined to end inflation. They have to stick with these harsh policies even if the economy starts to improve and inflation rates start to decrease. If they fail to do so, inflation will rise again and may lapse back into another phase 2 (as it did during the 1970s).

If central bankers and politicians can successfully tame inflation and continue unpopular measures, the inflation cycle moves into the final period: disinflation and normalization (phase 4). Top management needs to reverse current strategies to enable a company to deal with the many consequences of falling inflation. Once phase 4 has started, financing and capital strategies must be revised to account for falling interest rates. Long-term fixed rate loans should be avoided. Falling inflation rates make short-term variable rate loans much more attractive. Equity capital might be available again at more favorable terms than before. Companies that miss this final turning point in an inflation cycle may struggle with high debt costs on long-term financing agreements. The well financed and strongly capitalized company might find this time attractive for further consolidation efforts, such as acquisitions of business divisions of struggling competitors or takeovers of other companies.

Chart 32 summarizes a selection of important changes that occur in the four critical phases of an inflation cycle.

Chart 32: Changing environments and challenges in the four phases of an inflation cycle (select examples)

Pre-Inflation Period (Phase 1)	Inflation Shock/Surge (Phase 2)	Plateau (Phase 3)	Disinflation/Normalization (Phase 4)
• "False" economic booms due to fiscal deficits and excessively loose monetary policies • Rising equity markets • Artificially low interest rates • Plentiful credit available at low rates • High volumes of liquidity in the system • Majority of people feel confident and act complacent	• Significant fall of equity markets • Interest rates rise substantially • Banks tighten credit policies • Economy falls into recession, FX rate of domestic currency falls • Liquidity is channeled into real assets and contributes to further price rises (e.g., commodities) • Fear spreads among businesses and investors	• Fear reaches its highest level among businesses and investors • Uncertainty leads to paralysis among businesses • Equity markets reach bottom and trade at significant discounts to fair value • Interest rates peak • Credit availability is extremely limited (over-reaction by banks)	• Recovery occurs more quickly than anticipated by most companies • Equity markets boom • Interest rates fall quickly • FX rate of domestic currency recovers quickly • Economy grows strongly • Credit becomes more easily available; however, banks remain overly cautious for some time

FPIM is a simple and idealistic model of an inflation cycle. Variations from the model are possible and do happen. For example, during the 1970s, we witnessed two inflation shocks (1973–1974 and 1977–1980). Phase 2 occurred twice during that cycle. After the first inflation shock, inflation retreated, but it was not yet beaten. It re-emerged a few years later more aggressively. The reason for this re-emergence of inflation is simple. Central bankers and politicians were not sufficiently committed to implement and uphold the required, but unpopular, policies and reforms necessary to end high inflation. They relaxed monetary policies too early as they felt immense populist pressure due to high unemployment and a weak economy.

Those who anticipated an end to the inflation cycle in 1975 or 1976 were in for a dangerous surprise. After a short retreat, inflation returned during 1977–1980 and reached much higher levels than during the previous inflation shock. It was a repeat of a classic phase 2 of an inflation cycle accompanied by a severe and deep recession.

Beating inflation is like treating a dangerous infection with antibiotics. If patients declare victory over the infection too early and stop the course of treatment too soon, the infection is likely to come back even more viciously. If central bankers and politicians relax too early, inflation might return and create more damage than before (as it did in 1977–1980).

Managers need to assess when a victory over inflation is real and when it is not. This is not as difficult as it sounds. There is a distinct difference in terms of the determinedness and conviction with which Reagan and Volcker successfully fought high inflation in 1980–1982 versus the efforts made by previous administrations in 1975 and 1976. Careful examination should help most managers distinguish between false and real wins over inflation.

Another noteworthy variation from the generic FPIM model is Germany's inflation of the late 1910s and early 1920s. Then, phase 4 proved to be extremely abrupt as a successful currency reform put a sudden end to inflation. In the German hyperinflation cycle, the original currency (German paper mark) proved unable to survive. The government consequently replaced the Mark with the Rentenmark, a collateralized construct that was tremendously successful. Its success surprised many people who thought that the new currency would fail as did the old one.

The German inflation period is an example of an inflation cycle spinning out of control and creating irreparable damage to the economy, currency, financial markets, and society. This period provides a rich learning ground for understanding how to deal with extreme cases of high inflation.

Every industry within an economy has its own set of challenges and opportunities that arise during an inflation cycle. It is important to make inflation strategy as industry specific as possible. In the context of this book, it is not possible to provide a detailed discussion on how inflation impacts different industries. Some aspects regarding the banking and insurance sector are discussed. Based on work with my clients, an industry- and company-specific analysis can help develop efficient and effective strategies capable of reducing most severe inflation risks. They may also enable companies to unlock many opportunities to outwit the competition and to improve a company's strategic positioning.

Across all industries, there are many mistakes companies tend to commit that can result in significant costs and deterioration of competitiveness. Chart 33 lists a selection of typical mistakes. This list is neither complete nor sufficiently detailed. There is a long checklist of issues that I employ when working with clients on this topic. This level of detail, however, would go beyond the scope of this book. The selection of topics presented in Chart 33 enables us to recognize dangerous inflation traps.

Chart 33: A selection of inflation traps over an inflation cycle

Pre-Inflation Period (Phase 1)	Inflation Shock/Surge (Phase 2)	Plateau (Phase 3)	Disinflation/ Normalization (Phase 4)
• Miss one of the last chances to lock in long-term fixed rate financing at reasonable rates • Long-term delivery contracts with pricing not linked to inflation • Pension funds that offer generous inflation protection to employees	• Being trapped by floating rate debt (bank loans, bonds, swaps) • Overly short-term debt structure • Need to raise capital (when equity markets are likely to be weak) • Being hit by counterparty default (credit risk)	• Exposure to long-term procurement contracts that are based on continuously high inflation • Miss the chance to switch financing structure to floating rate/short-term debt	• Trapped by high debt leverage at fixed interest rates and long maturities

172

CHAPTER 10: THE FPIM MODEL IN ACTION—A RETRO-SPECTIVE CASE STUDY OF THE 1970s

The 1970s inflation cycle took most companies, investors, and individuals by surprise. They failed to anticipate a rapid and forceful increase in inflation and all the issues that came with it. As a result, the S+P 500 lost about half of its value within less than twenty-one months. If you adjust the losses for inflation, the stock market crash was even more terrifying, and its severity exceeded the losses experienced during the last financial crisis. Companies, investors, and individuals failed to understand that inflation will change almost all of the rules of business, financial management, and investing. This is very unfortunate as relatively simple strategies could have protected most of them from the severe losses and pain they suffered due to inflation.

The following case study will walk you through a complete inflation cycle. I chose the period of the U.S. 1970s inflation cycle as it provides a valuable richness of experiences and lessons learned. This was a very challenging period for businesses and individuals. Volatility of the economy and financial markets was extremely high. The FPIM model may help make sense of these volatile times. You will be better equipped to understand the volatility in the market as long as you engage in critical thinking and are willing to deviate from herd mentality and behavior when required.

The world was much less erratic during the 1970s than most businesses and individuals believed. A great deal of the volatility in the economy and financial markets could have been explained and anticipated by those who did their homework and understood the workings and economics of inflation. Inflation-beating strategies are not rocket science. Inflation cycles tend to show repeating patterns and elements. Understanding these patterns and elements provides businesses and individuals a competitive edge and might help you not only to protect yourself against the risks, but also to capture the many opportunities that inflation presents.

The application of logic to predict developments presents a tremendous opportunity. There are examples of companies and individuals creating fortunes due to their sophisticated handling of inflation. These are people who simply employed analytic rigor and discipline in their thinking and decision making and refused to uncritically follow the herd.

High inflation does not appear out of the blue. The same developments leading to EMEG Inflation and LOFIS Inflation typically begin a long time before high inflation appears. This is particularly true for LOFIS Inflation, which is usually preceded by a set of destructive policies implemented by governments, central banks, and regulators.

One prominent handler of inflation risks during the 1970s was Warren Buffett. Buffett generated impressive investment returns and shareholder value with his company, Berkshire Hathaway, during the 1970s inflation cycle. Like no one else, Buffett understood using inflation to his advantage. The value he created for his shareholders was impressive and outstanding. During one of the toughest periods of American business history, Buffett not only protected his shareholders from inflation and a loss of purchasing power, he actually made them rich. He was one of very few CEOs whose shareholder value creation beat inflation by a wide margin.

Past inflation periods hold valuable insights into the workings and economics of inflation. This chapter reruns the 1970s inflation cycle step by step. Good strategies to deal with inflation risks and to capture emerging inflation opportunities are presented. Obviously, this is an ex post analysis, and future inflation cycles might diverge from the 1970s period. Rerunning the 1970s and employing the FPIM model familiarizes you with successful anti-inflation strategies that might appear to be counterintuitive and differ from the herd of market commentators and experts.

We begin this case study with 1970–1972, phase 1 in our FPIM model. This is when the biggest mistakes are committed. If businesses and individuals fail to implement effective inflation management strategies at this time, they are likely to suffer severe consequences in phase 2 of the inflation cycle.

1970–1972: A DECEIVING CONFIDENCE BEFORE A BRUTAL STORM

The period of 1970–1972 can be described as one of unjustified overconfidence by companies, investors, and individuals. The S+P 500 index finished 1972 at an all-time high, reflecting this widespread confidence and positive expectations. Economic growth was strong again after substantial weakness in 1970. The U.S. dollar was trading at high levels against major international currencies such as the Deutschmark. Businesses and individuals expected the positive development to continue in the years to come. Few people realized that instead a brutal storm was building that was going to unleash its destructive powers very shortly.

As we will see, it was a false economic boom based on overconfidence and unsustainable monetary incentives. There were many reasons to be concerned about the economic outlook and overvalued stock markets.

Chart 34: 1970–1972: Calmness and unjustified confidence before the storm

Time: 1970–1972 The FPIM model: phase 1	
What happened?	**What would have been the ideal strategic response?**
<ul><li>Common belief that monetary policy can rule business cycle; expansionary monetary policy used to increase economic growth and reduce unemployment rate</li><li>Stocks increase substantially (S+P 500 June 1970: 76; December 1972: 118); P/E ratio increased to about 20</li><li>GDP growth picks up (70: + 0.2 %; 1972 +5.3 %)</li><li>Dollar starts its long phase of decline: average price in 1970: 3.65 Deutschmarks; in January 1980: 1.7 Deutschmarks</li><li>Credit markets provide last window of opportunity to refinance. For the next decade, it will be impossible for most companies and individuals to find such attractive rates</li></ul>	<ul><li>Diversify from U.S. dollar into Deutschmarks and other more stable currencies</li><li>Ride equity boom (knowing it is liquidity driven and likely to end), but exit early enough to avoid serious collapse; P/Es are a clear red flag!</li><li>Successful companies radically redo their liability structure; wherever possible, lock in long-term fixed rates; avoid short loans or variable rate loans</li><li>Conduct capital raising activities in a strong equity market (e.g., capital increase, IPO)</li><li>Avoid acquisitions if possible, but use high valuations for divestitures</li><li>Gold at $36 (1970) and other precious metals/commodities are attractive hedges against inflation</li></ul>

Policymakers before 1972 believed that they could fine-tune economic growth through monetary policies. Central bankers saw themselves as masters or directors of the business cycle. In their view, monetary policy could and should be used to shorten or avoid recessions and to reduce unemployment rates. The fatal mistake was that many policymakers and economists did not foresee the possibility of high inflation and low growth occurring simultaneously. Such a constellation, later to be known as stagflation, was not one of the possible outcomes of their economic models. They firmly believed that low growth would essentially limit the rise of prices and wages and would therefore eliminate the possibility for high inflation to appear.

Authorities seriously overestimated the slack in the economy (i.e., the extra economic capacity that is still idle and, according to classic theory, prevents rising prices). Overestimating the slack in the economy leads to wrong assessments of future price rises and to inadequate fiscal, economic, or monetary stimuli.

Astute observers would have realized that earnings were not rising in line with stock market increases. When the S+P reached a new high in December 1972, it was mainly due to rising price earnings multiples (higher confidence in the stock market) and not to better business performance by companies. In this context, the central bank's decision to adopt a looser monetary policy between 1970 and early 1972 worked as an artificial but unsustainable tailwind.[72] Given the economic weakness in 1970, the central bank felt obligated to support the economy with lower interest rates. It is important to differentiate between economic expansions and stock market rallies that are the result of structurally improved business conditions and the ones that are simply the result of unsustainable monetary tailwinds.

1973–1975: A RUDE AWAKENING

The rude awakening came in 1973 when CPI inflation jumped from 3.4 percent in 1972 to 8.7 percent in 1973 and 12.3 percent in 1974. This sudden jump in inflation rates changed the rules of doing business in almost all industry sectors.   It came so quickly that unprepared

177

companies and individuals had little chance to rectify their mistakes. Within twenty-one months, the widely diversified S+P 500 index lost about half of its value, the U.S. economy fell into a severe recession, and unemployment rates rose to about nine percent.

Companies were hit by several forces: lower demand, higher input costs, unavailability of affordable long-term financing, capital shortages, higher interest rates, and tougher credit standards imposed by banks. The collapsing equity markets made equity issuances (to strengthen capital levels) very challenging if not impossible.

Well capitalized companies could have identified many cheap acquisition targets at that time. It was a paradise-like business environment for acquisitions as companies were trading at extremely low valuations. Few companies found themselves in a position of strength when it came to capital and liquidity. Many companies had used their acquisition "gun powder" much earlier. During phase 1 of the inflation cycle, when valuations were much higher, companies were eager to buy expensive companies and businesses. When the S+P 500 index P/E ratio fell from about twenty to below eight, few companies could take advantage of historic low valuations for acquisitions. The enormous fall of the stock market scared many business managers and investors. They were insecure and doubtful about the future and so most of them preferred to do nothing. Media spread fear and angst. When equity investments presented one of the biggest opportunities in U.S. stock market history, business media announced the end of the cult of equities.[73]

The thinking of business managers and investors was clouded by fear and confusion. Just one year previously, they had chased big opportunities. Now it turned out that these opportunities were in reality big risks. Their fears and exaggerated risk aversion prevented them from exploiting real opportunities. This risk opportunity paradox provided exceptional opportunities for the few people who were willing to deviate from the herd mentality. People who practiced critical thinking and conducted fact-based analysis were the only ones who saw and captured the rich opportunities that arose in 1974. For decades to come, companies forming the S+P 500 were not available to be purchased at such low prices. The people who exited the stock market when it was expensive in late 1972 were the ones who could now load up on cheap stocks. When others saw opportunities, these people rightly saw risks. Now that stocks and businesses were actually cheap, they saw the opportunities that others mistook for risks. Not surprisingly, Warren Buffett was one of these successful people who took advantage of this risk opportunity paradox.[74]

The companies and individuals who anticipated high inflation and implemented effective corporate strategies to deal with these inflation risks did very well. These companies held higher inventory levels, negotiated long-term procurement deals before prices rose across the board, and adjusted their financial management strategies appropriately against inflation risks.

On the investment side, investments in real assets, commodities, and precious metals (e.g., gold) did quite well. Hedging cash positions through stable currencies such as the Deutschmark started to reap benefits. This should not have come as a surprise, as the German Bundesbank did not miss any opportunity to fight against inflationary tendencies. They made it clear that they were prepared to pay any cost to keep inflation contained. As a result, the German mark started a period of strengthening against the U.S. dollar.

On the financing side, companies that arranged their financing needs at relatively low (fixed) rates with long maturities during the first phase of the inflation cycle did well. All others were forced to refinance during phase 2 at extremely costly terms. For some companies, there was no refinancing available, not even at much higher rates. Banks immediately started to restrict lending practices and became extremely demanding with their lending standards. At that time, many businesses were either taken over or disappeared.

Time: 1973–1975 The FPIM model: phase 2	
What happened?	**What would have been the ideal strategic response?**
• As inflation rises sharply to 12.3% in 1974, U.S. economy slides into deep recession and unemployment rises sharply • Profit margins get squeezed • Interest rates rise, yield curve turns inverse, which hurts banks; real interest rates turn massively negative (issue for insurance companies and savers) • Stock market (S+P 500) loses almost 50% of its value at the bottom • Commodities, precious metals rise sharply • Financing costs and availability become highly problematic • Many companies get caught in need of capital and financing; capital increases extremely difficult to execute • Insurance companies get hit the worst and at the low point lose almost 60% of their value	• Stay invested in real assets (precious metals, commodities, real estate, nonperishable inventories) • Stay away from long-term bonds • Excellent time for acquisitions (M&A) for company with financing power/capital (i.e., bottom fishing); many companies available near/below book value • Stay hedged in more stable currencies (Deutschmarks) • Late 1974 at bottom ideal reentry period for stock investments as P/E ratios fall from about twenty to less than eight (S+P 500)

The inflation spike in 1973–1975 has often been misinterpreted. The surge of inflation was not caused by a spike in oil prices in 1973. The rise in oil prices may have later contributed to it, but there were other more important factors that initiated the inflation surge and forced inflation rates higher. Forgotten is the fact that in 1968, 1969, and 1970, the U.S. experienced high CPI inflation rates (4.7 percent, 6.2 percent, and 5.6 percent, respectively). Prices for products and services rose across the board. Inflation was high even if energy prices were excluded from inflation calculations. The 1973–1975 inflation shock (as well as inflation surges at the end of the 1960s) was the result of excessively expansionary monetary policies paired with insufficient structural reforms to increase productivity and efficiency in the economy. It was the result of not tackling the issues that led to the previous inflation period of 1968–1970.[75]

Structural issues forced inflation higher. Many contracts and agreements among companies, organizations, and individuals included standard inflation protection clauses that kicked in when inflation started to rise. They created a self-feeding mechanism that pushed inflation rates higher and higher. Inflation was therefore on autopilot, a self-reinforcing process that was hard to interrupt.

During the inflation period of 1973–1975, government officials also expanded the use of price controls in the economy. [76] These interventions, later withdrawn, contributed to a psychology of uncertainty that further fueled price rises. It is likely that some businesses that were not yet affected by government price controls did raise their prices in anticipation of being included in future rounds of mandatory price control actions implemented by the government.

Price controls are largely ineffective to fight high inflation. Governments are likely to introduce them anyway to win the support of voters in upcoming elections. To voters, it appears that governments take decisive action to fight inflation. In reality, things are worse, as we have seen in numerous examples in the past. Businesses have to prepare for irrational interventions from the government, more likely to occur in the retail sector than in wholesale markets. Anticipative pricing policies and other strategies are necessary to shield a company against such price control actions.

1975–1976: A FALSE PHASE 3—A HALF-HEARTED FIGHT AGAINST INFLATION

In 1975, the U.S. inflation cycle moved into phase 3 of the FPIM model with inflation rates peaking and later falling. Initially, many people believed that the fight against inflation was won as the CPI decreased from 12.3 percent in 1974 to 4.9 percent in 1976. Using our FPIM model in an uncritical way, people could wrongly assume that the inflation cycle would now move quickly into phase 4 (normalization). Such an interpretation of the situation is faulty. The fight against inflation has to continue until it ends. If monetary policies are relaxed too early and if needed structural reforms do not occur, there is a high chance that inflation will return more aggressively.

During 1975–1976, central bankers failed to fight inflation due to vehement complaints by businesses, politicians, and the general public. They relaxed monetary policies in an effort to quickly stimulate the economy and end the recession. At the same time, policymakers failed to implement needed structural reforms to raise efficiency and productivity in the economy. These were serious mistakes and as a result the U.S. did not proceed to phase 4 (normalization) in 1977, but repeated phase 2 (inflation shock). Inflation came back even stronger than before.

Time: 1975–1976 The FPIM Model: False Phase 3	
What happened?	**What would have been the ideal strategic response?**
• Monetary tightening of 1973–1975 pushes down inflation rates. Low growth and high unemployment motivates policymakers to return to expansionary policies too early • As a result, economy recovers (too) quickly in 1976 (+ 5.4 % GDP versus – 0.2 % in 1975) • Stock markets rise sharply after low in 1974 (S+P rises about 40 %) • Unemployment rate falls only slightly, which provokes more stimulus from policymakers (too much too soon)	• In general, the key was to keep inflation hedges in place as phase 3 was not a victory over inflation • Gold prices fall sharply due to (unjustified) belief of victory against inflation (opportunity to increase investments in precious metals) • Small window of opportunity available for capital increases and refinancing

The key factor of success in 1975–1976 was to understand that the fight was not over. This was not an easy call. Inflation is not yet over when the patient feels better. To eradicate double-digit inflation, a severe dose of restrictive monetary policy over an extended period is needed with structural reforms in the economy to boost efficiency and productivity.

There were many warning signs visible to the astute observer in 1976. Structural reforms to increase productivity and efficiency in the U.S. economy were rare. The Federal Reserve abandoned its anti-inflation policies too early and stepped too aggressively on the accelerator pedal to combat a weak economy and high unemployment. The result was an even weaker economy, higher unemployment, and higher inflation in

1977–1980. The Federal Reserve was about to lose its credibility. This was a very critical period for U.S. economic and monetary stability.

The 1970s show an important case study of ineffective central bank action and what it means for businesses. Investors grant central banks only a limited number of chances to prove their determination to fight inflation. Once these chances have been forfeited, a chain reaction of negative events is likely to happen. In a worst-case scenario, a country may experience horrific times similar to Germany's hyperinflation. Starting in 1922, after at least eight years of overly accommodating monetary policies, money printing, and fiscal deficits, investors decided that Germany was a hopeless case. Investors gave up hope for Germany and the country's central bank had finally lost all its credibility. One year later, the German currency was practically worthless.

Businesses should release their inflation hedges only after a careful analysis of the determinedness of central bankers and politicians to fight inflation to the end. Companies should not abolish their inflation hedges swiftly, but in a slow and steady way, prepared to reverse action if needed. Anyone who switched too abruptly from phase 2 strategies to phase 3 and phase 4 strategies paid a high price in 1975–1976.

1977–1980: THE RETURN OF THE INFLATION DRAGON

The half-hearted approach by policymakers and the Federal Reserve to beat inflation resulted in a return of the inflation dragon. The result was ugly for both businesses and individuals. I recommend reviewing magazines and newspapers of that time to appreciate the enormous pain of a second inflation shock. It is surprising that this did not lead to social unrest. Most Americans endured the bad times and worked even harder to make ends meet. This attitude of the American people at that time was both impressive and exceptional. It was probably a decisive factor in why the U.S. economy recovered so rapidly a few years later. I personally believe that very few countries in the developed world could have relied on such an unselfish, disciplined, and patient attitude from their populations. When other people might have resorted to protests and social unrest, the American people simply worked harder and endured the pain.

Companies should not take such disciplined behavior for granted. High inflation wears out a society. In many historic examples, society answered with either social unrest or political extremism and instability. It may then make sense for a company to seriously think about a quick relocation. When inflation ignites social unrest or political extremism, it may lead to a long and painful deterioration of economic conditions. Sitting it out might then be the wrong strategy for businesses that have the option to relocate to more stable environments.

Time: 1977–1980 FPIM model: phase 2 (repeated)	
What happened?	**What would have been the ideal strategic response?**
• Inflation returns in an even more severe way: CPI 1978: 9%; 1979: 13.3%; 1980: 12.5% • U.S. economy slides back into recession • Unemployment comes close to ten percent • U.S. dollar continues to weaken against hard currencies (e.g., Deutschmark); losses against DM exceed fifty percent at the bottom from pre-inflation period	• Keeping inflation hedges in place from the previous phase 2 (1973–1975) • Reduce financing needs to a minimum; secure capital base • Extra caution for industries that are impacted by government interventions (e.g., price controls) • Prepare M&A activities for competitors who need to exit the market and may be acquired at extremely attractive prices (only for capital-rich companies with strong cash flows/secure financing) • Commodity investments attractive; gold reaches new record level

At the end of 1980, there was a feeling of capitulation. Many people did not believe that inflation could be beaten in the near future. High unemployment rates, devaluation of savings, and rapidly rising mortgage rates weighed on the mood of the people. In the beginning of 1980, CPI inflation rates came close to fifteen percent. It was impossible for most people to protect the purchasing power of their savings.[77] Older people and retirees were exposed to strongly rising cost of living expenses at a time when the purchasing power of their savings declined rapidly.

The sad fact was that those who had behaved more conservatively in the past (in terms of savings activities and use of debt) were harder hit now by inflation. Retirees who had diligently prepared for retirement through long-term savings and avoidance of debt saw their financial health worsen. Many retirees needed to re-enter the workforce in lower paid jobs to preserve their retirement savings.

A number of businesses, however, seemed to cope better with high inflation during the 1977–1980 inflation shock than during the first inflation shock in 1973–1974. It seemed that many businesses learned from their mistakes and adjusted their business system and their strategic positioning to the new rules of the game. However, conditions worsened a few years later when the Federal Reserve started its assault on inflation and provoked a new recession in 1980 and 1982.

The enormous pain caused by three waves of inflation (1968–1970, 1973–1975, 1977–1980) led to an important outcome. Both the Federal Reserve and the U.S. government realized in 1980 that inflation was public enemy No. 1 and launched a massive and determined assault on inflation. The key to success was that the determined and unpopular central bank actions, introduced by Volcker, were fully and unconditionally backed by Reagan. Even though the public suffered tremendously for a short period of time and complained loudly about the hardships they had to endure, Volcker and Reagan kept the course and did not back down from fighting inflation to the end.

1980–1981: THE ASSAULT ON INFLATION

The period 1980–1981 was a true phase 3 (plateau of inflation) in the sense of the FPIM model. Determined actions launched by both Reagan and Volcker laid the ground for winning the fight against inflation. The price that businesses and individuals had to pay for this success was high. Interest rates were rising through the roof, mortgages became almost unaffordable, and unemployment rates in 1981 came close to ten percent. Economic growth came to a standstill and the U.S. experienced a recession in both 1980 and 1982. Houses were left unfinished, cars remained unsold, and many small businesses were forced to close down despite previously successful track records.

Reports in business media describe harsh times for businesses. Operating in a climate of no growth, high interest rates, low consumer demand, volatile prices, and general uncertainty was definitely a demanding challenge. There was a general feeling of despair and capitulation. The vast majority of people did not expect things to change for the better anytime soon.

The astute observer saw a distinct difference in the attitude of the current administration and the central bank in fighting inflation compared to previous years (i.e., 1974 to 1976). They were committed to keep up the fight against inflation to the end and were willing to stand firm against heavy criticism by other politicians, businesses, and individuals. Reagan and Volcker were aware that their measures were vastly unpopular and painful. They stayed the course, and this is what it takes to break the back of inflation.

That was a critical stage in the inflation cycle, requiring immediate preparation to adjust one's business inflation strategy. All elements of strategic and operational management, including financing, had to be revised to prepare for massive changes in the economic and financial environment for the years to come. Adjusting a company's inflation strategy from phase 3 to phase 4 is a dramatic U-turn that affects almost all functions of a company's value chain. Missing this crucial turning point can be fatal.

Time: 1980–1981	
The FPIM model: phase 3	
What happened?	**What would have been the ideal strategic response?**
• The beginning of the assault on inflation; Reagan declares inflation "public enemy No. 1" • Inflation growth rates have peaked, but not inflation expectations; bond yields are at high levels (1981: ten year treasury 13.9 %); mortgage rates (fixed rates) come close to twenty percent in 1981[78] • Volcker starts aggressive campaign against inflation; federal funds rate rises shortly to twenty percent in 1981[79]; clear signal to markets: this time inflation fighting is for real • Unemployment starts to rise rapidly and reaches 9.7 % in 1982 • U.S. dollar reaches its low point in 1980. It then rapidly reverses as financial markets strongly believe in the success of U.S. anti-inflation program (1980 annual average 1.80 DM, 1982: 2.43 DM).	• Start unwinding inflation hedges • Revise foreign exchange strategy and return to U.S. dollar • Long-term bonds become attractive investments • Reduce maturity spectrum of financing structure, avoid longer term fixed rate debt (i.e., take advantage of falling interest rates) • Prepare for attractive M&A opportunities • Exit precious metal and commodity investments • Ideal entry point for equity investments

The period 1980–1981 taught an important lesson in risk and opportunity management. When people feel the most fearful and depressed, the biggest opportunities are to be found. It was very easy back then to join the vast majority of politicians, business managers, and individuals who capitulated and thought that inflation and economic weakness were here to stay. But smart market participants like Warren Buffett looked at the facts, not at emotions, and realized that the future was more promising than financial markets and their valuations suggested.

The end of the 1970s inflation cycle came very rapidly. Phase 4 of the cycle lasted about one year. Inflation rates fell from 8.9 percent in 1981 to 3.8 percent in 1982. Short-term interest rates declined quite dramatically from their past peak. The federal funds rate fell from 19.04 percent in July 1981 to 10.12 percent in August 1982. Long-term rates, however, were much slower to adjust. This situation led to an instant need for companies to readjust their financing strategies to the new needs of falling inflation and falling interest rates.

FROM 1982 ONWARDS: PHASE 5—AN ASTONISHINGLY FAST RETURN TO NORMALIZATION

Many people consider the U.S. return to normalization a miracle. Starting in 1983, the U.S. enjoyed a long-lasting economic boom with real GDP growth ranging between 3.2 percent and 7.2 percent in the years to come. CPI inflation data fell like a rock from 12.5 percent in 1980 to 3.8 percent in 1982 and to 1.1 percent in 1986. Interest rates started a new downward trend that lasted (with short interruptions) into the present. Falling interest rates provided a constant tailwind for the economy and financial markets for many years to come. Few people would have thought that a return to economic normalcy could occur that quickly. It proved that the strategy pursued by Reagan and Volcker was the right one, even though there were obviously some lucky tailwinds aiding the overall economic recovery (e.g., favorable demographic developments, cost reductions through outsourcing).

Businesses and investors wrongly positioned to take advantage of the turning point in interest rates had to pay a high price. This includes businesses that took out long-term fixed rate loans before 1982, as well as investors who missed the chance to lock in extremely high long-term bond yields at the height of the inflation cycle. The perfect interest rate management strategy in phases 3 and 4 would have been exactly the opposite of what would have been required for phase 2. In both cases, counterintuitive decision making (based on critical thinking and fact-based analysis) and against the herd mentality were required to be successful.

Equity markets profited enormously from the economic recovery and started a long-lasting bull run that was only temporarily interrupted by the October 1987 crash. The S+P 500 index more than tripled from the end of the inflation cycle (March 1982) to the end of the 1980s.[80]

Chart 39: 1982 and later—A fast return to normalization and strong economic growth

Time: 1982 – end of the 1980s The FPIM model: phase 4 and beyond ...	
What happened?	**What would have been the ideal strategic response?**
• Economic normalization occurs with rapid speed: Inflation declines from 12.5 % in 1980 to 3.8 % in 1982 • Strong economic recovery starts in 1983 (real GDP growth 1983: 4.5 %; 84: 7.2 %) • Strong stock market recovery for the years to come: S+P 500 March 1982: 111; Dec 1989: 349 • Interest rates start a long period of decline, financing becomes available and affordable again (at a slow pace) • U.S. dollar gains substantially and comes close to pre-inflation levels (average FX 1985: 2.94 DM)	• Aggressive pro-growth activities including M&A activities and increase of debt leverage • Falling interest rates demand shorter term financing at variable rates • Ideal time for executing delayed business investments • Avoid precious metal, commodity investments; reduce raw material hedging • Rising P/E ratios might be used for delayed capital increases (if capital can be employed in expansion activities)

Eventually, the Federal Reserve and policymakers won the fight against inflation. The U.S. inflation cycle ended happily. Several benign developments helped achieve the rapid return to normalcy. First, the early 1980s saw the beginning of a massive production outsourcing trend that kept prices down for many years. While it is unclear whether this trend benefitted the U.S. economy in the long term,[81] it definitely helped to keep prices low. Second, demographics played a significant role in creating additional demand for products and services that supported the economic recovery of the U.S. Third, computer technology helped raise business productivity and provided an added protection against rising wages and prices.

Not every inflation period in the future will end on the same high note. Many of the factors that contributed to this happy ending of the 1970s inflation cycle are likely to be absent should high inflation return today. First, it is questionable whether today's policymakers and central bankers in the developed world have the determination and courage to pursue a course of action similar to the one Reagan and Volcker took in the 1980s.

Second, it is questionable whether societies in the developed world have a similar willingness to endure severe economic and financial pain for a few years in order to fight high inflation and avoid outbreaks of social unrest. We live in a feel-good society. The standard of living is high in the developed world. There is strong demand for instant gratification and a feeling of entitlement to government support. Today's standard of living is taken as a given by the last two generations. Many people view the current standard of living as a basic right and not an aspiration for which to work. The key question is whether people in the developed world are willing to endure the hardship of high inflation with a similar impressive attitude as the American population did during the 1970s.

Third, the additional factors that provided a strong tailwind for the U.S. economy in the 1980s are absent. We are facing a completely different demographic situation, and the outsourcing trend has reached its peak. It is questionable whether technology investments can produce a similar pricing discipline today as in the 1980s.

I personally doubt that people in developed countries today can endure the pain of high inflation and the measures necessary to fight it without massive protests and social unrest. If my assumptions prove to be correct, it will be much more challenging for future politicians and central bankers to end the next period of high inflation.

CHAPTER 11: NEW THINKING REQUIRED—DECOMPOSING THE EFFECTS OF HIGH INFLATION ON BUSINESSES

I am often asked: Is inflation good or bad for businesses? The answer is simple: It depends. In general, inflation causes significantly more headwinds than tailwinds for businesses. This is particularly true at the start of a new inflation cycle as most companies are unprepared for high inflation.

Sophisticated handling of inflation risks, however, can turn these risks into an exceptional opportunity. Well prepared companies will outperform their less prepared peers and gain a sustainable competitive advantage. Some companies may have the advantage that their business system naturally profits from rising inflation rates.

Managing inflation challenges is not rocket science. What is necessary, however, is to approach inflation challenges with a different type of thinking, as this chapter seeks to illustrate. I will look at conducting business from different angles and show how inflation changes the conduct of business in many ways. Approaching this new and challenging situation with a commitment to critical and rigorous thinking is the most important factor of success.

DIFFERENT THINKING REQUIRED

Since the end of the last inflation cycle in the developed world in 1982, we have been spoiled by very benign business conditions. With few exceptions, the developed world has been free of major disruptions such as severe economic crises, wars, catastrophes, periods of high inflation, and other serious risk events. Looking at the history of the developed world, it is amazing how prosperous the past has been. This is particularly true for Europe.

Financial risk events such as the 1987 stock market crash, the bursting of the internet bubble, and the last financial crisis did not lead to long-term disruptions or permanent losses. Most financial indices recovered their initial losses over a period of a few years.

It did not require sophisticated management strategies to operate in such a benign environment. Following mainstream business thinking and conventional management paradigms was, in most cases, enough to be at least moderately successful and to survive.

High inflation rates will end this cozy way of doing business. High inflation will lead to a period of extreme volatility and disruption. The financial and nonfinancial losses are likely to be permanent or to at least last a long time. Corporate strategy must become more dynamic, anticipative, and unique to deal with these challenges. This will require a new way of thinking, as Chart 40 illustrates.

The new thinking must challenge the status quo and conventional wisdom (critical thinking). It must consider the short- and, more important, the long-term effects of an organization's action (consequential thinking). It also must relate a company to the specific inflation cycle it is in (situational thinking). It must constantly look at absolute and relative competitive advantages (strategic thinking). Managers must anticipate future developments (anticipative thinking) and must then apply new strategies and solutions to problems caused by inflation (innovative thinking). If we look at best practice examples of success during periods of high inflation, we often find that conduct, intentionally or not, was the product of such new thinking processes.

Chart 40: Core elements of thought processes required to address inflation risks

Critical Thinking	Consequential Thinking
• What is the fact-based evidence for a recommended action? • Was a recommended decision based on rigorous analytic stress testing? • Did we challenge conventional thinking? • Are we clearly differentiating between hypotheses, opinions, theories, and verified statements?	• What are the likely consequences and second or third order effects of my actions? • What are the likely consequences of actions implemented by other parties or entities (e.g., policymakers, central bankers, competitors)? • Do we fully understand the consequences of being wrong?
Situational Thinking	**Strategic Thinking**
• Are recommended actions tailored to the specific situation? • Is our current strategy an appropriate response to our specific situation?	• What action is likely to enhance my competitive position? • How can I anticipate decisions by governments, central banks, and competitors to gain advantage?
Anticipative Thinking	**Innovative Thinking**
• Anticipation of future economic and business conditions • Application of scenario analysis to avoid surprises	• Development of new and innovative solutions to deal with changes brought by inflation in the business environment

Some may think that the core elements of this new approach to business described in Chart 40 are not new at all. Successful leaders in business, politics, and the military have practiced a similar approach for thousands of years. Great leaders of the past probably based their decision making on similar thought processes.

The point here is a different one. I want to alert business leaders that if we get into a period of high inflation, the price paid for wrong decisions will be exorbitantly high. Often there will be no second chance to make good on mistakes. A high inflation environment with all of its disruptions, volatility, and structural breaks is unforgiving. While most banks, companies, and organizations survived the last financial crisis that started in 2007, I am not optimistic that this will be the case during the next inflation crisis. Therefore, I advise my clients to start preparing for this potentially dangerous situation by practicing a substantially more rigorous and critical approach to business thinking. Debate and constant challenging of perceptions of reality and likely future scenarios must become a normal course of action in management circles.

Such new forms of management conduct are likely to be uncomfortable for many employees at the beginning. Pursuing a zero tolerance level may lead to uncomfortable questioning of thought processes, analyses, and suggestions. Testing the rigor and validity of analyses, opinions, and recommendations is now uncommon. Often, we tend to agree or withhold criticism to avoid confrontation. Consensus, participative, and harmony driven management styles are widespread and in many cases heated, but constructive debates on important issues are considered rude or politically incorrect behavior. Unfortunately, it is the analytical rigor that is often reached only by mutual challenging during heated debates that may lead to the decisions necessary to survive the next crisis. The basis for long-term success in business during times of volatility is not a cozy climate within a company, but a commitment to rigorous analysis, ruthless challenging of arguments presented by others, and critical thinking.

We should also apply such critical thinking to our personal lives. Making personal financial decisions in times of high inflation requires as high a standard as in big companies. Practicing this type of rigorous thinking may initially annoy people around you. Unintentionally, many of us outsource thinking and decision making to so-called experts. We often follow the advice of investment and sales people without demanding evidence for the correctness of their recommendations. We have become used to following others without questioning their approaches and the rigor of their arguments. Once we switch to a more engaged and critical thinking process, this change will annoy those around us. Few people today are used to being challenged on the rigor of their thinking and to being criticized if their recommendations are based on insufficient evidence. Therefore, annoying people with your new commitment to critical thinking may actually be a confirmation that you are on the right track.[82] The few people and organizations that flourished during the 1970s inflation in the U.S. were those who challenged conventional wisdom, deviated from groupthink, and implemented action based on their own rigorous analyses.

BUSINESS PROFITABILITY AND INFLATION

Inflation impacts business profitability in many ways, mainly negatively. This is not surprising, as periods of high inflation are often accompanied by severe recessions, high volatility, and widespread uncertainty. Chart 41 presents a selection of inflation-induced headwinds for businesses.

Chart 41: Headwinds for businesses during times of high inflation

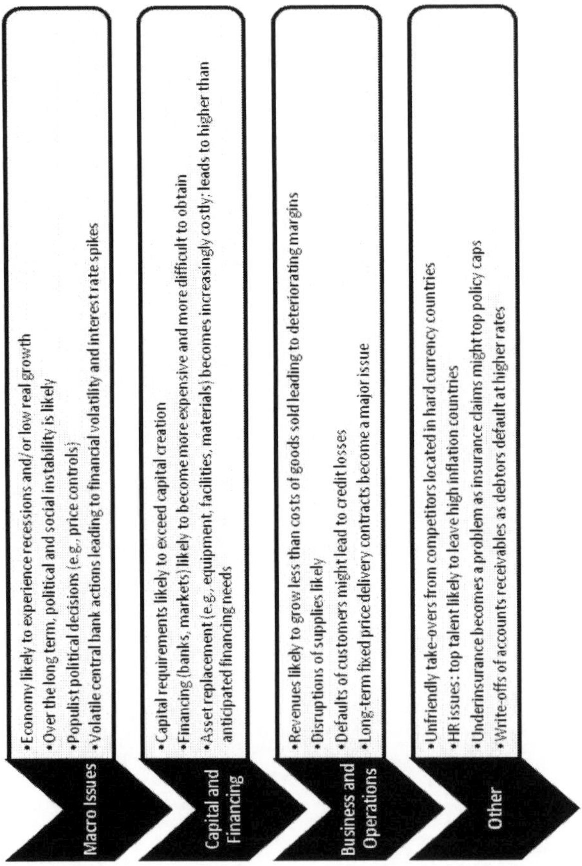

Macro Issues
- Economy likely to experience recessions and/or low real growth
- Over the long term, political and social instability is likely
- Populist political decisions (e.g., price controls)
- Volatile central bank actions leading to financial volatility and interest rate spikes

Capital and Financing
- Capital requirements likely to exceed capital creation
- Financing (banks, markets) likely to become more expensive and more difficult to obtain
- Asset replacement (e.g., equipment, facilities, materials) becomes increasingly costly; leads to higher than anticipated financing needs

Business and Operations
- Revenues likely to grow less than costs of goods sold leading to deteriorating margins
- Disruptions of supplies likely
- Defaults of customers might lead to credit losses
- Long-term fixed price delivery contracts become a major issue

Other
- Unfriendly take-overs from competitors located in hard currency countries
- HR issues: top talent likely to leave high inflation countries
- Underinsurance becomes a problem as insurance claims might top policy caps
- Write-offs of accounts receivables as debtors default at higher rates

It is generally safe to assume that these headwinds are normally stronger than the few positive effects a business might experience from high inflation. Unless top management is experienced in dealing with inflation issues, most companies will at least initially (meaning phase 2 of the FPIM model, inflation shock) experience a deterioration of business profitability due to inflation.

This might not be as bad as it sounds. Companies that successfully anticipate high inflation may succeed in gaining market share from other companies. Suffering temporarily from lower profit margins may be an attractive price to pay for leapfrogging into a significantly better competitive position.

THE CHARACTERISTICS OF A BUSINESS THAT BENEFITS FROM INFLATION

There are two ways businesses can profit from rising inflation. First, they can gain competitive advantages from choosing the right strategic responses. Second, some companies operate in an industry or sector that naturally profits from rising inflation rates. The latter will benefit from significant tailwinds during a period of high inflation without doing much for it. For example, mining companies could profit from high inflation as they are dealing mostly with fast-appreciating real assets. This is particularly true for companies focused on mining precious metals.

There are many companies outside the mining sector that may enjoy a significant tailwind due to high inflation. Chart 42 illustrates the characteristics of such companies.

Chart 42: Characteristics of a company that is perfectly positioned for inflation

Characteristics	Example
Sales volume independent of economic activity	Toll bridge operations, some utilities
Customers buy product (service) regardless of price (low price sensitivity)	Mandatory insurance policies, low price items, gasoline
Company has mostly long-term assets; replacement of assets occurs infrequently	Railway companies (trains, tracks, wagons)
All assets have a long-term depreciation schedule	Railway companies, utilities, infrastructure companies, real estate companies
All assets were financed long term with fixed coupon debt	Railway companies, utilities, infrastructure companies, real estate companies
There are no substitutes available for the product	Toll bridge
Any inflation related cost increases can be passed on to customers	Toll bridge, freight rates charged by railway companies

Companies that fulfill some or all of the criteria presented in Chart 42 may include infrastructure companies (such as railway companies, toll operators for private bridges, highways, and ferries), real estate companies, and, often, utility companies. Unless governments intervene in their pricing mechanisms, these companies may actually enjoy a substantial windfall profit from rising inflation.

During times of low inflation, many of these companies are considered to be boring investments. Employees tend to rank them as unattractive places to work. Nevertheless, these companies turn into stars when inflation causes headaches for others.

Large companies might consider investing in these businesses as an inflation hedge. They might go one step further and fully acquire an infrastructure or utility company. This strategy is particularly interesting if it is executed at the right time. These companies often trade at low valuations before inflation becomes a problem. In times of excessive liquidity and low interest rates, such a move could become a very efficient and effective inflation hedge.

Few companies have followed this path, probably because they are not overly concerned with inflation risks. The acquisition of Burlington Northern, a railroad company, by Berkshire Hathaway, is an example of such a strategy. It is unclear if inflation concerns were the main driver for this acquisition. However, the move may have been one of the most effective inflation hedges executed in the recent past.

WE NEED A DIFFERENTIATED VIEW OF INFLATION

Managers must understand that the impact of inflation on a business is not constant over time. Consumers' price sensitivity may decrease as they get used to higher inflation rates. Companies may be successful in passing on higher costs to consumers. At the beginning of a new inflation cycle, however, they may be unable to pass along the full extent of higher costs to their customers. Profit margins will suffer during those times.

Companies may be able to pass on price increases to consumers that go far beyond actual inflation rates. The longer inflation lasts, the less extreme are the reactions of consumers to further price increases. At a later stage of rising inflation rates, companies may be able to leverage inflation to increase their profit margins.

Managers also need to differentiate between EMEG Inflation and LOFIS Inflation when assessing the impact of inflation on their businesses. These forms of inflation have different patterns and consequences for the economy in general and for a business and its profitability in particular.

Generalizations are dangerous in times of high inflation. Management must adopt a differentiated approach to inflation and must change its thought processes and conclusions. Chart 40 is a starting point for this important requirement.

DEALING WITH IRRATIONAL BEHAVIOR IN THE ECONOMY AND FINANCIAL MARKETS

Economists often assume rational behavior of market participants in their models. We know that this assumption does not match reality. Financial bubbles, for example, are the result of prolonged irrational behavior of market participants. Customer decisions are often driven by emotional and social considerations rather than by rational analysis of the quality and functionality of a product.

During times of high inflation, this problem of emotional and irrational decision making tends to become more prominent than during normal economic times. When companies and individuals are confronted with new economic challenges that they did not anticipate, their behavior is often erratic, irrational, and myopic. At these times many individuals seem to suspend their own critical thinking and instead follow uncritical mainstream opinions.

Let me use an example from the financial world to illustrate this point. Investors who have been surprised by falling share prices (due to inflation) may continue to sell off their stock investments even though valuation levels may have reached historic lows. We saw this during the first inflation shock of 1973–1974, when the S+P 500 index fell about fifty percent. We also saw the same pattern when the S+P 500 crashed in 2009. Companies, investors, and individuals were overly confident and then became overly fearful.

There is a fear and risk aversion momentum when people have been caught unprepared by a major risk event. Fear feeds more fear and investment decisions will get postponed. Companies and individuals should expect this to happen and adjust their thinking and their strategies accordingly.

Successful strategists and investors not only look through these waves of irrationality, they also anticipate and exploit them. Equity valuations were extremely low in 1974. It was a once in a lifetime opportunity for well prepared businesses to implement acquisition strategies and expand market share or enter new businesses. People who did so, such as Warren Buffett, were not at all discouraged by the negativity, risk aversion, and fear expressed by other business people and investors. They trusted their own analyses and critical thinking.

ACCOUNTING VOLATILITY—PROFITS THAT ARE CAMOUFLAGED LOSSES

Most accounting systems in the developed world are based on nominal parameters and do not adjust their values and results for inflation. Modern accounting rules were developed in times of low inflation for times of low inflation. As inflation has not been a major problem in the developed world for at least three decades, this was not a major issue.

Once high inflation returns to the developed world, accounting data and figures will cease to reflect economic reality. A true picture of a company's financial situation may not be offered. Using accounting information uncritically is therefore a dangerous endeavor. Imagine that the definition of a meter or a yard would constantly change. Using a standard measurement tape would then get you into trouble if you do not adjust the measurement for the most recent definition of a meter or a yard. The same will happen with accounting measures and figures. Inflation will constantly change their meaning and implications. Misleading accounting information may therefore contribute to false and dangerous decision making by top management.

The accounting issues created by high inflation are actually even more complex. During past times of high inflation many books and articles were written about inflation-related accounting issues. Over the past thirty years, the topic has been neglected in management research. Chart 43 presents a selection of inflation accounting problems that management needs to be aware of.

During high inflation, companies tend to be surprised by the enormous cost increases for replacement investments. As old machines are depreciated over time based on their purchase value, they produce a decreasing charge to current earnings (both depreciation and current revenues profit from inflation). At the time when the machine has to be replaced, however, inflation turns into a headwind as the cost for the replacement is likely to exceed the number put into financial budgets in the past. This may catch management by surprise as both the actual purchase price of the new equipment and the subsequent depreciation charges may be beyond management's expectations.[83]

This is only one of numerous inflation traps that are buried in modern accounting systems that were not engineered to deal with times of high inflation.

Chart 43: Examples of problems regarding inflation accounting

Selection of issues regarding inflation accounting
• Higher costs for replacement investments than originally anticipated and reflected in current and past pricing decisions • Depreciation schedules possibly jump after replacement investments have been made at higher prices than anticipated • Value of tax loss carry forward structures • Goodwill amortization • Tax treatment of financial inflation hedges • Depreciation of cash • Advantages of high debt levels if debt was taken out at fixed rates • Foreign exchange rate issues (including government interventions) • Accounting for derivatives • Product price calculations on the basis of different depreciation and input cost scenarios

Management must anticipate these issues to avoid costly surprises. Ideally, management introduces alternative financial planning and accounting analyses based on different inflation scenarios. This might be quite cumbersome. It may, however, be the only way for a company to truly understand how rising inflation will impact the long-term economics of a business and its profitability.

GEOGRAPHIC CONSIDERATION—WHY LOCATION MATTERS DURING TIMES OF HIGH INFLATION

Companies headquartered in high inflation countries should be prepared to face substantial headwinds compared to their competitors in more stable countries. This is a huge problem for international and global industries. The geographic location of a company's headquarters and main operations can become a disadvantage during periods of high inflation.

Many factors contribute to this important issue. Being located in a high inflation country can lead to massive tax disadvantages. Since taxes are calculated on nominal aggregates (not on inflation adjusted terms), a company may pay high taxes even though it lost money in real terms. Foreign exchange considerations contribute to this issue as currency hedges are typically taxed on nominal terms in developed countries. It is very difficult for a company in a high inflation/weak currency country to hedge its inflation related risks. This may lead to an enormous disadvantage compared to competitors in more stable countries.

While some argue that a depreciating currency (result of inflation) may improve a country's competitiveness, reality seems to suggest a different outcome. I am not aware that any companies in high inflation countries such as Venezuela and Zimbabwe were able to take advantage of rapidly falling foreign exchange rates. People underestimate how many parts of a value chain are independent of domestic foreign exchange rates. Countries like Germany with strong currencies seem to be exporting powerhouses regardless of the strength of their currencies (e.g., Germany's economic performance during the 1970s or 1980s when its currency appreciated significantly).

There are additional issues that are related to the location of a company. From a human resources perspective, it is difficult to keep talent in a country suffering from high inflation (or other economic problems). Talented, well trained people are highly mobile. If the domestic situation continues to deteriorate, these people will leave. Adverse foreign exchange rates make it impossible to match the compensation that a talented manager is offered in more stable countries. High inflation and the negative implications that come with it are likely to induce brain drain in affected countries. Therefore, human resources issues must be addressed as part of an overall inflation strategy.

Companies in high inflation countries may also be exposed to the danger of unfriendly takeovers if they are publicly listed. As valuations for these companies tend to be low (from the perspective of an acquirer from a hard currency country), they become immediate targets for foreign competitors. For a country with high inflation, this problem may lead to a sell-off of its domestic productive companies and assets. This problem is referred to as the danger of foreignization. In relative terms, the assets of a high inflation country become cheap and this motivates foreigners to hunt for undervalued companies, businesses, real estate, and other real assets.

During the period of German hyperinflation, politicians and industrialists were concerned about a potential wave of foreign takeovers. The threat of foreignization risks was on top of the agenda for German politicians and business people. Foreignization did not materialize on the scale that German politicians feared it would. It is not quite clear whether foreigners simply missed an enormous opportunity or were scared by potential government action.

CHAPTER 12: THE PROCESS—HOW TO PREPARE FOR HIGH INFLATION

We do not have a crystal ball to look into the future. We do not know if, when, and how high inflation will return to the developed world. We do know that if high inflation returns, the consequences for the economy and businesses will be severe. This scenario can threaten the existence of a company.

The risk of high inflation must therefore be put on top management's risk radar screen and it must be a high priority. Companies cannot afford to gamble by hoping that high inflation will not arrive. Top management should start now to identify their exposure to inflation and prepare contingency plans to deal with it.

There are many ways companies can assess inflation strategies. Chart 44 shows a generic program that consists of four core activities and focuses on risk protection. Top management should make sure that both aspects of high inflation (risks and opportunities) are addressed. It is understandable that many top managers will initially focus on addressing inflation risks. However, companies should also devote sufficient time to identify inflation-related opportunities and to develop strategies to exploit them. At a minimum, companies should systematically collect all ideas on inflation opportunities that surface during workshops focused initially on inflation risk issues. Such a running list may later be valuable when a company moves to exploitation of inflation opportunities. Many inflation opportunities will be discovered accidentally and it would be a great loss if these opportunities are overlooked during the project.

Chart 44: The Inflation Preparation Program (IPP)—Four core activities to prepare for inflation risk

Core Activity 1: Identify all areas of vulnerability	• Scrutinize every business unit, product, and support function for areas of vulnerability • Constantly challenge your preliminary findings, assign people to play the role of a devil's advocate • Understand the mistakes of peers in past inflation cycles and relate them to your situation
Core Activity 2: Stress test your company with past and new scenarios	• Define stress-test scenarios (e.g., 1970s) to analyze your company's vulnerability • Prepare pro forma financial statements (balance sheet, P+L, cash flow analysis) based on these scenarios • Analyze whether current business strategy can deal with a surge of inflation
Core Activity 3: Identify risks that require action	• Define the most important areas of vulnerability based on the results of core activities 1 and 2 • Explicitly include issues of reflexivity and correlation into your analysis • Estimate the potential costs if high inflation returns and areas of vulnerability were left unaddressed
Core Activity 4: Develop strategies to mitigate/hedge these risks	• Develop inflation master plan and summarize all strategic and tactical moves in an inflation manual • Possible strategic moves include revisions of corporate strategy, financing and capital strategies, hedging strategies, M&A moves including defense strategy, product portfolio adjustments, accounting, legal, and tax strategies, procurement tactics

The four core activities are best executed as part of a company-wide inflation project supervised by top management. This inflation project should have a clearly defined organization with project teams and team leaders, projected milestones, and clear goals and deliverables. Responsibilities for each project team need to be clearly assigned.

The next step is to develop a project plan. Chart 45 shows a generic sample that can be used as a prototype for most companies. It should be tailored to the specific organizational requirements of a company.

Chart 45: The five steps to prepare for excessive inflation

Step	Activities
Step 1 (3 weeks)	• Establish project organization, time plan, and deliverables • Ensure that everybody in senior management understands the importance of the project • Secure external support if needed
Step 2 (8 weeks)	• Assign SWOT teams to analyze areas of vulnerability (core activity 1) • Stress test a company's financials and business model with past and newly created inflation scenarios (core activity 2) • In parallel, study past inflation cycles for additional lessons learned
Step 3 (4 weeks)	• Synthesize work of SWOT teams and identify hot spots/opportunities (core activity 3) • Explicitly address problems of reflexivity and correlations that could amplify negative implications of inflation • Engage external experts to discuss results on an as-needed basis
Step 4 (4 weeks)	• Identify areas of vulnerability that exceed management's risk appetite (core activity 3) • Develop strategies to mitigate or hedge unwanted risks • Consider adjustments of overall strategy if needed • Engage experts to support this work/stress test your thinking and conclusions
Step 5 (ongoing)	• Develop implementation plan and start execution of new risk strategy (core activity 4) • Work with experts to implement financial or technical aspects of new strategy (e.g., financial hedges, new financing structure) • Continuously monitor effectiveness of new inflation risk strategy and adjust if needed

It is mandatory that all business units and support functions of a company participate in this project. Fatal inflation traps can be found in any part of a company's value chain. Project leaders and team members must be educated on the importance of this project. They should examine case studies of companies that were crushed by inflation risks for which they were not prepared.

The financial crisis demonstrates how a small team of traders or risk decision makers (with admittedly excessive freedom in terms of risk taking) can bring down even the largest financial institutions. Even if risk management standards are excellent in all other parts of the organization, the deficiency of risk management practices in one unit can cause significant losses or the failure of a large institution. The same is true for inflation. Any business unit or support function can host a fatal inflation trap. Many companies detect the most dangerous inflation traps in areas of the organizations where they are least expected.

Given that the last inflation period in the developed world occurred more than thirty years ago, management should expect little experience in managing inflation <u>within</u> their company. This is obviously a problematic situation. One way to address this issue is to hire experts with relevant skills and prevent a time intensive and risky trial and error approach. There are different ways to accomplish this. First, companies can hire specialized consultants to guide them through these issues. There are, however, very few experts with credible experience in inflation management issues. Second, and this might be a preferable option, companies can rehire experienced managers who were in management positions during the 1970s inflation cycle. These managers most likely are in retirement. Rehiring such specialists could lead to a priceless acquisition of relevant skills that would be inaccessible otherwise.

It is important to always stress-test initial findings of the teams that are analyzing a company's vulnerability to inflation risks. A business unit or function initially classified as a low inflation risk may have substantial inflation risks once it is properly stress-tested and analyzed. Top management must avoid superficial or incomplete assessments of inflation risks. As business leaders are typically very busy with other (more short-term) issues, there is a tendency for hasty dismissal of inflation risks in a business unit. This may prove costly and needs to be avoided.

It is unlikely that any business function will be immune to inflation risks. If working teams claim that their area of analysis did not find specific inflation threats, it may make sense to double-check the assessments. Inflation traps are often difficult to find and may be visible only after a second or third analysis of a business unit or corporate function. A fresh set of eyes may sometimes be necessary to find the real risks.

CHAPTER 13: THE IMPORTANCE OF CONDUCTING ECONOMIC WAR-GAMING AND BUILDING AN ECONOMIC INTELLIGENCE UNIT

Successfully managing a company through times of economic volatility and high inflation requires superb economic analysis. Managers need to adjust their strategies to each phase of an inflation cycle. This is comparable to a sailor adjusting to wind and weather conditions. First-class economic analysis anticipates crucial turns in an inflation cycle and resulting changes in the economy.

Unfortunately, many corporate managers do not have access to high-quality economic analysis. This exposes managers to failure to anticipate adverse economic developments. The financial crisis of 2007 made this deficit painfully apparent. It is therefore crucial for top management to build first-class economic intelligence systems to guide and improve strategic decision making.

The limited use of economic insights is a big problem in the financial and corporate world. It is a problem not only for inflation management, but also for general management. A significant amount of shareholder value could be created (or preserved) if management would address these deficits. A strategy that is not compatible with economic developments or that fails to anticipate economic risks is a dangerous liability for a company and its shareholders.

This chapter discusses some of my ideas for setting up an economic intelligence unit and the analyses it would perform. There are two main objectives. The first is to improve management's capability to deal with economic volatility in general. The second is to enable management to deal with the specific challenges of an inflation cycle as outlined in Chapters 9 and 10.

THE IMPORTANCE OF GETTING ECONOMIC ANALYSIS RIGHT

Many people underestimate the importance of economic developments for long-term corporate stability and success. They fail to see that economic analysis can be both an important risk management tool and a business development tool. For example, the companies that anticipated booming emerging markets early secured a sustainable and decisive advantage over their myopic competitors.

Economic analysis today often is distracted by an abundance of irrelevant economic data. For most companies it is irrelevant whether GDP grew 2.7 percent or 2.8 percent during the last quarter or quarterly CPI moved from 1.7 percent to 1.8 percent. Short-term developments of highly aggregated and complex data are unlikely to be the basis of competitive advantages, especially since such highly aggregated data tends to be revised later. The main goal of strategically important economic analysis is not to predict short-term developments of GDP or other data points. The real goal is to understand the macro picture of the economy, its context, and the most likely scenarios that could unfold in the future. Managers need to be aware of the variability and volatility of an economy. This is essential to be prepared for changes and disruptions that require strategic adjustments.

For example, it was irrelevant for a German CEO in 1919 to have one base case prediction on the economic development of the next five years. Such a base case prediction would have been most likely a linear extrapolation of the most recent economic developments and would have distracted management from the more important and dangerous issues: the fragility of the German economic, monetary, and social situation. A stress test analysis of economic reality would have alerted managers to expect the need for radical risk management activities. Rational and critical thinking also would have uncovered the acute inflationary threats Germany was facing at that time.

What top managers need is a clear sense of the variability, volatility, and probability of different economic outcomes. We can reduce these issues to a simple set of questions: How would the worst and best future economic scenarios impact our company? What do we need to protect our downside or capture the upside? I am sure that companies that approached economic and financial volatility in such a way were significantly better prepared to deal with the financial crisis of 2007.[84]

The reality is that economic outcomes are rarely unexpected or erratic. In most cases, massive economic changes are the result of economic and behavioral forces that were apparent for an extended period of time. Even massive short-term changes in the economy such as the German hyperinflation in 1922–1923 or the economic collapse after the outbreak of the recent financial crisis in 2008 were the result of long-term observable developments. Any company that conducted sophisticated economic analysis would have had such adverse risk scenarios quite early on their risk radar screen. Risk events may unfold within a few weeks or months, but their buildup is typically the result of a multiyear process.

It is not possible to time economic risk events accurately. This should not be the focus of economic analysis. Economic analysis should focus on the identification of probable future economic scenarios and on the mapping of the underlying economic and behavioral forces that contribute to them. Economic analysis must ensure that all relevant risks and opportunities are detected and clearly communicated to top management, as Chart 46 illustrates. Such a process enables top management to develop contingency plans and adjust strategic decisions.

Chart 46: Two focal points for economic analysis

	Risk detection	Opportunity detection
Description	Identify possible economic scenarios that require preparation and contingency planning: Which economic scenarios could hurt us?	Identify possible economic scenarios that present exceptional opportunities: Which opportunities require strategic focus? Where are future growth regions?
Examples	• Return of high inflation • Reversal of interest rates • Long-term economic decline of a country (e.g., political shift) • Banking or financial crisis • Economic disruption	• Identification of regions with high growth potential (e.g., emerging markets in the 1980s) • Successful overcoming of an economic crisis (e.g., U.S. in 1982 after high inflation period)

The economic situation of a country is rarely an accidental development, but the result of many long-term forces.

It is important that a company's economic analysis is not based only on purely economic forces. The analysis must integrate behavioral forces as well. Social behavior is the origin of consumer spending patterns, which determine a significant portion of overall economic activity and growth. It is also responsible for an acceleration of CPI inflation or the buildup of financial bubbles. Economic and behavioral forces should be understood thoroughly to assess current economic conditions and likely future scenarios. Social behavior can be irrational and erratic for an extended period of time. Chart 47 shows a selection of topics that should be covered in a company's economic analysis.

Chart 47: Elements of a meaningful economic analysis

	Identification of economic forces	Identification of behavioral forces
Description	Identification of economic forces that result from economic trends, changes, and developments	Identification of current and future behavioral forces that result from beliefs, moods, and subjective assessments
Examples	• Demographics leading to higher economic growth • Deleveraging leading to lower consumer spending	• Demands for higher wages (enforced through actions such as strikes) • Strong beliefs in the attractiveness of an asset class or a particular investment (i.e., bubble building)

Companies must recognize that economic and behavioral forces are not independent. Short-term reality is a reflection of macro-behavioral forces no matter how rational the justification for these forces.

Top management is in a better position to make important strategic decisions if it has a good understanding of economic volatility and its main drivers.

VALUE CREATING ECONOMIC ANALYSIS: THE IMPORTANCE OF ECONOMIC WAR-GAMING

Traditional economics provides limited help in deriving the economic insights that are required for effective strategic decision making. Most traditional economists have a relatively poor track record in anticipating economic trouble, significant structural breaks, or attractive emerging opportunities. Their typical output is of limited use for top management in strategic decision making. For example, very few economists anticipated the last financial crisis. This economic risk event caught many companies by surprise. Most economists failed to anticipate the risk of rapidly rising inflation rates in the early 1970s. As a result, most companies were caught strategically and financially ill prepared to deal with strongly rising inflation rates in 1973.

Many economists practice their science in a theoretical and model driven manner. Economic theories are often based on restrictive assumptions and exclusions of important real world factors. These restrictive assumptions and exclusions create a world that is explained by challenging mathematical calculations. Such a model world, however, has very little to do with the real world.

To set up a value-creating economic intelligence unit in a company is not difficult. The key is to find staff that is knowledgeable in three skill categories: understanding of practical economics (zest to explain the real world), a superb understanding of the company's industry (the economics of an industry, its sensitivities, and its drivers for profitability), and extensive knowledge of economic history and cycles.

Chart 48: Three critical skills needed for a corporate economic intelligence unit

Practical Economic Skills	Industry Expertise

Understanding of Economic History

The first step is to eliminate the noise caused by irrelevant economic data. Economic data noise can be found in many places. For example, business media likes to hype meaningless weekly economic data such as job figures, housing statistics, or other frequently reported points. Weekly data points are hardly meaningful for the purposes of detecting either long-term economic developments or big structural changes that require top management's attention.

Another form of noise is created by highly aggregated and heavily adjusted data such as GDP figures and CPI inflation rates. The aggregation and adjustment procedures used by those who prepare such data sources are highly complex. They often camouflage important economic insights that are visible only when looking at the underlying raw or regional data.

Using short-term data to anticipate long-term economic developments is problematic. Short-term GDP and CPI data from 1972 would not have provided significant warning signs for the disruptive inflation shock in 1973. It was quite possible to anticipate the inflation shock of 1973 by looking at the many visible warning signs of economic and financial fragility (e.g., Federal Reserve monetary policies, end of Bretton Woods) and related economic and noneconomic forces.

The second step for creating meaningful economic analysis is to systematically identify long-term economic and behavioral forces and their impacts on economic outcomes. The key is to understand the forces and their interdependency. It is important to be aware of feedback loops, correlations, connectivity risks, and self-reinforcing trends. Economic and behavioral forces do not work in isolation; they show a high degree of mutual dependency and connectivity, particularly in complex and dynamic systems. Therefore, it is important to simulate how these forces interact and their current and future strength. Forces with negative momentum will lose their impact on the overall economic outcome over time. They may also dramatically change the balance of an economic system. In an extreme case, the waning momentum of just one economic force that was crucial for the overall balance of a system in the past might lead to a significant disruption or even the abrupt collapse of a system.

As an economy is a complex social system with many intertwined economic and behavioral forces working at the same time in many directions, economic analysis needs to simulate how these forces can create quite different future economic outcomes. Chart 49 illustrates how companies may conduct such analyses.[85]

Chart 49: The process of deriving meaningful economic scenarios

Economic analysis	Derive economic scenarios
• Identify economic and behavioral forces at work • Map interdependencies among economic and behavioral forces • Identify unsustainable market interferences (e.g., central bank or fiscal policies)	• Apply systems theory to simulate different economic outcomes • Describe a wide spectrum of different outcomes (scenarios) and assess their probability

One way to integrate practical economics into strategic decision making and risk management is the exercise of economic war-gaming. The task is to stress-test a company's current strategic course or a new strategy against a wide range of positive and negative economic scenarios.

When preparing for inflation risks, economic war-gaming can play an important role to protect a company as it reveals vulnerabilities to top management. Economic war-gaming exercises should stress-test a company's resilience to both historic inflation cycles (e.g. U.S. in the 1970s) and hypothetical scenarios. It is important to develop scenarios in great detail to include at least first and second derivative events or consequences such as raises in interest rates, recessions, reduced consumer spending, and restricted access to new financing. A dynamic economic war-gaming exercise might simulate interdependencies and connectivity risk consequences (spreading of volatility from one market to another).

Chart 50 illustrates the basic concept of economic war-gaming. Obviously, real-world applications are more elaborate and require greater detail. Chart 50 is sufficient to illustrate the basic concept for companies to begin this important activity.

Chart 50: Conducting economic war-gaming and economic stress testing

Create economic scenarios	Stress test your preparedness	Assess gaps and issues	Implement action steps
• Choose actual economic events of the past and hypothetical scenarios • Develop scenarios in detail including derivative developments	• Identify scenarios with pre-paredness issues for both risks and potential opportunities • Stress test your strategy against these scenarios	• Conduct detailed analysis of selected scenarios • Assess risk exposures and likelihood of scenario • Analyze scenarios that might provide you with attractive oppor-tunities	• Decide on action steps to address identified risks and opportunities • Review progress on implemen-tation of action steps

It is important that a company takes ownership of its economic analysis efforts and of the process of economic war-gaming. There is often a temptation for companies to outsource the entire process to external consultants. I recommend against this. Building up these skills internally provides a decisive competitive advantage. An external consultant may facilitate the process, moderate workshops, or assess the analytic rigor of your analyses, but he should not be in charge of your economic intelligence activities.

Companies should have their economic intelligence unit in place prior to rising inflation rates. As responding appropriately to phase 1 and 2 of an inflation cycle will be essential for the survival of a company, the required capabilities and skills for these analyses should be there at least two years before inflation becomes a problem.

ANTICIPATING STRUCTURAL BREAKS: HOW FORTUNES ARE CREATED AND DESTROYED

Structural breaks are extremely dangerous for a company and deserve special mention in the context of economic analysis. Structural breaks are abrupt and permanent changes in the economic situation of a geographic region, a trend or system. In most cases, structural breaks require significant strategic adjustments from management.

Structural breaks can be seen as important turning points that mark the discontinuation of economic trends. They will change future economic outcomes or results substantially and permanently. In those situations, the changes are unlikely to revert back to the mean, as with temporary disruptions (e.g., recession). The world is completely different before and after a structural break. Significant fortunes can be lost if top management fails to anticipate such structural breaks. Strategic planning exercises that are based on linear extrapolation of most recent trends will fail to anticipate structural breaks. This is a dangerous shortcoming.

The advent of high inflation is an important structural break. Price levels almost never revert back to the levels before high inflation. They remain permanently and significantly elevated. Losses due to a failure of anticipating high inflation are therefore permanent.

It is important to understand that high inflation can cause other wide-reaching structural breaks. For example, high inflation can lead to a shift of a political system (e.g., from capitalism to socialism or from a democracy to a dictatorship). Cases of high inflation are therefore not only financial risk phenomena, but also risks to the general long-term social stability of a country. Top management must take note of this.

Structural breaks require early and sophisticated preparation. Sticking to old strategies, thought patterns, or routines is a sure way to disaster. Berkshire Hathaway, for example, excelled at anticipating the new realities of high inflation during the 1970s and adjusted its strategies accordingly. The company was highly rewarded for doing so.

People who succeed in anticipating structural breaks and implement appropriate strategies can accumulate great fortunes. There are many examples of companies and individuals who leapfrogged to enormous prosperity by anticipating changes that most people ignored.

Certain economic, social, and business developments may continue for years, even decades, without experiencing any form of structural break. This phenomenon is thus dangerous for companies. Long-term calmness or linear developments may lead to a decreased effort in identifying possible future structural breaks. Because structural breaks are unforgiving, companies must always be on high alert to identify them as early as possible.

PART IV: PERSONAL WEALTH AND FINANCIAL STABILITY IN TIMES OF HIGH INFLATION

CHAPTER 14: YOUR PERSONAL INFLATION STRATEGY—CAREER, FAMILY, AND WEALTH MANAGEMENT CHALLENGES

In the previous chapters, we focused on the critical issues to weatherproof a company against inflation risks. Many of the concepts and ideas discussed in these chapters can be transferred to your personal life to develop effective inflation strategies. This chapter discusses specific issues regarding the effect high inflation may have on your personal life. You should familiarize yourself with these issues and develop appropriate strategies for you and your family.

Inflation affects many aspects of your life. Focusing solely on investment and wealth management topics will leave you exposed to other significant inflation risks. You also need to address inflation risks that are linked to your family life cycle stage. Those issues include future expenses (e.g., children's education), career issues, and specific macro issues of your environment (e.g., taxes, regulations, insurance, retirement planning). Therefore, your inflation strategy should be tailored to your specific life circumstances and inflation risks. Chart 51 suggests a minimum of five elements that need to be addressed by your inflation strategy.

Chart 51: Elements of a holistic personal inflation strategy

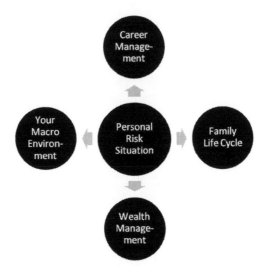

As you can see, there is a wide spectrum of issues that need to be addressed. These issues go far beyond traditional wealth management. For many people, a job loss during times of high inflation will have more severe consequences than a loss in their investment portfolios. A job loss not only eliminates a steady income stream but also robs you of an effective inflation hedge. Most salaries tend to rise during times of high inflation and even if these wage increases do not exactly match CPI inflation data, they at least reduce a significant part of inflation risks.

But even if you keep your job, there is another issue that often arises during long periods of inflation: underpayment. It is important not only to keep your job, but also to secure salary increases that at least match the rate of inflation of your regular expenses. That rate is likely to be higher than reported CPI inflation rates. For example, big ticket items such as education and healthcare costs in countries like the U.S. typically grow faster than reported CPI rates. Therefore, you must secure both a stable job and enough bargaining power to demand wage increases that match inflation rates.

The five elements of an inflation strategy shown in Chart 51 are now discussed in more detail. These are derived from the experience of selected past inflation cycles. Therefore, professional assistance should be sought to address all aspects of inflation risks. Obviously, future developments may create different outcomes than in the past and may therefore create a need for different strategies than those discussed in this book.

A) UNDERSTANDING YOUR PERSONAL RISK SITUATION

A good strategy—for companies and individuals—should balance risks and opportunities. Unfortunately, this is rarely the case. Companies and individuals tend to focus on opportunities and to neglect risks, which exposes them to an imbalance in risks and opportunities. They may get away with this in the short or medium term, but in the long term, they are likely to be caught unprepared by future risk events. Understanding and addressing these imbalances is of utmost importance.

You should link your inflation strategy to your specific risk situation. This is different for every person and family and depends on many factors. Some of these factors are discussed in the following paragraphs.

Many people wrongly believe that successful risk management focuses only on eliminating risks. This is incorrect. Successful risk management is about balancing risks and opportunities in a way that creates the best value for you (given your risk taking preferences). Avoid the risks that do not have an attractive opportunity associated with them or risks with which you are uncomfortable. In an ideal world, you want to pursue opportunities that have a value potential that exceeds risk costs. Fortunately, there are many strategies available to change the risk and opportunity balance of an activity.

This may sound a bit theoretical. Let us transfer these important points into reality using a simple example. If you do not enjoy riding a motorcycle, why would you take the risk of riding one? Why choose an activity that does not create a meaningful opportunity for you while it exposes you to significant risks? However, if you enjoy motorcycling, you may pursue this activity as it creates happiness and enjoyment for you. In this case, you would focus on making motorcycling as safe as possible. In other words, you seek to improve the risk opportunity balance for this activity. You can do so by wearing high-quality protective gear, choosing a motorcycle with top-notch security systems (e.g., double disk brakes, ABS), or by taking classes to improve your riding skills. By doing so you will have decreased the risks of motorcycling, while keeping the joy of doing so (i.e., the opportunity) at the same level. The same principle applies to management of inflation risks in your personal life as discussed later.

Successful risk management and assessment requires that you know your personal risk situation. At a minimum, you should be clear about the following three aspects: your risk appetite (how much risk do I want to take?), your risk management capabilities (how good am I at managing risks?), and your risk absorption capacity (given my resources, how much risk can I absorb?). Chart 52 explains these three aspects of assessing your personal risk situation in more detail.

Chart 52: Understanding your personal risk situation

Risk Topic	Examples
Risk Appetite	<ul><li>How much risk do I want to expose myself or my family to?</li><li>What are the key risks that I consider catastrophic or severe and which I should avoid at any price (e.g., loss of job, X percent loss of savings)?</li><li>At what risk level would I have problems sleeping well at night?</li><li>Am I emotionally prepared to accept the potential negative consequences if a high-risk strategy I chose fails?</li></ul>
Risk Management Skills	<ul><li>Do I have the qualification and experience to deal with the risks I am exposed to? Do I need external advice to do so?</li><li>What is my past risk management track record? Did I correctly assess my risk management skills or do I tend to over- (under-) rate them?</li><li>Collect past examples of well managed risks and risk management failures. How is the balance between the two? Do I have a positive track record?</li></ul>
Risk Absorption Capacity	<ul><li>Do I have fallback options available if my risk strategy fails (e.g., additional sources of income, savings)?</li><li>For how many dependents am I financially responsible? What does this mean for my risk absorption capacity?</li><li>For what future cash expenses will I need cash reserves (e.g., education, health care, significant house repairs)</li><li>How many months would my savings support me and my dependents in case of job loss and rising price levels? Am I comfortable with this situation?</li></ul>

When it comes to inflation risk management, you have to answer the following question: Do I want to approach high inflation defensively (main goal is to protect my current standard of living) or offensively (main goal is to beat inflation and make it significantly improve my standard of living)? Do not jump too quickly to the offensive strategy. It requires a higher risk tolerance, higher risk absorption capacity, and more sophisticated risk management skills. Do not implement a personal strategy that exposes you to unreasonable or undesired risk levels. Exceptional businesses and individuals regularly fail during periods of high inflation. Beating inflation is possible, but it is a challenging endeavor. Do not pursue opportunities for which you lack the necessary risk management skills. Deciding on whether to pursue a defensive or offensive strategy is a personal decision for which you should seek professional advice.

B) PROFESSIONAL CAREER ISSUES

The period of German hyperinflation (1922–1923) had a disastrous impact on most middle- and lower-class families. Many of these families ended up in severe poverty, including many highly educated individuals with respected careers.

For example, university professors, high school teachers, museum directors, and senior public servants were trapped by high inflation. The issue was that their employers did not raise their salaries in line with inflation rates.

High inflation treats people brutally. Past achievements and status do not guarantee future prosperity and success. The more intense inflation becomes, the greater the importance of bargaining power vis-à-vis employers. Your problem is not only keeping your job. You must also ensure that your job compensates you for lost purchasing power due to inflation. Otherwise your income will not enable you and your family to maintain your lifestyle and standard of living.

Bargaining power comes from a variety of sources. In general, bargaining power correlates with the importance of your job to the overall success of a company and the difficulty of replacing you at lower cost. Ideally, your job is mission critical to a company and you are hard to replace. A plumber in a plumbing business is mission critical, an administrative aide in the same company is not. A plumber with special training and skills can demand salary increases that match or even exceed inflation rates. The administrative aide can be replaced easily at lower cost. If you are the only person in a company familiar with its complex computer systems you have significant bargaining power. Highly trained engineers in charge of critical infrastructure maintenance for a city have bargaining power; employees at the city's cultural institutions do not. They may not lose their jobs due to inflation, but they lack the bargaining power to demand inflation beating salary increases.

The situation can change dramatically when specific skills come into play. The same administrative aide has a high degree of bargaining power if he or she is the only one who knows how to run the company's complex customer scheduling computer program. The answer is: make yourself irreplaceable and be prepared to always have a new job lined up in case you lose your last one. This is one of the most effective inflation protection strategies you can choose.

There is a lot you can do to increase your bargaining power in your company prior to the outbreak of an inflation cycle. Most employees neglect the important function of weatherproofing their careers for inflation purposes. They simply believe that the good times will continue. They miss a unique chance to increase their competitive advantage in the job market and face an even higher inflation risk. You and your dependents will pay a hefty price if you fail to have built enough bargaining power in the job market.

To raise your personal bargaining power, you can pursue a number of strategies and tactics. These strategies include acquiring language or computer skills, having a track record of exceeding expectations and reliability, being responsible for a significant amount of revenue, and having a large number of critical client relationships.

It does not hurt to have a contingency plan in place. High inflation typically comes with abnormally high unemployment rates. Therefore, you can never rely on being secure from getting fired, regardless of your performance. Your employer might simply default due to a severe recession or the company might get taken over by a competitor. You should have a Monday morning plan in case you lose your job on Friday. There are many tactics to line up alternative job opportunities. You can build a good rapport with clients and suppliers of your current job and you can get to know people at competitors' organizations.

Your contingency plan might also include a temporary relocation to another country. Being internationally mobile might be one of the most effective inflation hedges available to you. Getting paid in hard currencies in a country with low inflation is a significant advantage. To do so, you will need language and professional skills that are transferable. Ideally, you have already established some connections to another country (e.g., relatives, friends, business relationships). Relocating to a more stable country can have tremendous advantages. Given that periods of high inflation and the associated economic hardship may last for many years, it is often an unattractive strategy to sit out the problem in your home country. This is particularly the case if inflation rates seem to accelerate and start to destabilize social order. For example, Germans who relocated to other countries prior to the extreme phases of inflation in the early 1920s managed to escape the deteriorating situation caused by hyperinflation, chronic economic weakness, and the breakdown of social order. They managed to establish new professional careers in stable and prosperous environments. They were paid in a strong currency that created significant wealth effects.

Engaging in activities that secure your current job and increase your bargaining power is one of the most important inflation hedges available to you. The good thing about these career-related inflation strategies is that they also work during times of low inflation. Therefore, there is no reason to postpone the implementation of such activities.

C) FAMILY LIFE CYCLE ISSUES

Your personal inflation strategy must incorporate specific family life cycle issues. Your risk exposure, as well as the spectrum of available strategic options, is determined by your family's life cycle phase. Are you working; are you close to retirement; are you retired? If the latter, you have lost a natural inflation hedge (i.e., salary increases). Do you have children? Are you financially responsible for dependents?

It is probably not wise to engage in an aggressive inflation strategy that seeks a high return (while exposing you to high risks) when significant family expenses are in the near future (e.g., children's education, healthcare costs). A retiree might prefer a more defensive strategy to avoid financial losses due to a failed aggressive investment strategy. Retirees are among the hardest hit by high inflation. Their living expenses are met by pension payments (that tend to rise less than actual—not reported!—inflation rates do) and by personal savings (whose purchasing power disappears due to inflation). Retirees are normally quite limited in their ability to absorb risk events in general and inflation risks in particular. They may not have the option to go back to work to replace a loss of savings due to a failed inflation strategy.

On the other side, young single individuals who have finished their education and are entering the job market are in a more attractive position. Student loan debt (if at fixed rates) can quickly disappear due to high inflation. In cases of very high inflation, such loans will be later repaid with pocket money as the inflation adjusted value of the outstanding loan principal decreases year by year. Debtors are typically advantaged in a high inflation environment while savers are not.

Young professionals profit from high inflation. Not only are they likely to feel a significant tailwind as high inflation erodes their debt levels, they do not have to worry about investment losses as their savings and retirement accounts are relatively empty. They have many years of working ahead of them and their salaries will most likely reflect high inflation rates. Young professionals have the advantage that when they are eligible for government entitlements, government debt levels will have been reduced by inflation. At that time, governments are again fiscally healthy as inflation wiped out most of their outstanding debt. Consequently, they may receive more generous subsidies and government services (including infrastructure investments) after a period of high inflation. As unfair as it is, retirees may have paid substantial taxes and social security over their work lives, but inflation may be why only a fraction of this money (in terms of purchasing power) is returned to them.

Families with young children need to take extra care to avoid the perils of high inflation. Some of their major spending categories are especially impacted by inflation: education, health care, housing, and insurance.

Owning a house may turn into an inflation liability when it prevents you from exercising your bargaining power in the job market. Refinancing issues and illiquid housing markets may prevent relocating to a place that offers better career opportunities. This is a particular risk for owners who have invested in houses that are hard to resell or rent (e.g., "B-locations").

There are many proactive strategies individuals and families can pursue to protect themselves from the hardship of inflation. It is crucial that you realistically anticipate how inflation may impact your specific life circumstances. As companies should prepare war-game exercises regarding inflation risks, families should do the same. Cash flow, financing, and contingency planning are valuable not only to companies, they are required tools to protect your family.

If you plan to send your children to top universities, you should assume that these schools will be less generous with scholarships (they suffer from inflation too) and that they will raise their tuition levels higher than official CPI rates. In the U.S., for example, high inflation could raise education costs by a multiple. This is a serious risk to families as it may make top quality education unaffordable for many of them.

There is no reason to panic. The key is to understand your financial situation and the impact different inflation scenarios may have on you. If you start your preparatory work early enough, you will have a wide range of options to mitigate inflation risks. Chart 53 illustrates some risk mitigation strategies for families.

Chart 53: Selection of ideas for families to address inflation issues

Select Inflation Issues	Possible Responses
Education expenses	• Analyze special tax-exempt education savings programs • Have your children develop special skills that make them eligible for scholarships and grants • Consider quality of public schools when choosing your residence • Consider international education programs that are often more cost-effective or government sponsored. This is particularly attractive if your children are multilingual or interested in foreign languages (international experience will be an attractive asset later in life) • Being an employee at a private school or university may entitle you to a significant tuition discount
Healthcare costs	• Include inflation considerations when selecting your health insurance plan • Consider lifestyle changes that may reduce your overall healthcare spending in the future (and may lower health insurance costs as well)
Insufficient income	• Consider structural changes to your house that enable you to rent out some space • Consider swapping a big house (with unneeded space) for a smaller house and a rental property (income) • Consider cost-cutting investments: solar energy or better insulation to cut (inflated) utility bills (consider financing these investments through fixed rate debt) • Develop a skill that gives you additional income (e.g., tennis instructor, editor, math or language tutor, piano teacher)
Other actions	• Grow your own vegetables and fruits • Take advantage of multiyear prepayment options for certain expenses (e.g., car and house maintenance, insurance contracts, tuition payments). Lock in attractive discounts and inflation protection, but carefully watch counterparty credit risk issues[86]

You have to be creative when looking for ways to escape the hardship of high inflation. There are many smart moves available to you. You must use your first mover advantage. Once inflation rates have increased, many options are unavailable.

D) WEALTH MANAGEMENT ISSUES

Protecting your savings and wealth during times of high inflation is a difficult challenge. Inflation cycles go along with headwinds in the economy and high volatility in financial markets. Under such conditions, it is not easy to achieve a return greater than inflation, particularly when you need to factor in taxes on nominal capital gains.

Investors who familiarize themselves with the particularities of high inflation and who study past inflation episodes should be well prepared to face the increased levels of volatility that are likely to accompany a return of high inflation. They are also likely to avoid the mistakes of companies and individuals that get caught unprepared by inflation. There are many recurring patterns to be observed from past inflation cycles that give us some ideas of what might or might not work. Such knowledge is not a guarantee for the future since we cannot predict the behavior of governments, businesses, investors, or individuals in the future.

However, knowing past patterns of irrationality and wrong decision making is important. History does not repeat itself in every aspect, but it often does show remarkable patterns of repeat mistakes and stubbornness about learning from past misconduct.

At times, the behavior of governments, companies, and individuals will be irrational or at least surprising. Emotional outbursts reduce or eliminate rational thinking. Such conditions typically lead to extreme disruptions and irrational market outcomes. Even though such irrationality is typically temporary, as rationality tends to win over irrationality in the long term, irrationality may persist longer than many of us anticipate. You must pay close attention to the situational context during an inflation cycle and differentiate between irrational behavior and long-term rational developments. The positive exaggeration of the U.S. stock market in December 1972 (prior to the inflation shock) and the exaggerated negative reaction as a response to the inflation shock in 1974 are both examples of irrationality and emotions overcoming rationality. What followed 1974 was a more rational response to a difficult economic situation. Stock markets later reverted back to normal levels.

To draft successful investment strategies, seek professional advice. Ideally, you will find a group of advisors who have experienced high inflation or are aware of the particularities of inflation cycles. This will not be a simple endeavor since the last inflation cycle in the developed world occurred several decades ago. Try to add people to your personal advisory group who have some practical and hands-on inflation experience. These people may include friends, colleagues, or acquaintances. Some of them may have lived and managed through the 1970s in the U.S. Others may have gained priceless experiences during times of high inflation in South American countries. Do not make the mistake of relying on only one person or one book. Try to access as many diverse sources for external knowledge and experiences as possible. Just as you are likely to diversify your investments, you may diversify your advisory group or sources of information as well. Do not be shy about approaching retirees in your neighborhood to have them talk about their experiences of high inflation in the 1970s. I am sure many of them will be eager to talk about it.

Before we address inflation issues of some high profile asset classes, I direct your attention to five important caveats that may impact the success of your inflation strategy.

First, you must pay attention to local regulations, tax regimes, and other specific circumstances. Some successful strategies that worked in the past might not be available or effective in your country or region due to local circumstances. Some countries exempt investments in certain real assets from capital gains taxes; others do not. Tax and regulatory rules may impact your success significantly. As taxes typically are levied on nominal gains (regardless of inflation rates and loss in purchasing power), tax regimes have a significant impact on the performance of your inflation strategy. You must seek professional help for these and all other issues.

Second, expect phases of irrational behavior to occur in financial markets. Keep in mind that the vast majority of investors are neither Nobel Prize winners nor experts in inflation management. Most are likely to be only superficially aware of inflation risks and challenges. Expect governments, investors, and business managers to repeat the same or similar mistakes of the past. When people are surprised by a risky and uncertain situation, irrationality can feed irrationality. As a result, financial markets may experience extreme levels of volatility. In past inflation cycles, these situations often turned out to be exceptionally attractive investment opportunities. Therefore, your inflation strategy may lead to short-term losses due to such irrationality by market participants. This may not necessarily be an indication that your strategy is wrong in the long term.

Third, in almost all past inflation cycles, governments intervened in the business world, financial markets, and everyday life. Governments may introduce price controls for a select group of products or prohibit landlords from raising rents in line with inflation. Often these interventions made the situation worse. Governments intervene in markets either to protect the country's financial stability or to calm the majority of people (voters). The first issue often leads to severe controls on foreign currency transactions, trade, and mobility. We have seen this in the past (German hyperinflation). Currently, there is far-reaching government intervention in high inflation countries such as Argentina and Venezuela.

The fourth caveat addresses the unprecedented scale of the problem and the complications that could arise from it. Never before in history have we seen such a massive and concerted effort by so many countries to engage in pro-inflationary policies. Because of this scale, it may be more difficult to rely on past inflation experiences that typically occurred in only very few countries by comparison. In addition, past inflation cycles occurred at a time when the volume of outstanding derivatives agreements was negligible.

The world is different today and we may experience different and more volatile and vicious outcomes in the economy, financial markets, and society. We should not underestimate the potential for severe forms of social unrest and disorder that could emerge from future episodes of high inflation and its derivative effects on the economy and financial markets.

The fifth and last caveat addresses the severity of an inflation cycle. High inflation can have different outcomes ranging from a return to normalcy (U.S. 1970s inflation period) to a total blowup (German hyperinflation of the 1920s). Chart 54 illustrates the different levels of severity. Your strategy must adjust to the severity of the inflation cycle and the potential endgame that may follow. The severity is mainly a function of the effectiveness and courage of authorities in governments and central banks to fight inflation, and the willingness of people and voters to absorb a period of economic and social pain that is necessary to end a period of high inflation. Analyzing the situational context appropriately is highly important in anticipating the endgame of inflation.

Chart 54: Assessing the intensity of the inflation cycle

Level 1: Low inflation	Level 2: Elevated inflation	Level 3: Excessively high inflation	Level 4: Inflation spirals out of control
•Inflation at or below target levels •No significant threats to economy or financial markets •Does not guarantee future low inflation	•Inflation has started to rise and is above target rates of central banks •Inflation rates begin to have negative impact on economy and financial markets •Example: U.K. post 2008	•Inflation substantially above target rates and continues to rise •Process of "inflation feeding inflation" in place •Inflation creates significant damage to economic, financial, and social stability •Example: U.S. in the 1970s, Venezuela in 2013	•Central banks and governments lost fight against inflation •Currency collapses •Chaos in economy, financial markets, and society •Political stability at high risk •Example: German hyperinflation in the 1920s

The simple FPIM model presented earlier may help companies steer through disruptive times of inflation. It may also be helpful to individuals. This model can act as a framework helping to relate price movements of asset classes to the phase of an inflation cycle and the respective situational context.

Asset classes are likely to behave differently in each phase of an inflation cycle. Choosing the right asset is less of a problem than choosing the right timing for an investment. As Chart 55 illustrates, there is always a right and a wrong time for any asset over the course of an inflation cycle.

Chart 55: Making investment decisions depending on the stage of an inflation cycle (illustrative example)

Asset Class	Phase of inflation cycle			
	Phase 1 Pre-Inflation Period	Phase 2 Inflation Shock/Surge	Phase 3 Plateau	Phase 4 Decreasing Inflation/Normalizati on
Stocks	+	- -	+	++
Bonds	+	- -	+	++
Gold	+/-	++	+	- -
Commodities	+/-	++	++	- -
Real estate	+/-	+/-	+ +	+
Long-term fixed savings accounts	+/-	- -	- -	++
Cash	+	+/-	- -	-
FX investments in safe harbor countries	+/-	++	++	--

Legend: ++: highly attractive; -- highly unattractive (illustrative assessment)

Judging from history, there are two critical periods of an inflation cycle that deserve special attention. The first is the initial inflation shock when the majority of people are likely to get caught unprepared for rising inflation rates. The second critical period occurs around the peak of an inflation cycle when the economy starts its journey back to normalcy. These two periods require particular substantial strategic and tactical adjustments. These adjustments constitute significant changes compared to the previous period. If you fail to anticipate these critical periods, your punishment may be quite severe.

I hope that these concepts will help you to draft your own personal, tailor-made wealth management strategy. In the following paragraphs, I present a selection of issues concerning many popular assets and financing topics. Please note that this is a general discussion of possible issues and ideas around asset classes during times of high inflation. It is not meant as a recommendation or advice.

The stock market

Stocks are real assets, but do not expect that a simple buy and hold strategy of a diversified equity portfolio will protect you fully against the perils of inflation. During the 1970s period of high inflation, investing in the S+P 500 stock index would have yielded an accumulated return of about eighty-nine percent (including dividends, excluding tax considerations and transaction costs).[87] Accumulated inflation, however, would have required a return of more than 130 percent.[88] If you include taxes on nominal capital gains and dividends, the stock market performance constitutes a substantial failure as an inflation hedge.

There are two reasons for the substandard performance of passive buy and hold strategies in times of high inflation. First, high inflation creates substantial headwinds for companies and their profitability. These headwinds include:

- Recessionary developments (negative GDP growth, more difficult business climate)
- Rising unemployment rates and decrease of real (inflation adjusted) disposable income
- Falling demand for nonessential products and services
- Rising interest rates and unavailability of affordable financing and credit
- High level of economic uncertainty negatively impacts demand and business investments

- Erratic government interventions into the real economy (price controls, FX controls)
- Higher replacement costs for machines, equipment, and other production factors
- Higher input costs for raw materials

None of these conditions are positive for companies, particularly if inflation comes as a surprise to companies and investors. Companies caught strategically unprepared to deal with high inflation may face additional headwinds.

Second, stock prices are more volatile than underlying business factors suggest. Stock market valuations tend to oscillate between unjustified exuberance and exaggerated despair. Before the beginning of an inflation cycle, stock markets may be at high valuation levels reflecting past expansionary monetary policies by central banks (the behavior that will later fuel inflation) and unsubstantiated euphoria among investors. Once inflation sets in, the exuberance in stock markets may quickly disappear and despair may spread among investors. As a consequence, stocks may move from exaggerated high to exaggerated low levels. A passive buy and hold investment strategy does not deal with this type of volatility.

A good example to illustrate this point is the beginning of the 1970s inflation cycle. Propelled by accommodating central bank monetary policies, the S+P 500 index increased from 74 in June 1970 to a record level of 118 in December 1972. All of these gains were eliminated when the S+P 500 index subsequently fell to 65 in September 1974 due to an unexpected increase of inflation. The S+P index lost about fifty percent of its value in just twenty-one months. It is hard for any investor to recover from such a loss and beat inflation. A large part of these losses was probably caused by adjustments in investors' expectations. The price/earnings ratio fell during the same period from over nineteen to under eight. Investors probably overreacted before and during the inflation shock period.[89]

Behavioral interference with share prices is real and must be considered during times of high inflation. Some investors are good at taking advantage of this. The share price of Berkshire Hathaway rose about 870 percent during the 1970s inflation cycle. This outperformance was not accomplished by a passive buy and hold strategy, but by a dynamic strategy that was tailored to each phase of the inflation cycle. This strategy proactively linked investment decisions, financing decisions, and corporate governance decisions to the respective situational context and the stage of the inflation cycle. When everyone was selling, Berkshire Hathaway expanded its equity portfolio, taking advantage of extremely low valuations.

A key challenge for such dynamic strategies is to deal with behavioral factors in financial markets. Overshooting and undershooting of fair values can persist for a prolonged time. This may lead to temporary periods of irrationality that an investor must deal with. The key is not to be emotionally influenced by the majority opinion of markets, but to stay the course and focus on real forces determining the economy and financial markets in the long term. Berkshire Hathaway seems to have done this successfully during the 1970s.[90]

Stock markets showed some forms of irrationality during the period preceding German hyperinflation. Feldman points out that the total market value of Daimler shares during the early 1920s was the equivalent of the sale price of 327 cars.[91] At that time, share prices of many German companies were extremely low as equity markets, despite high inflation rates, failed to attract investors. Only at a later stage of the disastrous German inflation cycle did investors return to the German equity market. Due to a lack of reliable data, it is hard to determine exactly if stocks were a successful inflation hedge during this time.[92] German equity markets did, without question, better than paper money or fixed income bonds that later became practically worthless.[93]

For the equity markets, the initial inflation shock is likely to be the most dangerous period, as stocks often revalue from exaggerated high to extremely low valuations. Inflation shocks tend to lead to radical reassessments of general valuation levels and parameters of stocks. The 1970s inflation cycle created two inflation shocks. The first shock led to a fifty percent decrease in equity prices; the second (1977–1982) led to rising nominal equity prices (not adjusted for inflation). Overall, the price increases of U.S. stocks during the 1970s inflation cycle did not match the loss of purchasing power incurred by high inflation. Consequently, shareholders that followed buy and hold strategies were likely to lose money in real (inflation-adjusted) terms.

Companies can learn to deal with inflation. It is safe to assume that most will be caught unprepared again if inflation rates rise. There may be similar patterns in equity markets as during the 1970s inflation cycle. People who are familiar with these patterns may gain significant advantages. The FPIM model may assist you in developing dynamic equity strategies that incorporate typical inflation patterns and the associated volatility.

People who prefer stock picking over investments in diversified index funds (such as the S+P 500 or equivalents in other countries) face two additional difficult tasks. First, they need to understand how an industry sector in general and a company's business system in particular will be affected by the respective phases of an inflation cycle. Second, they need to understand whether a company and its management are knowledgeable and prepared to deal with these exceptional challenges presented by an inflation cycle. A company's unfamiliarity with inflation management issues may prove to be a costly liability to its shareholders during times of high inflation.

Chart 56 presents a selection of issues investors may include in their stock selection analysis to address the critical period preceding an inflation shock. Typically, this transition period is extremely challenging for all companies. Not many companies will fulfill the criteria of an ideal inflation investment. This example is meant to be illustrative. Remember to adjust your analysis for each phase of the FPIM model.

Chart 56: Attractive and unattractive company features for the transition period from phase 1 to phase2 [94]

Attractive	Unattractive
• Low price to book value ratios (i.e., real assets constitute a substantial part of a company's valuation) • Very low financing needs over the coming years, long-term business assets and production facilities with limited need to upgrade investments • Revenues correlate with inflation rates, high pricing power • Revenue streams are recession proof • High fixed rate debt leverage (under certain circumstances) • Products/services are unlikely targets for government price controls or other interventions • High export ratio to countries unaffected by inflation	• High price to book value ratios • Significant financing needs over the coming five years • High exposure to interest rate risk (e.g., variable rate loans) • Revenues do not correlate with inflation rates and are not recession proof • Constant high investment needs (e.g., high technology dependency) • Products/services likely targets for price controls by governments • High pricing power/high margin products • Business assets (e.g. machines) are short term and need to be replaced/upgraded frequently

Chart 56 illustrates the ideal company in times of rising inflation rates. An example is a toll bridge or a private street operator that has financed the infrastructure investment (i.e., bridge, street) with a high level of long-term fixed rate debt. The company that owns the toll bridge could easily increase tolls to match current inflation rates. Once the toll bridge has been erected, there would be minimal additional investment needs. High inflation would over time diminish the debt of the company while steady toll income would provide an attractive inflation protected revenue stream.

Investors have to take particular care when an inflation cycle moves from phase 3 to phase 4. This is when companies must reverse many (if not all) elements of their inflation strategies. This requires changes in areas such as financing, procurement, and marketing. Companies that fail to anticipate the new environment of falling and normalizing inflation suffer equally as during times of rising inflation. Their investors are likely to suffer from this management failure.

A critical approach is justified when considering stock market investments in times of high inflation. Stocks are not a perfect inflation hedge, even though they are considered real assets. Profitability issues, investors' behavior, and management mistakes may depress share prices. A simple buy and hold strategy during an inflation cycle is therefore questionable. Preliminary evidence suggests that a dynamic investment strategy better addresses the ups and downs of share prices during an inflation cycle. Companies' management needs the same dynamic approach to sail safely through the challenges of an inflation cycle. The FPIM model may support drafting such an investment strategy.

Residential real estate

Most people believe that real estate is a wise investment to beat inflation. This can be a serious misperception. Real estate investments can backfire leaving the investor with significant losses. A more balanced analysis is required to judge the suitability of real estate investments as part of an inflation strategy.

In most cases, real estate investments work well if inflation spirals out of control (i.e., level four situations illustrated in Chart 54). When money rapidly loses its purchasing power, old paper savings accounts and long-term fixed income bonds are unwanted. Only real assets are likely to protect against a significant loss of purchasing power.

History suggests that real estate investments in certain situations create problems for investors. There is a long list of caveats investors need to consider before they use real estate as their main inflation hedge and investment vehicle.

A real estate investment can bring on significant cash expenses: real estate taxes, insurance fees, maintenance and repairs, home owner association fees, utility bills, financing charges, transaction costs for buying or selling. Most of these expenses are positively correlated with inflation rates. A house may increase in value during times of high inflation, but so do related cash expenses. Do not underestimate these expenses. In some areas of the world, they can easily run at three to five percent of the assessed value of a house. In the U.S., real estate taxes per year are often the equivalent of about two percent of the assessed value of the house or apartment. This raises several issues. Sufficient income must be generated to pay for these recurring (and, due to inflation, increasing) cash expenses. This can be a problem during times of high inflation when many people lose their jobs or when salaries do not meet inflation rates. Also, the increase of the value of a house is a noncash gain that, unless sold, is inaccessible for paying the running costs. Therefore, the effectiveness of real estate investments for inflation purposes may vary significantly depending on financial circumstances and geography. Financial cash flow analysis is needed to avoid cash flow bottlenecks due to rapidly rising real estate expenses.

If a real estate investment is used to generate rent income, additional problems can arise. Experiences from past inflation periods suggest that governments can get involved in the rental market to set caps to control rent increases. These caps typically lag actual inflation rates quite significantly. Germany introduced such caps during the 1920s and, as a result, rents became ridiculously cheap. These measures are highly attractive to politicians to secure votes. During the 1920s, many homeowners in Germany struggled to meet the rising maintenance expenses of rental properties as rental income—due to the introduction of rental caps—proved to be insufficient to cover these expenses.

This problem is present today, even though government reported inflation rates are very low. For example, German politicians currently discuss caps on rental price increases ("Mietpreisbremse") as they feel that rents have increased too rapidly. Imagine such discussions when inflation really becomes a problem.

The next caveat concerns the leverage in real estate transactions. Financing a real estate transaction with long-term fixed rate debt may turn out to be a very attractive strategy, particularly if the mortgage is secured at currently historically low interest rates. Most of a thirty-year mortgage's principal payment basically dissolves when there is a significant boost in inflation rates. During the 1920s inflation period in Germany, a landlord who bought properties financed by long-term fixed rate mortgages paid very little for his investments as fast rising inflation rates reduced the real (i.e., inflation adjusted) value of the mortgage principal substantially. As these windfall profits were in some cases dramatically high, the German government later introduced a special tax on property owners who profited from inflation. [95]

During times of high inflation, it is possible that the financing of real estate transactions will provide greater opportunities than the real estate itself. This is the case only if a mortgagee chooses a long-term fixed rate mortgage. Real estate investments are made up of at least two transactions: purchasing and financing. The attractiveness of a real estate transaction as an inflation hedge may be determined significantly by financing. High debt leverage at long-term fixed rates can make real estate investments extremely profitable. Deciding on the appropriate leverage in real estate transactions is therefore an important decision and must be carefully reviewed. Risks (e.g., liquidity risks to pay for taxes, interest, or maintenance) must be carefully balanced with opportunities (e.g., long-term real price appreciation, decreasing real value of outstanding mortgage).

In general, the scale of house value appreciation is often overestimated. Boeckh points out that the trend growth rate for real house prices was about 0.4 percent between 1890 and 2010.[96] As house ownership comes with enormous risks, as I will point out later, this is a modest return. However, it beat inflation rates and it comes with other benefits, such as independence from rental markets. Over the short and midterm, house prices can be quite volatile as the last housing boom and bust cycle in the U.S. demonstrated.

During the 1970s inflation cycle, the track record of U.S. residential real estate as an inflation hedge was questionable. For example, FHFA data suggests that house prices in the U.S. rose from 61.2 index points in 1975 to 111.6 in 1982, an increase of about eighty-two percent. There is no reliable data for the period prior to 1975. The price increase between 1975 and 1982 may have been insufficient to match inflation rates.[97] It is questionable whether the savings in terms of rental expenses were sufficient to match the costs arising from home ownership. House price appreciation on its own did not match inflation rates. Interestingly, U.S. real estate prices performed better during the low inflation (and mostly low interest) period from 1996 to 2006. As most people finance a substantial part of their real estate investments through mortgages, the importance of availability and costs of mortgages for house price appreciation may not be that surprising. In fact, interest rates may be more important for real estate prices than actual inflation rates.[98]

The next caveat real estate investors should consider is the specific set of risk management challenges that are associated with this asset class. Real estate is not a risk free asset. It exposes most investors to a wide spectrum of significant risks. Chart 57 lists a selection of these risks.

Chart 57: Risks associated with real estate investments

Risk	Description
Concentration	• Value of real estate constitutes a significant portion of an individual's asset portfolio • Difficult to eliminate through diversification (due to size of a single investment)
Liquidity	• Real estate investments are typically illiquid; sales may take some time to settle, particularly during market troughs
Selection	• Real estate investments may come with significant faults that require expensive repairs (e.g., structural damages, mold, termite damages) • Even the most careful inspection cannot detect all faults
Legal/Liability	• Wide range of liability risks (e.g., injuries on property, lawsuits by tenants, damages to third parties)
Fungibility/Mobility	• Real estate sales or purchases have high transaction costs and can take time to execute • May restrict owner from relocation to pursue new job opportunities
Maintenance	• Future repairs may exceed budgeted amounts
Investment expenses	• High cash expenses (e.g. taxes, insurance, fees, repairs) • Expenses correlate with inflation rates

An additional caveat has to do with demographic challenges. Many countries experience low birth rates, which will impact the demand for real estate in the future assuming no significant changes in migration or household formation patterns. While top locations are likely to continue to achieve high prices, there may be fewer demands for less desired locations. In such situations, prices for real estate may fall despite rising inflation rates.

Despite all of these caveats, real estate may still be a good investment and a decent inflation hedge. It is important to reflect on these issues and caveats and to seek professional advice before making an investment.

Gold

Gold is one of the investments most consider a perfect or near perfect inflation hedge. Fact-based analysis shows that this is only partially true.

In times of high or extreme inflation, gold investments seem to have protected investors. Whether you look at the German hyperinflation of the 1920s, the U.S. high inflation period of the 1970s, or more recent examples of high inflation in Argentina and Venezuela, gold showed a remarkable track record of dealing efficiently and effectively with the perils of high domestic inflation. When the value of paper money starts to come close or converge to that of scrap paper, gold will shine as an investment. This assumes that gold is protected against theft and government confiscation, an important consideration.

For example, during the inflation cycle of the 1920s, the German government required citizens to turn in gold to the government at low prices. It is believed that most Germans ignored the call to turn in their gold. In March 1933, U.S. President Roosevelt prohibited the possession of gold for U.S. citizens. His famous executive directive 6102 specified that all citizens hand over their gold to the government within ten days or risk substantial fines and imprisonment.

Gold possession (often held by domestic central banks) is an assurance to international investors that governments are able to meet their obligations and that paper money is at least indirectly backed by real assets. During times of trouble, governments tend to sell hard assets to finance war expenses. Germany abandoned the direct backing of its currency with actual gold at the start of World War I. This enabled the government (via its central bank) to print money to meet war and government expenses. The value of the German paper mark started to deteriorate and the overall monetary policies ended later with extreme hyperinflation. As war and other expenses were met with printing more money, the German currency started a tremendous downward spiral. During these times, people referred to the new currency as paper mark and the old currency, which was backed by gold, as gold mark. Gold, gold marks, and gold coins helped their owners escape the process of paper money deterioration. Back then, it was a successful inflation hedge.

An additional caveat for gold investors is the risk of fraud. It is difficult for an individual to determine the gold content of a piece of gold (or jewelry). Therefore, fraud is a risk for buyers of gold.

During periods of low or moderate inflation, gold's track record as an inflation hedge is miserable. This is an extremely important observation. For example, between the end of the last U.S. inflation period in 1983 and the beginning of a new gold bull market in early 2000, accumulated inflation reached a level of about seventy-eight percent for the CPI.[99] During the same time, the price of gold declined substantially. Not only did gold fail to protect against inflation, the possession of gold during this period actually produced a substantial loss in nominal and real terms for the investor. Gold may work well during severe cases of inflation and uncertainty, but it is unreliable as an inflation hedge during times of low or moderate inflation.

The World Gold Council estimates that about 174,100 tons of gold has been mined and is presently available.[100] In addition, there are an estimated 54,000 tons of gold reserves available to be mined.[101] This might sound like a lot, but it is not. If all the gold in the world that has been mined until today was melted and formed into a cube, one side of a cube would measure a little less than 21 meters[102] (about 23 yards). The total amount of gold mined is the equivalent of about 25 grams per person. This is the equivalent of about six wedding bands.[103] In today's prices, the amount of gold available per person is less than $1000.[104] However, significant amounts of gold are off the market in the form of art, jewelry, central bank reserves, and long-term reserves held by individuals. These reserves are not accessible to investors.

Some experts estimate that only about 70,000 tons of the world's mined gold are available for investment purposes, as gold used in art, jewelry, industrial or dental applications, or held by central banks (or other long-term investors) is off the market.[105] This is the equivalent of less than US$3 trillion in today's prices.[106] This estimate of gold available to investors is, in my opinion, still too high. For example, the amount of gold held by Exchange Traded Notes (ETNs), a popular instrument for gold investments, was, as of April 2015, only 1,622 tons.[107] This corresponds to a value of about US$63 billion in early May 2015 prices. Although there is more physical gold available to investors, it is fair to believe that the liquid gold market for direct investment purposes is much smaller than 70,000 tons. This will be even more the case once inflation rates start to rise and potential sellers of gold refuse to let go of their physical gold. However, for the purpose of this book, let us assume that the number offered by the World Gold Council is correct.

Even in this case, the size of the gold market is tiny in comparison to the size of monetary markets, such as the fixed income market, or monetary assets invested in checking and savings accounts. The amount of outstanding bonds and securitized debt alone is more than US$100 trillion.[108] In times of rising inflation, bonds are typically a bad investment. In other words, the gold market seems to be much too small to absorb even a small fraction of the money currently invested in bonds. Gold prices per ounce may have to increase to levels of US$5,000 per ounce or more to provide some absorption capacity for investors looking to protect their monetary assets from inflation.

Gold is scarcer than at any point previously. The ratio between monetary assets (e.g., cash, savings, fixed income instruments, stocks, derivatives) and the size of the physical gold market seems to be out of synch.[109] It is fair to assume that if inflation rates start to increase significantly, there will be a demand and supply mismatch in the gold market, which is likely to lead to extreme forms of price volatility. To make matters worse, the increasing amount of wealth held in emerging markets may further deteriorate the imbalance between demand and supply in the gold market. Currently, many people in Asian countries are still underinvested in gold or other precious metals. For example, China has become one of the top buyers for gold as its central bank and individuals are catching up to trends in developed countries. China's inhabitants have just started to diversify their wealth into precious metals and it is likely that this investment trend is going to accelerate with greater wealth accumulation.

Gold investors should be aware that the price of gold can be quite volatile. The tightness of the market may lead to wide swings of gold prices. Even during high inflation, gold investments show patterns of extreme volatility.

Chart 58 shows select examples of gold prices during the 1970s inflation period. Any change of investor expectations or any new rumors, regardless of how unsubstantiated, can lead to such massive price swings.

Chart 58: Select gold prices during the 1970s inflation period[110]

Date	Price per ounce (USD)
Dec 4 1972	63
Apr 29 1974	168
May 27 1974	172
Aug 30 1976	104
Nov 27 1978	198
Jan 21 1980	850
Feb 4 1980	670
Mar 17 1980	484
Sep 22 1980	710
Mar 22 1982	321

Gold has a stable track record over thousands of years to protect from high inflation and failing currency systems, but potential investors must be aware of its volatility over the short and midterm.

The volatility of gold prices has increased during the recent past due to the introduction of exchange traded gold funds (e.g., Gold ETNs) that allow investors to enter and exit gold investments within seconds. While these investments have become very popular, they can lead to an enormous increase in volatility if the physical gold market is unable to absorb the high-speed transactions of these funds.

In the very long term, gold seems to be one of the few reliable mediums that allow for successful wealth transfer over several generations. For example, gold is likely to be the only available asset that a family could transfer from the Middle Ages to descendants today that kept its value. Houses can be destroyed by war or decay over time. Forest and land possessions face confiscation during political and military conflicts. Equally, stocks, bonds, and family businesses have a low chance of wealth preservation over several generations.

There are three key attractions for investing in gold as an inflation hedge, a disaster protection, and family wealth protection for the long term:

portability, ease of storage, and fungibility. Almost all of us could easily carry our net worth in gold. If you filled two one liter milk boxes (i.e., 0.53 gallon) with gold, the content would be valued at about US$1.5 million.[111] In times of uncertainty, this is an enormous advantage. Gold is easy to store and produces minimal (if any) storage costs.[112] Gold will survive fire and water damage. It is practically indestructible and extremely fungible. Gold coins are easily exchanged for domestic currency in any country.

Gold investments can be made in a wide variety of forms. Examples are gold barren or coins, exchange traded funds backed by physical gold, and derivative contracts. You can also buy stocks in gold mining companies. Each form of gold investment has advantages and disadvantages and should be discussed with a qualified professional. You can also invest in gold in the form of jewelry. However, jewelry investments are typically inefficient. The retail price for a piece of jewelry is often about four times the value of the actual gold used.[113] The gold price must quadruple in order to break even on the actual gold investment. On the other hand, you get some value out of your gold investments as you may enjoy wearing a piece of gold jewelry.

Gold and other precious metals have a good track record in severe inflation, extreme economic uncertainty, and preserving family wealth over very long periods. It is often claimed that the same amount of gold could have bought you a set of clothes (be it a toga or a fashionable suit) during the Roman era as today. Gold, however, seems to be an unreliable inflation hedge for periods of low or moderate inflation rates. Also, its high price volatility in the short term is not suited to everybody.

Foreign exchange (FX) investments

High inflation is likely to weaken a country's currency. Therefore, foreign exchange (FX) considerations should be included in an inflation strategy. This may include a diversification of your FX exposure into currencies of more stable and robust countries.

Such a strategy of FX diversification showed promising results during past inflation cycles. Germans who diversified their wealth into more stable currencies (e.g., dollar, pound) during the German period of inflation reduced their inflation risks substantially. As the German mark deteriorated from 4.1 marks prior to World War I for one dollar, to 4.2 trillion marks for one dollar in late 1923, effective FX strategies were needed to deal with domestic currency deterioration.

The 1970s high inflation period in the U.S. and U.K. provides a more recent learning experience. During the early 1970s, officials in both countries were much less concerned about inflation than their counterparts in Germany. Once it arrived, they were also less committed to fight inflation. German central bankers were adamant not to allow inflation to spread. Even if the necessary measures weakened the economy, German authorities would not compromise on their commitment to fight inflation.

The U.S. dollar weakened substantially against the German mark. This weakening continued as long as market participants did not sense any form of strong commitment and determination by U.S. policymakers and central bankers to end high inflation. Consequently, between 1970 and 1980, the dollar lost half of its value against the Deutschmark. An investor who incorporated FX diversification into more stable currencies like the Deutschmark would have limited the impact of inflation on his net worth considerably. The execution of such a strategy would have been quite simple. For example, an investor could have switched part of his investments in U.S. treasury bonds to German securities or cash. While Germany also experienced some inflation during the 1970s, its commitment to fight inflation limited its CPI rates to relatively low levels.

Chart 59: Deutschmark as an effective inflation hedge in the 1970s[114]

Year	Circumstances	U.S. CPI in %	German CPI in %	USD/DM FX rate: 1 USD is...
1970	Expansionary monetary policy	5.6	3.6	DM 3.65
1972	Expansionary monetary policy	3.4	5.4	DM 3.19
1974	Strong rise of inflation	12.3	6.9	DM 2.41
1979	Strong rise of inflation	13.3	4.1	DM 1.73
1980	Peak of Inflation	12.5	5.4	DM 1.97 Low: 1.70

Foreign exchange strategies are particularly important in severe cases of inflation as Chart 59 illustrates.

The good news is that FX investments are very easy to execute. Today, retail investors in almost all countries of the developed world have access to FX investment instruments. These include savings accounts denominated in foreign currencies, access to investment in foreign government bonds, mutual funds that cover foreign stocks and bonds, and many other forms of international investments.

Governments tend to limit accessibility of investing in foreign currencies during times of high inflation. They do so to protect the value of the domestic currency and to avoid additional inflation increases due to higher import prices. We have recently seen such interventions in both Argentina and Venezuela. Also, we have seen foreign exchange restrictions during the 1920s in Germany and during the 1970s in the U.S.

Investors are reminded that foreign exchange markets are very volatile and may react swiftly to changes in inflation expectations. The dollar lost about half of its value against the Deutschmark during the 1970s inflation period. Under Reagan and Volcker it quickly regained most of its lost value. In fact, the market was surprised by the determination of U.S. officials to accept temporary economic weakness to win the fight against inflation.

Bank stability

Bank stability may be challenged again if high inflation returns to the developed world. In general, banks seem to have problems dealing with high inflation. Bank and insurance stocks were among the weakest performers during the 1973–1974 inflation shock in the U.S. [115] As explained in Chapter 7, we should assume that a return of high inflation will have much more severe consequences for the financial sector than in the past.

The financial sector seems poorly prepared to deal with high inflation and its second and third order effects, such as rising interest rates and shifts in interest rate yield curves. An interest rate shock of the magnitude of 1973–1974 could create severe risks to the financial sector. As banks are extremely interconnected, any weakness of only a few institutions may send out shock waves across the sector. These shock waves can destabilize the whole system as they did during the recent financial crisis.

One key concern is the gigantic volume of derivatives transactions. It is questionable how these products in general and interest rate derivatives in particular will behave during rapidly rising inflation and interest rates. Past inflation cycles in the developed world occurred at a time when derivatives volumes were negligible and insignificant. Today's gigantic derivatives market has never been tested during times of high inflation.

Bank customers should prepare for similar or worse episodes of bank instability than during the last financial crisis. Therefore, it may be advisable to have more than one bank relationship, particularly with a substantial amount of savings that exceeds common bank insurance limits. Keep in mind that even though there are bank deposit insurance schemes in place in most developed countries and that their limits were raised during the last financial crisis, cash payouts from these insurance schemes may take some time in some countries. Scrutinize banks and diversify your savings across several robust banks and financial institutions.

A major financing need in the near future should be addressed now. Once inflation hits, interest rates on loans and mortgages will rise. Banks may be forced to curtail lending activities. High inflation typically forces banks to focus on short-term loans or charge excessive fees and high interest rates for multiyear lending facilities. In a period of rising inflation, do not rely on short-term mortgages or loans or variable rate facilities.

Interaction with financial institutions such as banks, insurance companies, and brokerages should be conducted with great caution and a skeptical attitude. Even financial institutions with long-standing track records and excellent reputations may get into financial trouble. Assume the worst, to avoid costly surprises. Phases of high inflation are severe risk events and they may hit the financial sector quite severely.

Debt leverage

Periods of high inflation change the rules of the game for financing. What is prudent in periods of low inflation becomes risky and dangerous during periods of high inflation. The concept of employing debt leverage changes dramatically when an economy moves from low inflation into high inflation.

During the German hyperinflation, many who increased their debt leverage to invest in real assets made a fortune. Some of them, like Hugo Stinnes, were called kings of inflation. Their recipe was simple: Buy real assets with reliable and inflation protected cash flows and finance these acquisitions with ideally long-term fixed rate debt. Continued inflation increases the value of the assets and decreases the (real) value of the debt. Later in the German inflation cycle, the value of the debt converged to practically zero. This was a dramatic case in which some highly leveraged speculators and investors made great fortunes on the back of high debt leverage. Inflation favors speculative debtors and punishes conservative savers. While this is grossly unfair and unjust, it is the reality of most inflation cycles.

The lesson learned is simple. Companies and individuals must carefully adjust their financing strategies to anticipate a changing playing field introduced by high inflation.

It must be noted that debt-based strategies are very risky, particularly for people with limited financial skills and experience. Many things can go wrong. A liquidity bottleneck could prevent meeting interest payments or other cash expenses. This can easily happen with real estate investments when associated ongoing expenses rise more than expected.

The period that follows high inflation (phases 3 and 4 of the FPIM model) can create significant challenges for the over-indebted. The economics of employing debt changes dramatically. The Stinnes business empire ran into trouble in 1924–1925. Stinnes' successors did not adjust their financing strategy to the new environment of low inflation and low economic growth referred to as a "stabilization crisis."[116] Tight monetary policies caught many companies and individuals unprepared as they struggled to obtain refinancing. The lesson learned is simple: Falling inflation rates in phases 3 and 4 of the FPIM model can be as dangerous as rising inflation rates in phase 2 if one gets caught unprepared.

The risk of high inflation (and later in an inflation cycle, the risk of disinflation) requires close attention to financing needs and financing strategies. Addressing these complex issues will require professional help. Individuals must make sure that their advisors are fully educated about the impact of inflation (and later disinflation) on financing and other issues.

Diversification

Periods of high inflation are periods of high uncertainty. Governments might intervene in certain asset classes and markets. This may change the attractiveness of an investment considerably. For example, during past episodes of inflation or economic weakness, governments prohibited the possession of gold, reduced access to foreign currencies, and restricted the availability of foreign investments. Governments introduced various price controls covering rents, food products, and general consumer prices.

Any of these measures of intervening into free markets can occur during a return of high inflation. New price controls or intervention may be introduced by governments or regulators. Investments and inflation hedges should be diversified across a wide range of markets and strategies. Doing so may help reduce exposure to unforeseen developments, government interventions, and market failures. Expect that uncertainty and volatility will be a reliable companion during future episodes of inflation.

PART V: SOME MORE THINKING ON INFLATION—THE NEED FOR A NEW ECONOMIC PARADIGM

CHAPTER 15: HIGH INFLATION CAN BE DYNAMITE TO SOCIAL AND POLITICAL STABILITY

It would be wrong to close this book without discussing the social implications and dangers of high inflation. Inflation has been analyzed from the perspective of a company and an individual, focusing on economic, financial, and business matters. Strategies to address issues and to explore opportunities have been discussed.

Inflation is not only an economic, business, or financial danger; it is a social danger as well. We tend to forget this. The more severe an inflation period, the higher the chance that it will negatively impact society and political order.

Such disturbances may last for a long time. They may open the door to political extremists who misuse the economic chaos and social distrust to take over a country or contribute to deterioration of social order. This is a serious issue; the interdependency among the economy, financial markets, and social order can lead to uncontrollable chain reactions.

I wonder whether politicians, central bankers, or other experts who support ultra-loose monetary policies and demand higher inflation rates to address economic issues are aware of these issues. Are they aware that they punish conservative savers (such as retirees) and reward in many cases irresponsible speculators? Are they aware that they fundamentally change the risk culture of a country?

If inflation occurs as a result of such monetary and fiscal policies, it is likely to lead to frustration and a feeling of injustice among ordinary people. This not only leads to a deterioration of a country's risk culture (as conservative acting people will stop being conservative) it will also lead to a destabilization of social and political order, as ordinary people who are the anchor of democracies will feel betrayed by authorities.

It is naïve to believe that politicians and central bankers have the instruments, knowledge, and power to prevent inflation from overshooting once it has begun. The belief in the ability to fine-tune inflation rates is not only naïve, it is outright dangerous. The mechanisms that link inflation to monetary policies are complex and sometimes irrational and erratic. There are serious time delays between cause (monetary policies) and results (rising inflation). It is like driving a car in which all mechanisms work with an erratic time delay. Most likely, any driver would have to struggle with avoiding over-acceleration, over-steering, and over-braking.

Monetary policies should be used as cautiously and infrequently as possible. Germany's long-term and sustainable economic success since the 1950s has been substantially aided by the steady, calm, and hypoactive management style of its central bank, the Bundesbank. The Bundesbank's monetary policies have enabled the development of a robust economy. On the contrary, a hyperactive monetary policy would have seriously distracted businesses and management from their core function: inventing, engineering, producing, and selling high-quality products. Even more dangerously, hyperactive central banking can promote excessive speculation and unproductive forms of financial engineering. This, in turn, is a huge liability and danger to social order and peace.

HIGH INFLATION CREATES SOCIETAL LOSERS

High inflation produces more losers than winners in society. Losses are not measured in only financial terms. Many people will also experience emotional losses due to periods of disturbing uncertainty, fear, and hopelessness. Retirees will fear having insufficient funds for their retirement. Families may struggle with managing insufficient household budgets in an environment of rapidly rising prices. Foundations may see the purchasing power of their endowments disappear quickly. Their management may have to discontinue the provision of funds to worthwhile social causes that were supported in the past. Long-standing family businesses may have to close their doors due to deteriorating economic conditions. These patterns have been seen many times in the past and there is no reason to believe that the next inflation cycle will show a more benign face.

As most of these people will suffer severe financial losses and emotional pain through no fault of their own, there will be anger towards authorities and the few people and groups that managed to gain from high inflation (e.g., speculators, financial "wizards"). Politicians will be accused of incompetence, betrayal, and lying, just as during and after the German hyperinflation.

The brutality of a possible devaluation of fixed income assets (such as bonds and savings accounts) during times of high inflation, the principal investment tool of the general public, becomes apparent upon consideration of a law from 1924 (the first year after the hyperinflation) in Germany. This law freed the government and other state authorities from their obligation to pay interest on old debentures, as the costs of administering and paying interest on the outstanding bonds were higher than the actual interest payments. [117] While the government, industrialists, and clever speculators profited from their high debt leverage, those who provided the funds for these often irresponsible or speculative debt strategies were left with practically nothing.

It is obvious that such a development leads to enormous discontent with the government and the political system. Herein is the biggest danger of high inflation. A population of disgruntled and angry savers is extremely susceptible to the seduction of new, charismatic political leaders who propose extremist positions camouflaged in populist wrappings. Those demagogues tend to be experts in exploiting such situations of past social injustice for their own purposes.

INFLATION CAN BECOME SOCIAL AND POLITICAL DYNAMITE

The dramatic asymmetry between winners and losers of inflation and the many cases of social injustice can unleash a power that works like dynamite on the social and political stability of a country. The majority of people tend to feel betrayed and robbed by their government and the so-called elites. They feel the pain while the government has magically shed its indebtedness. Inflation rewarded the irresponsible behavior of prior governments and lets them now appear as "cheating winners" who exploited and misled ordinary people for their own success.

Such a situation creates enormous resentment towards governments. The same politicians who marketed government debt securities to innocent families and retirees will later be silent when it comes to the pain suffered by these people due to inflation, whose prior trust in the government (and the debt securities they sold) was seriously abused. This situation is an ideal breeding ground for extremist political parties and leaders. Due to frustration, anger, and economic despair, many individuals start listening to and sympathizing with alternative leaders from the left or right political spectrum. The problem is that at this point in time even moderate people tend to gravitate to extreme positions. If they favor socialist ideas, they gravitate to the extreme left. If they tend to favor conservative policies, they may follow extreme right-wing leaders. Inflation may therefore lead to a process of radicalization and disintegration of a society. At that point, building a social consensus on issues becomes impossible.

Democracies are in great danger during such situations. Within a short period of time, charismatic extremist leaders might be able to gather a significant following and create a disastrous momentum to spread their ideas. After reaching a certain tipping point, it is extremely hard to reverse this process of radicalization and disintegration.

Germany after World War I is a warning example of this important issue. In 1913, it was a solid, orderly, and culturally diverse country with a very good standard of living.[118] Germany was a country respected for culture, art, education, and science. Education was a central element of the country. School teachers and university professors were highly respected and were addressed by their respective titles.

Less than ten years later, the country was financially, politically, and socially debilitated and partly destroyed. The chaos after World War I and, in particular, the economic misery that increased with accelerating inflation turned Germany into an internal battleground of extreme left and right-wing politicians and ideologies. Moderate politicians were attacked from both extreme ends of the political spectrums. As a consequence, many high ranking politicians were assassinated by their political enemies (e.g., Germany's Foreign Minister Walther Rathenau, 1922). Eventually, the young democracy of the Weimar Republic collapsed and made way for what would be a brutal and barbaric dictatorship.

As always in history and social sciences, it is hard to prove cause and effect, in this case the causality between inflation and the collapse of democracy that led to the establishment of a dictatorship. There is an intense debate on this issue. At a minimum we may state that the period of hyperinflation contributed considerably to the circumstances that facilitated the rise of Hitler and his party.[119]

INFLATION MAY RESULT IN LOST DECADES

Companies and individuals need to understand that severe cases of inflation do not end with central banks' succeeding in restoring financial normalcy. Even if central banks push back inflation rates to more normal levels, the negative implications are felt for a considerable time.

Periods of high inflation generally create permanent, not temporary, losses. After periods of moderate or high inflation, prices may stabilize, but they are unlikely to go back to pre-inflation levels. Therefore, anyone with monetary assets is likely to suffer permanent losses (in terms of purchasing power of savings). Only a period of considerable deflation would prevent this. This is bad news for retirees and savers. In simple terms, we will never see a gallon of milk priced at fifty cents. We will never fill our gas tanks with gasoline priced at thirty cents per gallon. These were the prices in 1960 but steady inflation has almost continuously pushed up living expenses year after year.[120]

High inflation creates a long list of secondary issues for a society that includes uncertainty around retirement planning, misallocation of capital, and overuse of debt instruments.

The situation is particularly grave right at the end of an inflation cycle. It may take a country a decade or longer to overcome the effects of high inflation. Unfortunately, the problem may be even worse. High inflation can lead to a debilitating exodus of talent that is likely to be permanent. This brain drain may constitute a significant problem for a country trying to rebuild itself after a period of high inflation. We have also observed that periods of high inflation can lead to young people being undereducated as economic hardship requires them to quit high school or college and start working. Finally, periods of high inflation may lead to insufficient investments in crucial research and infrastructure projects.

Another negative implication of high inflation is a general distrust in money, monetary aggregates, and financial markets. On a macro level, high inflation can lead to a suboptimal allocation of capital; on a micro level, individuals may make poor financial decisions. Both effects can be a serious liability for a country trying to rebuild itself.

For example, Germans during the 1950s and 1960s may have been tempted to keep their wealth in dollars or pounds, even though both currencies have experienced a long-term decline compared to the Deutschmark. It is easy to understand why some Germans behaved that way and may still do so today. Depending on the city of birth, some Germans experienced seven or more different currencies in their lifetimes. [121] Several of these currencies either became practically worthless or led to substantial losses of purchasing power.

People who experienced high inflation and their descendants may become excessively risk averse or became the victims of a distorted risk culture. As a result, they may forgo attractive opportunities in their careers or with the management of their investment funds. Once the Deutschmark was established as the first trustworthy German currency since the goldmark in 1913, Germans held most of their wealth in checking and savings accounts. Not many Germans have benefitted from the impressive appreciation of the German stock market over the past decades. The majority of Germans focuses on the preservation of capital and the elimination of uncertainty and volatility and do not allocate a significant amount of their wealth or retirement savings to the stock market. Despite the significant amount of wealth held by Germans, a large number of listed German companies are owned by a majority of foreigners. Excessive risk averseness is still holding back many Germans from investing in the stock market.

DEVELOPING BETTER STRATEGIES

Inflation is in most cases the result of poor and myopic fiscal, political, and monetary policies. It is a problem that is self-inflicted and could be easily avoided. The danger of high inflation is typically underestimated by politicians, central banks, managers, and citizens. Despite countless case studies, decision makers stubbornly fail to understand that irresponsible fiscal and monetary strategies can bring down even the strongest countries within a short period of time. Past greatness is no insurance for future stability. It took politicians less than ten years to turn Germany from best practice to total chaos (1913 to 1923).[122]

Governments that want to avoid the disruptive danger of high inflation should focus on at least two issues. First, they should avoid pursuing unsustainable strategies that are based on excessive debt and that require positive inflation rates to keep the pseudo-economic value creation going. Governments should revise their views on deflation. Mild deflation is much better than currently thought. A country with low debt levels may actually profit from mild deflation as it helps reduce uncertainties, disciplines the usage of debt and thus avoids the emergence of bubbles, and supports social stability. Second, the balance of risks and opportunities must change. Governments are overly focused on pursuing short- or medium-term opportunities without explicitly understanding their associated (long-term) risks, which is why the actions of regulators constantly lag the markets they are regulating. This unbalance is the reason for the accelerating frequency and increasing severity of financial and nonfinancial risk events.

Addressing these two issues is a prerequisite for social stability and for producing sustainable prosperity.

CHAPTER 16: HOW PAST INFLATION CONTRIBUTED TO AN ECONOMIC GROWTH ILLUSION

I have argued that over-indebtedness, fiscal deficits, ultra-loose monetary policies, and gigantic derivatives markets have created a world that is extremely complex, fragile, and hard to manage during times of economic stress. We are in a terrifying situation. How did we get to this point? And what does this mean for our future?

Many would like to blame banks. The majority of people believe bankers were solely to blame for the financial crisis of 2007 and want to hold them accountable for the current economic and financial malaise. However, a more detailed analysis shows that the causes of today's fragility are more far-reaching. It is important to avoid repetition of past mistakes.

Western society missed an exceptional chance to create a more robust and sustainable economic order at the end of the last inflation cycle in 1982. There was the chance to build an economic and social system that was robust, solid, and based on real and meaningful growth. In the early 1980s, debt levels were low and central bankers realized the perils of playing with monetary policies to encourage short-term (unsustainable) growth. Demographics provided an attractive economic tailwind to the developed world. Society, recovering from the hardships of high inflation, was longing for a period of stability and willing to do anything to avoid renewed inflation pain.

Decision makers in most developed countries, however, took a completely different path. Starting in the 1980s, most developed countries pursued strategies of using debt to push up economic growth beyond its natural level. In other words, they leveraged the economy to pull forward future growth. Given low debt levels during the 1980s, this strategy initially worked very well. Total debt to GDP ratios for most developed countries were a fraction of today's. Also, a significant portion of new debt was initially spent on future investments. Governments invested in infrastructure and families invested in new homes and the education of their children.

The perceived success of the debt-based paradigm led to an acceleration of debt issuance. Unfortunately, a growing portion of the new debt was used for noninvestment purposes, such as consumption expenses or other nonproductive or unsustainable purposes. At the same time, businesses realized that outsourcing production and manufacturing increased profit margins. A growing portion of income was transferred from developed countries to emerging markets as companies shifted their production facilities. As spending was not cut accordingly, new debt issuance was necessary to fill the gap between income and spending in developed countries.

Today a high portion of new debt is going into entitlement and subsidy programs, complex administrative functions (governments), consumption (consumers), and financial engineering[123] (companies). As a consequence, there is an excessive amount of new debt accumulation, and most of the new debt is not spent in areas that will create sustainable future growth.

Few people understand the role of debt in our macro systems. Many believe that the past few decades, with the exception of the financial crisis of 2007, showed impressive economic achievements and progress. Many experts postulate that we should return to the pre-crisis mode of economic growth. This is dangerous, as the growth experienced over past decades was not real or sustainable. It was mostly the result of increasing debt borrowed irresponsibly from our children's generation. Our children will have to deal with the debt racked up by today's decision makers, if the problem is not solved by excessive inflation in the meantime.

The immoderate ambition to increase GDP growth, the key benchmark in today's society for economic prosperity of a country, led to extreme levels of debt. Two significant mistakes were made. First, we failed to understand that GDP is a poor indicator of real economic strength and prosperity. Second, decision makers used debt as an easy way to pump up GDP and to achieve short-lived popularity with voters. Debt was a drug to which many became addicted. Not surprisingly, GDP did grow as a result of the accelerated use of debt, and it made many economies look like super-athletes in the arena of economic competition. Unfortunately, these improvements were false and unsustainable. Let me explain this with a sports analogy.

Imagine a country totally obsessed with the athletic discipline of running a one hundred meter race. Track meets are always sold out and the crowds enjoy the hype around athletes running faster and faster. The domestic athletic association of that country feels compelled to ensure steady progress in shortening the athletes' times to keep the interest alive and growing. There are two options: a hard way and an easy way. First, they can invest in better training facilities, improve training programs for coaches and athletes, and increase the workout intensity of the runners. Second, they can use (manipulative) shortcuts to improve track times. For example, build tracks with a negative slope, provide artificial tailwind through ventilators positioned behind the start blocks, or shorten the track. All these measures would undoubtedly lead to better track times and make spectators happy and interested in the sport, but they do not result in better performance if measured objectively. Eventually, when competing against foreign athletes under objective terms, the illusion of progress will become apparent.

Economic development in the developed world has a lot in common with this analogy. Real economic growth requires real progress in terms of inventing and making better products, developing new solutions, and creating value to society in meaningful ways. Such growth is based on creation preceding spending. Unsustainable growth seeks to spend (with the help of debt) before a meaningful value creation has occurred.

Examples for creation of real economic growth are activities such as making cars more efficient and more reliable, developing new or more effective drugs for diseases, producing healthier food, and generating sustainable and environmentally friendly energy. These activities lead to real progress and real economic advancement. This is the equivalent of having the runners practice more efficiently and effectively to become faster instead of engaging in manipulative and unsustainable shortcuts.

Any country can manipulate the rules to make a situation look better. We can change the arithmetic rules to calculate GDP or CPI figures or we can use debt to make up the shortfall in real economic growth and progress. However, we must understand that such behavior is nothing more than manipulative shortcuts as described above. One day, the bluff will be called and on that day, people in that country will have a rude awakening.

The sad reality is that most developed countries have taken a path over the past decades that is similar to this sports analogy. Economic growth increasingly has been achieved by unsustainable measures, shortcuts, and, by some forms, manipulative trickery of accounting procedures. Few understand that the type of economic growth we are experiencing at the moment will come to an abrupt stop when these strategies cease to work. We used these strategies as drivers of an economic growth illusion, but as Chart 60 illustrates, these drivers may cease to work in the future.

Chart 60: Drivers of the economic growth illusion (1982–2014)

Driver	Description
Excessive use of debt in absolute and relative terms	• Total debt increased in almost every dimension: absolute, relative to GDP, to savings, or per employed person
Steadily falling interest rates	• Since 1982, interest rates have trended downwards • Many countries currently enjoy record low interest rates, which makes debt service very affordable
Presence of positive inflation	• Inflation targeting of two or more percent reduces the risk to borrowers and provides a constant tailwind to debtors
Financial innovations	• Structured credit, collateralized debt obligation, and other techniques helped to find new buyers for fast rising debt issuance volumes • Derivatives helped repackage debt that is otherwise unsalable
Changing definitions of important measurement aggregates	• Redefining and recalculating important economic measures served the economic growth illusion • GDP, CPI calculation methodologies have undergone significant changes in some countries

If economic growth produced over the past decades in the developed world is decomposed, the result is sobering. A significant portion of that growth is the direct or indirect result of an accumulation of government and private debt. We did not earn the money we spent. Instead, we borrowed it from our children. Total debt in relative and absolute levels is at historic record levels for peacetime. In fact, global total debt levels are now higher than before the start of the last financial crisis. McKinsey & Company estimates that global debt levels have increased by US$57 trillion between 2007 (start of the last financial crisis) and 2014.[124]

What is concerning is that we seem to get less economic growth out of every unit of debt we raise. In other words, we need in relative terms more debt to achieve the same level of economic growth. The effectiveness of the "debt medicine" is decreasing at an alarming trend. Compare the additional GDP created since 1980 with the debt accumulation during the same period for intervals of five years. It seems that the economic growth impact of each additional unit of debt is decreasing significantly over time.[125]

When the Euro currency was introduced, the member countries accepted the so-called Maastricht agreement to adopt and enforce a set of parameters to ensure the Euro's long-term stability and longevity. One of the key parameters was a limit on government indebtedness, which was seen as a major threat to the Euro's stability. As a consequence, the participating countries set a limit of sixty-five percent for the ratio of government debt to GDP. The Euro member states, including countries with known appetites for debt, believed that a debt to GDP ratio of sixty-five percent or worse in any of the many member countries was not sustainable, and such a situation would constitute a danger to the stability of the Euro. Today, almost every European country has failed to keep debt below the agreed-upon level. Adjustment of the indebtedness with innovative accounting gimmicks or unsustainable fiscal strategies (e.g., unfunded future liabilities, postponement of critical infrastructure investments) makes the situation even worse.

These excessive debt levels have been sustained by the forces described in Chart 60. First, the trend line of interest rates has been steadily falling since 1981 in almost all developed countries. The U.S. federal funds rate was as high as twenty percent in 1981, while it is near zero in 2014. During the same period, yields of ten-year U.S. government bonds have decreased from over fifteen percent in 1981 to under two percent in 2015.[126] Today's debt load would be unmanageable for both government and private debtors if today's interest rates were closer to their long-term average. However, they are not due to excessively loose monetary policies. Thus, the developed world for now can manage such an unprecedented level of debt.

Second, an almost constant presence of positive inflation facilitates debt management. Even inflation rates as low as two percent lead to a substantial reduction of principal repayment obligations for debtors. U.S. accumulated inflation between January 1983 and March 2015 was 141.4 percent. This increase constitutes a strong tailwind for debtors and a great headache for savers. Central banks' explicit commitment to keep inflation targets at positive levels and fight deflation risk at its earliest signs eliminates the risk for debtors to be caught by deflation, which would make debt repayments more difficult. Central banks hand debtors an unconditional guarantee or a carte blanche.

Third, the explosion of financial innovation since 1982 also helped manage existing debt and paved the way for temporarily absorbing even more debt. The introduction of credit derivatives and structured credit products enabled financial institutions to find new buyers for additional debt. Collateralized debt or loan obligations (so-called CDOs or CLOs), for example, introduced new (often international) buyers to a country's new debt issuance. Credit derivatives made it possible to separate credit risks from debt investments. Credit default swaps made it possible to transform lower rated debt into investment grade debt for which it is easier to find a buyer.

Changing critical definitions, such as GDP calculation methodologies, also contributed to the unsustainable strategy of pumping up economies. GDP calculations in many countries have undergone major transformations that often lead to an overstatement of actual real economic growth. It is beyond the scope of this book to describe this point in more detail.[127]

Because of these developments, it is not an exaggeration to call a substantial part of economic growth experienced over the past decades an illusion. This growth was the result of borrowing from the next generations' bank accounts to finance past consumption. Such a debt-based approach may still continue for a while without major disruptions. However, financial markets may eventually become unable to absorb additional debt. This will be the time when trouble arrives and major debt defaults will occur.

Some readers may object to these statements and may argue that technological innovations are an important part of past economic achievements and will pay substantial dividends. An economic growth illusion, it may be argued, misses the substantial present and future impact of these innovations.

There were indeed remarkable examples of technological innovation over the past decades. However, how much real economic value is created by these technological innovations?

The balance between positive and negative effects of technological innovation may have declined into negative territory over the recent past. This trend will not reverse itself over the next years. Despite all the impressive technological innovations, the most basic goals for the economy and society have not been met; that is, to make products and services better by increasing their longevity, reliability, effectiveness, efficiency, human health impact, and environmental compatibility. Chances are high that today's refrigerators, for example, will have a much shorter life span than the same products sold a generation ago. In addition, they are likely to cost more in terms of repairs. Also, the health impact of many food and nonfood products may have significantly deteriorated over the past decades.

Real technological progress should provide us primarily with products that have a longer life span, are more reliable, and are more environmentally friendly than their predecessors (while not exposing the user or society to any health risks). Providing products that are less reliable, but have more fancy gimmicks is not my definition of real technological progress. Unfortunately, the latter issue increasingly describes reality today.

Decision makers are far from understanding the danger and risks of a continuation of the leveraged debt economy. Few are concerned about rising debt levels and the quality of growth an economy produces. It seems that the majority of decision makers prefers higher growth rates even though the underlying forces and elements are not sustainable and may lead to serious disruptions. The longer we wait before we return to sustainable and robust growth, the more disruptive the inevitable U-turn will be.

A new economic paradigm that focuses mainly on creating long-term and sustainable prosperity and robust systems and processes in the economy, businesses, financial markets, and society is needed. The next chapter provides highlights of such a new approach.

To believe that the debt-based economic growth paradigm could continue is like believing that the one hundred meter runners will be able to get away with their tricks. The point of reckoning will come and then it may be too late to prevent very serious disruptions in the economies of developed countries.

CHAPTER 17: AN ALTERNATIVE ECONOMIC PARADIGM— HOW AN ECONOMY BUILT ON THREE DIFFERENT PILLARS CAN PRODUCE FUTURE PROSPERITY AND STABILITY

Successfully addressing our economic and financial problems in the developed world without causing serious disruptions and volatility is unlikely. There is no reason to believe that the developed world can simply grow out of its current problems. Economic growth has been very weak for years and it is difficult to imagine that the developed world can return to the strong growth of the past that is necessary to start bringing down debt levels. In addition, we must not forget that the growth experienced before the last financial crisis was mainly a product of excessive debt issuance.

In my view, the most likely solution will involve a combination of inflation and debt forgiveness. Both paths will lead to substantial volatility and disruption in the economy and financial markets. This is hard to avoid. In fact, I would not be surprised if the scale of the disruptions and volatility that we will experience during this adjustment period exceeds those observed during the last financial crisis. This is the price we may have to pay for our excessive and irresponsible behavior.

When the rebalancing process is accomplished, then the debt-based economy must be replaced with a real growth economy. The goal is not short-term growth that produces long-term instability but long-term stability and prosperity. To accomplish this, we need a new economic paradigm that guides businesses and financial markets and ensures long-term stability of our economies and societies. As Chart 61 describes, there are at least three pillars to this new economic paradigm.

Chart 61: The three pillars of a new economic paradigm

Pillars of Economic Prosperity and Stability		
Absolute price stability (targeting mild deflation)	Robust systems and processes (targeting robustness)	Creation-based economy (targeting real growth)
• Long-term preservation of purchasing power • Decrease uncertainty and volatility • Required to ensure stability of fiat money systems over the long term • Disciplines the use of debt	• Systems, solutions, and processes that focus on longevity, reliability, stability, efficiency, and effectiveness	• Economy based on creating real products and solutions, not on debt, financial engineering, excessive consumer spending, or trading • Engineering, building, manufacturing, and producing are vital elements of an economy • Long-term sustainable economic growth that does not lead to boom/bust cycles or mega bubbles

Some countries have pursued economic policies similar to these. Germany's economic rebirth after World War II and its economic reinvention after the introduction of a radical reform program, Agenda 2010, introduced in 2003, were both based on principles that resemble in many ways those of the proposed economic paradigm. Pursuing this new economic paradigm is not exclusive. World economic growth is not a zero sum game in which one can win only at the expense of someone else. There is room enough for all countries to achieve improved prosperity and stability.

The transition period required to adopt the new economic paradigm will be an enormous challenge for many developed countries. The introduction of Agenda 2010 in Germany was accompanied by massive protests. It took some time until the first fruits were to be seen. However, years later Germany found itself in a much improved economic position. It managed the transition from the "sick man of Europe" to a global economic powerhouse.[128] Any country that is willing and disciplined to accept the short-term pain that comes with them can introduce similar programs.

During the transition period countries will face two key problems. First, politicians have to be aware that the economic and social situation will become worse before it improves. Therefore, the first problem is that decision makers must be courageous and strong willed to hold the course when the going gets tough. Similar to the exemplary leadership shown by Reagan and Volcker during the early 1980s, they must be tough when populous demands call for a postponement of needed reforms.

Second, politicians will have to deal with the rise of political extremism at both ends of the political spectrum. Economic weakness and tough reform agendas are the ideal breeding ground for demagogues. Extremist leaders have exploited such situations, gaining momentum that can derail an economy, crush political stability, and disrupt social order.

PILLAR I: ABSOLUTE PRICE STABILITY

The first pillar of the new economic paradigm postulates absolute price stability. Absolute price stability is incompatible with the aim of having constantly positive price inflation, a goal pursued by most central banks. Prolonged periods of constantly positive price inflation—even if the rate of inflation is low—are likely to lead to excessive indebtedness and fiscal irresponsibility in the long term. As soon as the possibility of deflation has been eliminated by a central bank's inflation guarantee, governments and households have a great incentive to increase the appetite for debt issuance. Therefore, the need is to target mild deflation, not mild inflation. This is the only way to achieve long-term price stability and prosperity. It forces market participants to create growth primarily through value creation and not through additional issuance of debt or financial engineering.

What is so bad about mild deflation (if an economy is not experiencing over-indebtedness)?

Most experts condemn any form of deflation. Central bankers, politicians, and experts warn about deflation. Even though prolonged deflation has not materialized in most parts of the developed world (with the exception of Japan), it is treated as public enemy number one. The possibility of inflation rates moving closer to zero causes central bankers and politicians to ring alarm bells. Extremely loose monetary policies will be implemented to attack even the most remote signs of deflation.

 Most agree that deflation is bad, but no one can provide an indisputable argument on why. There is no question that very high levels of deflation are as disruptive as high levels of inflation. Also, high levels of indebtedness are incompatible with deflation, but a general rejection of mild forms of deflation is not acceptable.

In some cases, the concept of mild deflation may be misunderstood. The Japanese period of poor economic growth and deflation was at least partly the result of a previous period of excessive inflation (particularly in financial assets and real estate) and over-indebtedness. The lack of structural reforms and demographic deterioration made the matter worse. Deflation experienced in the following decades was the result of these problems and not the cause.

Equally, the Great Depression that started in 1929 was caused by excessive financial inflation (e.g. stock market bubbles) and over-indebtedness. Back then, deflation was the result and not the cause of problems experienced later. The Great Depression was preceded and, at least partly, caused by unsustainable excesses and unjustified exuberance.[129] As deleveraging helped the U.S. economy to return to normalcy and to eliminate excessiveness seen in asset markets and in the use of debt, deflationary trends had to occur. Did authorities back then implement overly restrictive measures to enforce a period of normalization? Maybe. Were these restrictive measures the sole reason for the tough years that followed 1929? In my opinion, this argument has to be rejected, even though it is widely shared. I doubt that an overly loose monetary policy back then would have prevented the normal adjustment process that was needed to guide the U.S. economy from a state of debt-driven growth and speculation to a new equilibrium.

In the absence of excessive debt, asset bubbles, or uncontrolled speculation, mild deflation can create enormous value and stability for society and the economy. It can anchor paper money currencies, encourage risk management discipline, and guide an economy to high-quality, long-term growth and sustainable prosperity. Mild deflation can be beneficial and should not be generally considered as a threat. In fact, periods of real productivity gains and innovations should experience some forms of deflationary price developments.

For example, the period between 1870 and 1898 produced annual real growth of four and one half percent in the U.S., while consumer prices fell annually by two and one half percent.[130] The driving force of this economic bonanza was not an excessive use of credit or expansionary monetary policies. Instead, economic growth was the result primarily of productivity gains due to innovation, also known as the Industrial Revolution. These productivity gains were real, not the product of financial engineering and innovative accounting. It would be great to experience such a period of real productivity growth, high degree of innovation, and falling prices again. I believe that most people would highly welcome such an economy.

Deflation is not compatible with a situation of high debt leverage, which may be why many central bankers and economists today fear deflation. Deflation is a threat to debtors, and today's situation is that of overly indebted governments and economies in the developed world. Such a situation requires inflation, and central bankers these days do everything possible to invite inflation back to our world.

However, a productive and well working economy does not need inflation. Most people would be better off in an economy focused on the successful creation of new solutions, innovations, inventions, new products, and the associated process of making, manufacturing, and producing these solutions and products. If this is accompanied by stable prices or even mild deflation, prosperity would be enjoyed not only by a few successful business people or financiers, but also by the vast majority of people, including retirees and those close to retirement. Therefore, as Chart 62 illustrates, we should target mild deflation to achieve long-term price stability. We need to err on the downside and aspire for mild deflation to eventually arrive at a stage of absolute price stability, thus avoiding the emergence of excessive debt leverage and misallocations of capital.

Chart 62: Types of deflation and inflation[131]

Deflation Falling Prices		Price Stability	Inflation Rising Prices	
Medium/High	Mild		Mild	Medium/High
	Suggested new focus		Past and current focus	
Disruptive	Preferred case		Long term: Disruptive	Disruptive
• Should not be pursued	• Promotes risk management discipline as it discourages excessive debt leverage • Rewards conservative investment policies and discourages excessive and unproductive speculation • Supports long-term stability of an economy and society • Often the consequence of real productivity gains and innovation		• Tends to encourage debt-based strategies • Rewards speculation and excessive debt leverage • In the long term, may lead to boom/bust cycle when debt levels become unmanageable • Continued devaluation of paper money; problematic for retirement	• Should not be pursued

Even mild inflation can deteriorate the risk management culture of a society

The risk management culture of a society determines how it balances risks and opportunities. It is therefore an important determinant for a country's long-term stability and prosperity. In the long term, countries will have to pay the price of excessive risk taking by going through a period of painful adjustments and disruptions.

When it comes to inflation, the situation is similar. Low positive inflation rates may well create short- or mid-term opportunities and economic growth, but they encourage the use of debt. This can quickly get out of control and create an addiction to debt to fuel future growth. This process undoubtedly leads to a deterioration of risk management

296

standards. Very soon the risk management culture of a country is in danger.

This is what happened prior to the last financial crisis of 2007 and thereafter. The accumulation of such gigantic proportions of debt would have been impossible in a world of mild deflation, in which a debtor is confronted with the risk of rising real principal payments. The risk of occasional periods of mild deflation would have disciplined governments and market participants in the use of debt instruments.

Today, we underestimate the scale of the problem presented by a deterioration of risk management culture. The last financial crisis punished the conservatives, not the speculators. In fact, it led to grotesquely unfair situations. Retirees and those close to retirement, who depend on interest income from savings accounts or annuities, were hit the hardest as a prolonged period of low interest rates pushed them into severe financial problems. Highly indebted speculators, on the other side, not only were bailed out, they also enjoyed an enormous rise of asset prices, fueled by a policy of excessive liquidity provision to financial markets by global central banks. Simply put, reckless speculators profited twice: first by the depreciation of the real value of their debt (and lower interest rates) and second by the fast appreciation of the value of the assets they invested in.

The parents and grandparents who are in that unfortunate group of undeserved losers are most likely changing their message to children and grandchildren, which is likely to have a more negative view on conservative risk management practices. Most likely their message will be that saving money does not really pay off. Some may even encourage their children to take on debt and enjoy life or to speculate. It is hard to defend the merits of saving and conservative financial management when savings rates do not even match already low inflation rates and speculators are vastly and undeservedly rewarded.

The depressing experiences of this conservative group will have a decisive impact on the future risk management culture of the developed world. It will likely increase the imbalance between pursuing opportunities and addressing responsibly the risk management challenges that emerge. This unfortunate development plants the seeds for the next financial and economic crises, moving us further away from stability and prosperity.

Mild deflation does not automatically lead into a prolonged recession

Many opponents of deflation claim that deflation automatically leads to economic deterioration. Following their logic, deflation motivates companies and people to postpone spending and hoard money.

While such arguments could be valid during times of high deflation, they seem implausible for the case of mild deflation. Many examples suggest that mild deflation can persist for extended periods of time without compromising economic growth. Any period with significant productivity growth typically comes with a general downward pressure on price levels (e.g., computers). In most cases this has not been linked to economic weakness.

Sound business investments will be made regardless of low inflation or low deflation. If a company has a new product, it will not postpone market introduction until the machinery that is needed to produce it is one percent cheaper in the year to come.

Thus, people are unlikely to postpone consumption because mild deflation may lower the price of a bottle of red wine, a toy, or a movie ticket by one percent over the next year. Also, required household investments such as a dryer or a washing machine will be bought independent of mild inflation or deflation.

The same argument could be applied during times of positive real interest rates. Neither companies nor consumers tend to postpone expenditures when nominal interest rates are significantly higher than inflation rates.

If they did, there would have been substantially lower economic growth. Consumption patterns in the U.S. indicate that the positive spread between savings rates and CPI inflation had no significant impact on consumer behavior prior to the financial crisis of 2007. Savings rates were falling while consumption expenditures were increasing.

PILLAR II: ROBUST SYSTEMS AND PROCESSES

Today's world is fragile, complex, highly connected, and, at least during times of stress, close to being unmanageable and uncontrollable. This problem has been ignored for some time. However, the financial crisis of 2007 and more recent risk events such as the outbreak of Ebola and its spread to the developed world have demonstrated this quite clearly.

Risk management capabilities do not match the challenges. The risk management approach has relied too often on hope and luck, not control and preparedness. In many aspects, the world is actually at the edge of experiencing a serious catastrophe or collapse.

A return of high inflation is one of the many trigger points that could set off a chain of deteriorating events that eventually will end in debilitating collapse. While high inflation is already a serious challenge for countries with simple systems, solutions, and processes, it becomes a completely different ball game in complex and connected countries. When high inflation returned to the U.S. during the 1970s, there were relatively simple systems and processes. There were no gigantic volumes of financial derivatives or complex financial structures. Economies, financial markets, and production systems were not overly connected or dependent on each other. Nevertheless, high inflation in the 1970s created substantial damage and was hard to contain. In today's complex and fragile world, this will be a different story. It is easy to imagine how high inflation may start unmanageable chain reactions that will destabilize economic, financial, and social systems leading to massively larger scale damage to the economy and society.

Decision makers must replace complex and fragile systems, solutions, and processes with robust ones. Wherever possible, priority should be given to robust solutions to improve manageability, reliability, efficiency, and effectiveness.

Robustness should be a core principle applied to the developed world. Robustness in this context is defined as systems, solutions, and processes that can withstand high levels of stress without losing the ability to function reliably, predictably, efficiently, and effectively. For example, robust financial markets and banks are expected to function well even during periods of elevated stress. Robust systems, solutions, and processes do not offer all the bells and whistles of more complex ones. Sometimes they might be a bit Spartan regarding the options they offer. Therefore, some people might consider robustness a step back. However, robust systems, solutions, and processes are the backbone of a functioning economy, financial markets, and society. They are essential to ensure stability, protection, manageability, and prosperity, even in rough times. They are the provider of stability and not the source of volatility.

The tragedy is that in the past many developed countries were robust. Their systems, solutions, and processes were designed to withstand natural and man-made volatility. This was particularly true for the decades following the end of World War II and parts of the nineteenth century. It was probably in large part robustness that made these times so successful, stable, and prosperous. In contrast, the past decades were driven by financial engineering and an application of innovation and computer science that prioritized functionality and optionality over robustness. Modern products offer a wide spectrum of uses, comfort, and entertainment at the expense of reliability, robustness, cost efficiency, and longevity.

When I was a student, I preferred to buy very old (cheap) cars as they fulfilled efficiently and effectively the main purpose of owning a car: getting me safely and reliably from location A to location B. In the unlikely event that the car broke down, it was easy to repair myself or by a local mechanic. In short, the cars were robust solutions to my specific objectives.

Since the mid 1990s, the automotive industry has undergone a major process of digitalization and technicalization. Most automotive systems, processes, and solutions have been redesigned. An abundance of new features and functionality has been added. Many of these features have nothing to do with the primary purpose of a car (getting reliably and efficiently from A to B). Mechanical systems have been replaced by electronic ones, independent systems by connected ones. A computer[132] connects and regulates the high number of systems and processes. Gone are robust mechanical knobs and levers. They are replaced by fancier, but more vulnerable, touch pads and sensors.

Without a doubt, it is a pleasure to drive these cars, but they are more complex, more fragile, more expensive to maintain, and need an expert with special equipment to fix them. As the inexpensive mechanic around the corner likely does not have this special equipment or the training needed to fix modern complex cars, the downtime and repair costs can be much longer and more expensive than that of past robust cars. My student strategy of buying old cheap cars is therefore likely to fail in the future.

The developments seen in the automotive industry are similar to those found in all aspects of economic, financial, and social life in developed countries. The world has morphed from being dominated by simple, robust, reliable systems and processes to a world with amazing possibilities created by technology and innovations that are unfortunately complex, unstable, costly, and fragile. While initially technological progress made systems, solutions, and processes more robust, this has changed over the past years. Now robustness of products and solutions seems to be a thing of the past. It seems that further technological progress brings more complexity, fragility, and risks. The systems, solutions, and processes are often associated with significantly higher costs.

The financial world exemplifies this metamorphosis. Until the early 1980s, banking products and processes were easy to understand, manageable, and controllable.

Over the decades since, with the help of modern technology, banking has been transformed into one of the most complex and fragile sectors to be found. Simple investment and lending products have been turned into complex structured solutions. A much wider spectrum of options and solutions are now offered to a bank's clientele. Complex derivatives allow tailor-made risk management and investment solutions for every single client. Repackaging of financial products allows more far reaching distribution of credit products and a significant expansion of credit issuance. Unfortunately, these innovations come at a high price. During times of stress, financial markets can become disruptive, volatile, and, at times, unmanageable.

As a result, the ability of the financial sector to deal with stress events has decreased over the past decades in an alarming way. The financial crisis of 2007 clearly showed that the sector is not only highly vulnerable to stress events, it is close to unmanageable. The connectedness of financial markets and the complexity of the products can easily unleash undesired chain reactions that are difficult to contain.

The automotive and financial industries are only two examples of a frightening trend in the developed world, which replaced robustness with complexity and fragility. A mushrooming zest for regulation, the introduction of new products, materials, and services without proper risk management, and the exponentially growing connectivity of systems and processes of all kinds have created a dangerously complex world. Compliance, tax, and legal regulations have taken over and contributed to an enormous, but underestimated, risk management challenge. In addition, expenses for navigating through such a complex world have risen dramatically. This trend has not been limited to the economic and financial world; it has also spread to society. Signing up a child for an organized activity used to be a three minute event. Today, such a procedure requires filling out countless release, information, health, and indemnity forms.

Fifty years ago, a bank CEO understood all products and processes in a bank in great detail. He could have performed any job in the bank with very little training. In other words, top management knew very intimately the risk situation of a bank. Today, few (if any) top managers are able to do this. Products and processes have become immensely complicated and specialized. Bank management is dependent on armies of specialists for each business and support function. Today's top managers in banks are coordinators of an army of specialists. This has become quite problematic in terms of the risk management issues and challenges.

The drivers of complexity and fragility, which are also the destroyers of robustness, can be hard to identify. It is crucial to understand these drivers. Chart 62 illustrates a selection of the most prevalent killers of robustness.

Chart 63: The drivers and forces of the modern world's complexity and fragility (killers of robustness)

Drivers and forces for complexity and fragility	Comments
Massive proliferation of rules and regulations not controlled or managed	• Tendency to over-regulate increases complexity and decreases local risk management responsibility and competence • Regulation standards focus on case-based rules rather than general principles (micro versus macro managing approach)
Increasing connectivity among systems and processes	• Connecting an increasing number of systems making them dependent on other systems • Understanding all forms of connectivity becomes increasingly difficult and eventually impossible
Introducing increasingly new functions and features to existing systems, solutions, and processes	• Exponential increase of functionalities, options, and features included in systems, solutions, and processes
Uncontrolled digitalization	• Trend of digitizing and computerizing regardless of actual needs, efficiency, and effectiveness
Pursuing new opportunities without understanding or assessing associated risks	• New systems, solutions, and processes as well as changes made to existing ones neglect to identity and assess risk management impact • Society prioritizes the exploitation of new opportunities over risk management issues

Complexity and fragility are in many ways problematic. First, they tend to reduce the life span of solutions. For example, modern constructions or products are not expected to have the same longevity as those built or produced in the past, despite all the technological progress. An extreme example can be seen in Trier, Germany. The so-called Roman bridge[133] is built on pillars from the first century. Even today, this ancient bridge construction carries modern car and bus traffic, despite its age of almost 2000 years. It is quite unlikely that any one of today's modern bridges will be in use in 2000 years. Roman engineers stressed robustness and purpose; thus, many of their buildings are or could be in use today.[134]

Second, complexity and fragility make products less reliable and require significant expense for maintenance and repairs. Refrigerators and televisions, for example, were simple appliances that could be repaired inexpensively locally. Today, all consumer electronics and appliances have more complex systems and need expensive experts to fix and maintain.

Third, complex systems tend to have more downtime. Car repairs are unlikely to be done quickly while the owner waits.

Finally, and most important, complex systems increase the risks for substantial and uncontrollable chain reactions that spread to multiple locations, witnessed in the recent financial crisis. Loss of manageability is therefore a key concern.

Because of these issues, complex systems are likely to push up actual inflation rates in the future. This effect tends to be overlooked in many inflation statistics.

The trend of including risky and inefficient complexity and fragility in our systems, solutions, and processes must be stopped. A return to the principle of robustness is a gigantic step toward a more stable, manageable, and prosperous world. Efforts should be made to start this process as soon as possible. Robustness of systems and processes is a needed pillar for a new economic paradigm that seeks to avoid the mistakes of the past and that reintroduces manageability to our economy.

Economic growth is not a luxury for modern economies in developed countries. It is absolutely critical for achieving prosperity and maintaining social stability. Countries that have been derailed by political revolutions or political extremism typically went through a period of insufficient economic growth. Therefore, decision makers have to do everything in their power to avoid prolonged economic weakness and economic volatility. By doing so, decision makers must focus on sustainable economic growth and avoid boom/bust cycles, witnessed many times in the past. The key is not to strive for just economic growth per se, but to aspire to high-quality and sustainable economic growth. High-quality economic growth is the gift that keeps on giving. Poor-quality growth will eventually lead to severe problems in the future including massive disruptions and volatility.

What constitutes safe and high-quality economic growth and how is it measured? In today's developed world, most people look at overall aggregates such as gross domestic product (GDP) or unemployment rates. GDP figures after adjustment for inflation, so-called real GDP growth, are seen as the most important and are most frequently used to assess and measure the activity and health of an economy. This is a dangerous misperception. GDP-based measures are often inaccurate and misleading.

A full discussion of all the problems surrounding GDP measures is beyond the scope of this book. Note that GDP is nothing but an accumulation of all sensible and nonsensical activities in an economy. Meaningful activities contribute as much to the GDP measure as negative value activities. For example, businesses investing in training of their employees, in research and development, and in new machinery have a positive impact on GDP. On the other side, people spending money on unhealthy food or on activities that deteriorate the environment equally contribute positively to GDP calculations. It does not matter whether an activity creates or destroys value to society; for GDP calculation purposes, every activity is treated the same way.

This can lead to quite grotesque results. Buying unhealthy foods may push up GDP not only in the year of consumption, but also in following years when unhealthy people pay for medical treatments. As the price for medical treatments tends to rise faster than CPI rates, unhealthy living may even over-proportionally contribute to future GDP figures (and to CPI data as well).

GDP measures are based on complex adjustment processes and calculation rules. Therefore, there are no meaningful comparisons possible across countries (which the media does every day). A one percent GDP increase in the U.S. means something very different than a one percent increase in a country such as Germany or China.

If one is willing to exclude long-term effects from economic policies, it is quite easy to increase GDP figures for an extended period of time. Governments, companies, and individuals can do so by using extensive amounts of debt to push up current spending levels. Obviously, there will be a rude awakening to this irresponsible behavior, particularly if additional debt is mainly used for non-investing expenses (such as consumer spending or nonproductive entitlements). In these cases, GDP measures are likely to mislead the observer in his assessment of the health and strength of an economy.

Therefore, it is of utmost importance to focus on high-quality GDP growth. More specifically, elements contributing to GDP growth should originate predominantly from innovations (new or improved products), productivity improvements, infrastructure or other meaningful investments, manufacturing, and education. The current world offers ample opportunities for high-quality economic growth. There is need for new and better clean energy and environmental and health friendly solutions. Upgrading all residential and commercial buildings and their contents (e.g., furniture, appliances, infrastructure) to healthier and environmentally friendlier standards would provide substantial opportunities for economic growth. Upgrading outdated infrastructure would also constitute a significant pool of future economic demand. And finally, adding the positive demand effects originating from the transition of emerging market countries to new populous economic powerhouses will create growth potential for decades to come. Switching to higher quality growth does not lead to lower economic growth and lower standards of living.

What governments and other authorities fail to understand is that switching to a high-quality growth strategy will lead to double benefits. First, it provides economic growth and stimulus for the present. Second, it will have positive secondary effects in many ways: cost savings as future secondary costs will decrease (e.g., addressing environmental pollution), higher growth due to infrastructure or education investments, positive benefits resulting from higher degree of financial, fiscal, and monetary stability. Let me add one more perspective: If higher investments in education today lead to graduates achieving twenty-five percent higher salaries and companies that employ them will achieve higher productivity and higher profitability, the impact on tax revenues can be beyond the wildest dreams of politicians.[135]

Often, governments do not have to do much to enable the creation of high-quality growth. In fact, more often than not, governments and other authorities hinder quality growth as they burden businesses with excessive (and often ineffective and counterproductive) regulations, rules, and compliance duties. Governments must set the boundaries for the playing fields and define the direction for business. But then they should try to get out of the way of business. I have never encountered an example in which governments succeeded in micromanaging society, the economy, or individual businesses. Countries bloom when liberated from unproductive, unwise, or overly burdensome rules. In fact, China has been prospering over the past decades due to a constant and intelligently devised strategy of deregulation and pro-business policies. Germany has started to prosper again after the Schroeder government implemented courageous structural reforms.

Simple changes can have great impact on moving to a higher quality growth economy. For example, balancing the treatment of debtors versus savers is an easy first step to prevent excessive debt accumulation or debt creation for unproductive purposes. Today's world sees an extreme asymmetry between the ways debtors are pampered and savers are punished. In some countries, governments financially punish parents who take on debt to pay for children's education (which will produce higher tax revenues in the future). However, if the parents use the debt instead on speculative efforts such as flipping homes, debt is often fully tax deductible. Such rules are the opposite of what is needed to achieve high-quality growth.

Another important lever for achieving long-term sustainable growth is the strengthening of small and medium sized companies (SMEs), often the epicenter for innovation and quality growth creation. A large part of Germany's economic success, for example, is rooted in this sector. SMEs have been a crucial stabilizer for Germany's economic growth, employment levels, and social stability. In many countries, however, these companies cannot realize a fraction of their actual potential. Often, they are crippled by excessive compliance and regulatory costs and time-consuming bureaucracy. There is also little help from government agencies in the form of education support for young employees in these SMEs.[136]

In an ideal world, governments would protect and promote these SMEs comparable to the way a gardener protects young seedlings until they reach a meaningful size. To get to this point, radical thinking might be required. For example, to allow SMEs to "ignore" any regulation or compliance activity[137] demonstrated to be unreasonably time-consuming or burdensome.

The new economic growth paradigm will be distinctively different from the past in developed countries. Chart 64 illustrates some of the most important differences.

Chart 64: Comparing the new and old economic growth paradigms

New economic growth paradigm (safe and sustainable economic growth)	Traditional economic growth paradigm (debt and financial engineering-based)
• Focus on efficient and effective education and transfer of practical real world skills • Education seen as a continuous process of highest importance	• Despite huge investments, education outcomes not impressive (e.g., low PISA)[134] • Missing link between education and real world
• Strong focus on making and inventing things (i.e., revival of manufacturing, production, and engineering)	• Focus on financial world, trade of imported products (distribution) and services
• Focus on innovation and constant improvements of existing systems, solutions, and processes • Objective is measurable improvements for society (environment, health, safety)	• Innovation focused on financial engineering, entertainment, or low value creation activities
• Real value accounting— understanding and managing the long-term impact of economic activity including environment, health, and social stability	• Focus on financial accounting • Value creation measured in purely financial terms
• Balancing of incentives given to debtors and savers (to avoid excessive accumulation of debt)	• Preferred treatment of debtors at the expense of savers (e.g., asymmetric tax treatment)
• Export success proves quality and competitiveness of domestic products and services	• Import-driven economy as manufacturing base has been neglected and has become uncompetitive in terms of quality or costs
• Long-term view on economic growth issues	• Short-term view on economic growth

Many countries might claim that they are following these requirements. For example, most developed countries would claim that they have invested heavily in education or that their schools are among the best in the world. The key is to differentiate between unsubstantiated claims of greatness (often derived from past achievements) and current evidence for outperformance and superior achievements. How can a country credibly claim the best education if it is not among the top ten nations in the PISA ranking for high school students?[138] How can economic growth and prosperity continue if a country's PISA results are at best mediocre in math, science, and literacy? Most developed countries are not among the top ten nations in the most recent PISA rankings. Some of them do not even make it among the top twenty in some categories. It is more than striking that current economic strength of a country seems to correlate with its ranking in the PISA studies. For example, Asian emerging market countries not only enjoy a vibrant period of economic growth, they also show positive momentum in the PISA rankings with the top five positions almost exclusively being occupied by Asian countries. This should be a loud wake-up call for developed countries.[139]

WRAPPING IT UP: COUNTRIES THAT ARE CLIMBING UP AND COUNTRIES THAT ARE FALLING BEHIND

Pursuing the three pillars proposed in this chapter is an important prerequisite for ensuring future economic growth, prosperity, and social stability. Exiting the current path of debt leverage, low-quality economic growth, and excessive complexity will likely be rewarded with substantial economic and social improvements in the future.

If we look at the situation of today's countries and their progress towards these requirements outlined above, we see an alarming dichotomy. On the one side, we find countries that are on a positive and encouraging growth trajectory. Many emerging market countries belong to this group that I call the CLIMBERS. Chart 65 illustrates the characteristics of a typical CLIMBER nation.

Chart 65: Characteristics of successful countries (CLIMBERS)

	Characteristics	Explanation
C	Comprehension and zest for critical thinking	• Education focused not only on degrees, but on critical thinking and holistic comprehension of matters
L	Leadership	• Leadership devoted to long-term stability, high-quality economic growth, and sustainability • Thought through solutions preferred to "quick and dirty" fixes or short-term solutions
I	Invent and engineer	• Focus on invention, innovation, and engineering • Engineers and inventors more highly regarded than bankers and lawyers
M	Make and manufacture	• Manufacturing and making things core to a country's economic mission; outsourcing limited to true commodity products or noncore processes
B	Become better in any aspect of life at any time	• Zest for constant improvements • Complacency and arrogance seen as key enemies of long-term economic success
E	Efficiency and effectiveness	• Every system or process geared to highest possible efficiency and effectiveness
R	Robustness and stability	• Robustness is a key principle in any form of conduct be it engineering, manufacturing, system design, or other activities

On the other side, we find a group of countries that are clearly struggling to stay competitive. This group seems to be somewhat lost when it comes to the challenge of achieving high-quality and sustainable economic growth. They are caught in an addiction to debt and unsustainable policies seeking to stabilize fiscal, financial, and economic conditions that are far from stable. Their excessive focus on short-term goals prevents them from implementing programs geared at re-establishing long-term prosperity and stability. Many developed countries belong in my view to this group that I will call the LOST countries. Chart 66 provides the characteristics for a typical LOST country.

Chart 66: Characteristics of struggling economies (LOST countries)

	Characteristics	Explanation
L	Legal, administrative, and regulatory excessiveness, ineffectiveness, and complexity	• Exponential growth of complexity created by fast rising number of rules and regulations in all aspects of business and society • Complexity hinders businesses to reach their full potential and stifles entrepreneurship
O	Outsourcing paradigm	• Widespread neglect of the importance of domestic manufacturing, engineering and production • Talent wasted in support activities such as finance or legal. Primary activities such as engineering, manufacturing, and construction starved of qualified and trained talent
S	Self-delusion about real strength and competitiveness	• Own competitive position vastly overestimated • Widespread complacency and arrogance; reluctance to accept the need for radical structural change • Biased view of reality; distorted self-perception
T	Trade imbalances	• Multiple trade imbalances: persistent trade deficits, imbalance between volume of trading activities versus domestic manufacturing and production activities (paradigm of trading and distributing what other nations produce)

LOST countries seem to be following the wrong course. This does not mean that they cannot return to the right path and transform themselves into a CLIMBER nation. However, this transformation is likely to lead to a period of disruptions, volatility, and pain. As I have pointed out, many of these countries may have to go through a period of high inflation as their actions and policies have led them to a point at which rising prices is a logical consequence of past behavior and necessary to clean up imbalances and misallocations.

While the period of high inflation and/or debt restructuring may be painful, it provides a chance for a new beginning and the introduction of new economic policies that stress long-term safe and sustainable economic growth. There is an attractive future ahead if we manage to get safely through the hard and painful period of transformation.

PART VI: FINAL DISCUSSION AND OUTLOOK

CHAPTER 18: FINAL DISCUSSION AND A LOOK INTO THE FUTURE

You have reached the end of this book on inflation. It is now up to you to assess the validity of my concerns and to determine appropriate next steps for your professional and personal life. As I have mentioned, this book is only a starting point on a journey that seeks to address inflation risks and opportunities. Some readers may not agree with the points I make. Others may agree, but feel that there is still plenty of time until inflation requires targeted actions. Before you decide on next steps, I would like to remind you of my key messages.

First, high inflation is a very serious threat for businesses, individuals, and society. If you get caught unprepared, you may risk the survival of your company or may expose yourself and your family to severe threats. Second, if inflation returns to the modern developed world, its consequences will be much more severe than during past periods of high inflation. We are living in a complex, interconnected, and fragile world that has never been tested by high inflation. Our monetary reality looks very detached from economic realities. Our systems, solutions, and processes in the developed world have been developed during times of low inflation and are made for times of contained inflation. Therefore, we should not be surprised if the dimensions of the next financial crisis go far beyond what we experienced during the financial crisis of 2007. Third, there are many strategies, concepts, and tools available to companies and individuals that may help mitigate inflation risks. You can prepare to deal with high inflation. Some companies and individuals might even be able to turn inflation risks into attractive opportunities. Warren Buffett, CEO of Berkshire Hathaway, capitalized enormously on his superb understanding of the new economics of high inflation and produced astonishing returns for his shareholders during the 1973–1982 U.S. inflation period.

While writing this book, I came across an increasing number of absurdities in the economy and financial markets of developed countries. How can it be that countries such as France, Italy, Spain, Japan, and the U.S. enjoyed record low yields on their government debt in early 2015 despite struggling with record levels of debt, immense fiscal deficits, deteriorating demographics, suboptimal or deteriorating education systems, and frightening, extremely loose monetary policies? How can it be that politicians and central bankers talk openly about the need to raise inflation or the need to weaken their own currency and only a few people seem to be concerned about these intentions? Did we forget that those very same policies brought great harm to societies in the past?

Is this the calm before a major storm? Are we sleepwalking into the next crisis? We know from history that the vast majority of experts and decision makers in politics, finance, and business have failed at anticipating major risk events in the past. It seems that we are caught by the magnetism of following blindly the momentum of the recent past. Our assessment of reality seems to be dangerously out of sync with the pools of emerging risk threats that have grown significantly, but have not yet materialized. We should be highly skeptical if current reality (i.e., the confidence and complacency of most experts and decision makers) does not match the facts that our analyses provide. We need to escape the magnetism of a momentum- and herd-based interpretation of reality or we will be caught unprepared when major risk events occur. Is our assessment of reality backed by the facts and evidence that our analyses provide or is it the product of behavior that is rooted in the uncritical extrapolation of the recent past into the future?

Changing course is not a trivial thing. Short-term reality is the product of our collective thoughts, decisions, and behavior, regardless of how substantiated and justified they are. Our short-term reality can deviate significantly from what fact-based analysis and critical thinking would suggest as likely long-term outcomes.

LOFIS Inflation that I have described as a likely outcome of current and past economic, financial, and monetary realities is behavior driven and will occur once a critical mass of people change their assessment of inflation risks and subsequently change their behavior. At that point, they will shift increasing parts of their wealth from monetary assets to real assets. At this tipping point, inflation is likely to accelerate quickly. While it is impossible to accurately predict the timing of this change of behavior leading to inflation, its occurrence should not surprise us and should be seen as a logical consequence of past behavior.

LOFIS Inflation is discussed from the perspective of the developed world, as many emerging markets seem to enjoy improved economic, financial, demographic, and fiscal conditions. It is the developed world where monetary reality is most widely detached from economic reality. LOFIS Inflation risks may be severely aggravated by EMEG Inflation risks, originating in emerging market countries. The billions of people living in these emerging market countries, upgrading their living standards to become modern consumers, will create substantial demand for commodities, products, and services. A simultaneous appearance of LOFIS Inflation and EMEG Inflation could lead to a perfect inflation storm that most certainly will lead to devastating and disruptive economic and social volatility in the developed world.

It is conceivable that a return of high inflation might trigger reversed roles. That is, today's emerging markets will become the new developed world, while developed countries will be on a road to long-term decline. We should not forget that in the long term not a single country managed to keep its super power status forever. The typical course in history is that countries rise, bloom, peak, and eventually fade away.

Maybe some kind of exceptional constellation, economic innovation, or miracle will prevent high inflation. Maybe there is a magic solution for the current economic malaise. The world sometimes does take surprising turns. Reliance on hope or luck, however, cannot be a basis for responsible risk management. Doing nothing in terms of understanding the threat of high inflation is, in my view, negligent and irresponsible. Sophisticated risk management anticipates possible turns in circumstances and develops contingency plans before the new reality materializes. At a minimum, all of us should form a basic understanding of the economics of inflation and how these new economics will impact us. Ideally, all of us will have well prepared contingency plans in place that will help to lessen the negative impact on our professional and personal situations if or when inflation returns to the developed world.

Such contingency plans can become a decisive competitive advantage for companies once high inflation starts to materialize. It may be the source for sustainable outperformance over competition and lead to significantly improved competitive situations.

It is better to prepare for the worst and be relieved when it never materializes than to prepare for the best and pray that the worst will never happen. I hope that this book motivates you to take inflation risks seriously. It is now up to you to turn concern about inflation into effective risk management strategies for your company and your personal situation. I wish you the best of luck in this important task.

FOOTNOTES

[1] When we analyze cause and effect of the economic malaise in Japan, we may quickly learn that the real cause of the problems is not deflation, but a combination of highly inflationary property and equity markets during the 1980s ("bubbles"), the inability to clean up the banking system after the bubble burst, unaddressed demographic issues, and the lack of structural reforms.

[2] There is one exception. If governments can convince people to increase their savings and invest in government bonds (or put money into savings accounts with banks who then use the funds to invest in government bonds) and to accept low interest rates (in absolute and relative terms), then we might experience an extended period of low inflation (or even deflation) and high or rising indebtedness at the same time. Such a situation requires that almost all government debt is issued in the domestic currency. However, this will most likely create problems in the future. As debt levels continue to rise, people will eventually look at alternative currencies to protect their savings.

[3] Economic growth in developed countries is not only low in absolute terms, but also relative to growth rates in emerging markets.

[4] There are also cases when governments experience continued LOFIS Inflation even though radical currency reforms have taken place. The most recent history of Venezuela is an example.

[5] Bernholz (2003), p. 19. In the same book, the reader will find a very detailed historic compilation of hyperinflations.

[6] Bernholz (2003), p.37. Bernholz points out that metallic currencies were also victims of debasement, but the resulting inflation was rather moderate.

[7] Compare Reinhard (2009), p. 181.

[8] Source for data: BIS Statistics; McKinsey (2011), Bain (2012), my estimates and calculations. A more detailed discussion of the issues related to the stability of the financial world can be found in Chapter 7.

[9] The reader might object by saying losses and gains are a zero sum game. However, as banks and the financial sector are heavily intertwined, the losers might weaken the winners through these interconnectivity problems. For example, if some writers of credit derivatives had not been bailed out by their respective governments during the last financial crisis, several major banks would have been destabilized as well.

[10] Source for data: U.S. Department of Labor.

[11] Source for data: Berkshire Hathaway Annual Reports; U.S. Department of Labor (CPI data). Note: Berkshire performance: book value per share. Share price performance was up about 870 %.

[12] Loomis (2012), starting p. 9.

[13] Obviously, during the U.S. 1970s inflation period, one would have picked currencies such as the German deutschmark as stable. Critics may claim that in

retrospect it is easy to make such assumptions. However, during the 1920s and earlier, it was suggested by U.S. authorities that they would not follow the German pro-inflation strategy. Equally, Germany made it very clear during the 1970s that it would not accept rising inflation and would fight it even at the expense of higher unemployment and lower economic growth. There will always be countries that refuse to play the inflation game to get rid of excessive indebtedness. These countries tend to be safe harbors during times of excessive inflation.

[14] CNBC Website, January 12, 2015: China's auto sales slowed in 2014 but reached 19.7 million vehicles.

[15] As an example, think about standardized software packages that can be sold thousands of times without leading to noticeable amounts of extra demand for (inflation increasing) commodities, employees, or other resources. In a developed economy, billions of dollars of revenues originate from sales of products with such scalable properties.

[16] U.S. CPI-U; U.K.: Retail Price Index (RPI).

[17] U.S. Department of Labor.

[18] Source for data: U.S. Department of Labor; Worldbank data (GDP).

[19] Source for data: U.S. Department of Labor; Worldbank data (GDP), Samuelson (2010); Bureau of Economic Analysis (website).

[20] Feldman (1997), p. 5.

[21] Ehrlich (1987), p. 36, provides more background to the context of Caesar's quote.

[22] In my view, it is a myth that debasing a currency will solve any economic problems. In fact, such a strategy might aggravate the problem. First, importing commodities becomes much more expensive. Second, debasement of currencies does not make any product better in terms of quality or functionality. Third, a significant portion of the total costs of an exported product does not occur in the domestic currency. Transport, distribution, marketing, and service costs make up a huge portion of total costs and occur in the export country. If such debasement strategies worked, then Venezuela and Argentina would be the top exporting nations.

[23] Many traditional economists would deny this problem, claiming that higher exchange rates encourage domestic production of imported goods in developed countries. However, such thinking may miss some important developments. Emerging markets' competitive edge is no longer solely confined to cheap production or labor cost advantages. It is based on a multitude of strengths, including enormous production know-how, quality improvements, better education systems, and enormous depth of engineering talent. In my view, the developed world is much more dependent on imports and production from emerging markets than many of us might realize.

[24] Charlie Rose interview with economist Niall Fergusson on June 19, 2013, on Bloomberg TV.

[25] Note: This is a fictive example. However, similar transactions such as these do happen in the real world.

[26] Obviously, such derivative transactions may yield advantages in terms of regulatory, rating, or other capital requirements.

[27] For example, Germany decided after the event at Fukushima to phase out nuclear power altogether.

[28] Many experts and observers warned early on that risk-taking excesses without appropriate risk management activities could lead to severe problems for the economy and the banking sector. For example, I warned as early as 2000 in a *Financial Times* interview of a possible banking crisis if serious credit risk management deficits were not addressed in time (see bibliography).

[29] For example, inflation rates in the U.S. were 12.6 percent in 1916, 18.1 percent in 1917, 20.4 percent in 1918, and 14.5 percent in 1919. Source: U.S. Department of Labor Statistics.

[30] The U.S. experienced three consecutive years of fiscal deficits of enormous dimensions reaching a level of 11.9 percent in relation to GDP in 1918 and 16.8 percent in 1919. Data from website: USgovernmentspending.com.

[31] Source: U.S. Department of Labor Statistics.

[32] Bresciani (1937), p. 196.

[33] Calculations based on data from Bresciani (1937) page 47 and 437–438. Starting 1919 numbers based on Goldmark (to adjust for inflation). Note that years 1916 to 1922 were based on April to March data for the respective years (not calendar years).

[34] Bresciani (1937), p. 30.

[35] Bresciani (1937), p. 30.

[36] Calculations based on data from Bresciani (1937), p. 30.

[37] Feldman (1997), p. 5. Source of original data: Statistisches Reichsamt Zahlen zur Geldverwertung in Deutschland 1914–1923, Berlin 1925.

[38] Source for data: CPI-U: U.S. Department of Labor; U.S. GDP: U.S. Department of Commerce; World GDP: World Bank (all: website information).

[39] PISA stands for Program for International Student Assessment conducted by the OECD (Organization for Economic Cooperation and Development). It is a global assessment of the scholastic capabilities of fifteen-year-old students.

[40] This is a major problem if you receive payments that are directly or indirectly linked to CPI data. Retirees or holders of inflation linked securities may suffer from this issue.

[41] I have not yet touched on product longevity issues that make this problem even more serious.

[42] I define "simple technology standard" as the equipment and service subscriptions necessary for a normal household to fulfill family requirements. This includes repair and maintenance fees. Equipment purchase prices should be spread over the life span of a product (which seems to continue to decrease).

[43] Please note that in this context I use the term "quality" not to describe technical features or performance data, but to measure the robustness and longevity of a product.

[44] Most methodologies do not sufficiently include self-repairs or increased maintenance time (whether by consumers or paid specialists/repair men). Also, costs of extended warranty programs - in lieu of providing maintenance - often are not fully included.

[45] This is also an inflationary effect as clean up and disposal costs will continue to increase over time.

[46] Ideally, CPI would divide the purchase costs (including all service and maintenance costs) through the expected years of service for consumer goods, explicitly reflecting shorter product life spans and costlier repairs. This would be fair, as most CPI methodologies adjust for performance improvements of products.

[47] The effects of higher base values of GDP can create inflation problems at lower GDP growth rates than those observed prior to the financial crisis.

[48] For example: GDP growth or consumer spending.

[49] We should not expect that this will occur in a linear way. Instead, expect increasing volatility of valuations and markets along the way.

[50] In the meantime, the price differentials among European government bonds have decreased again.

[51] Hammes (2010): Presentation at the Guy Carpenter Insurance Conference, Munich, Germany. Based on sector samples.

[52] Hammes (2010): Presentation at the Guy Carpenter Insurance Conference, Munich, Germany.

[53] Estimates for 2010–2012. Sources for data: Bank capital (equity) based on lower range of my estimates (as reliable data was hard to obtain); World GDP: World Bank; Global Securitized Debt: estimate based on data from McKinsey Global Institute (2011); Total Financial Assets: My estimate including notional value of outstanding derivatives and all other financial assets.

[54] Schroeder (2008), p. 733.

[55] Bank for International Settlement: Statistical Release – OTC derivatives statistics at end December 2014, April 2015, page 15.

[56] World GDP in 2013 was reported to be US$75.6 trillion (report on Worldbank website dated April 14, 2015).

[57] Contracts that are used for netting procedures rarely are completely identical. Therefore, netting procedures may also leave a user with some residual risk, which grows with the magnitude of valuation swings in the market.

[58] Data based on Federal Reserve website for secondary market rates for three-month treasury bills on May 19, 2015.

[59] A recent Bloomberg article claimed that U.S. banks possess US$2 trillion of mainly government bonds ("U.S. Banks Hoard $2 Trillion of Ultra-Safe Bonds," February 22, 2015).

[60] Hammes (2010): Presentation at the Guy Carpenter Insurance Conference, Munich, Germany. Based on a sample of listed insurance companies.

[61] Due to the significant differences in life insurance products and regulations in different countries, this discussion is more general.

[62] An excellent description of Buffett's conduct during the 1970s inflation cycle can be found in Loewenstein (1995), pp. 140–161.

[63] The FX rate between the German mark and the U.S. dollar is a good indicator of inflationary developments.

[64] Based on Feldman (1997), "The Great Disorder," p. 5. Note: Due to the German language and its inclusion of milliards (in German: Milliarde), there is sometimes confusion about and misinterpretation of 1923 exchange rates.

[65] The strengthening of the German mark occurred between February 1920 and July 1920. As Chart 27 focuses on yearly figures, the reader cannot see this phenomenon.

[66] Source: U.S. Department of Labor (U.S. figures); Office of National Statistics (U.K.).

[67] Greenspan (2007), p. 66.

[68] Compare Lowenstein (1995); inflation indirectly also enabled Warren Buffett to execute many attractive investments between 1973 and 1982.

[69] The FPIM model has been developed to guide strategic decision making for both businesses and individuals before and during inflation cycles. In this chapter, the tool is described from the perspective of a corporate user. However, it can also be used to guide decision making for individuals and to cross-check personal inflation protection strategies.

[70] For a more complete discussion of the inflation strategies employed by Hugo Stinnes and the fate of the Stinnes empire after his death, see Domberg, Rathje (2009): *Die Stinnes – Vom Rhein in die Welt*. The most complete discussion on the life of Hugo Stinnes can be found in Feldman (1998): *Hugo Stinnes*.

[71] This chart is based on earlier presentations by the author on inflation management. Compare to Hammes (2010). It has been refined to reflect additional research gathered from the study of past inflation cycles.

[72] The federal funds rate declined from 8.98 percent in February 1970 to 3.29 percent in February 1972. Source: Federal Reserve Website.

[73] Lowenstein (1995), pp. 157–159.

[74] Lowenstein (1995), pp. 159–161.

[75] Looking at historic federal fund rates illustrates the key source for the three inflation shocks in 1968–1970, 1973–1975, and 1977–1980. Hyperactive central banking gravitated quickly between excessively loose and restrictive monetary policies.

[76] Compare e.g., Greenspan (2007), p. 62.

[77] This is particularly true if one includes bank fees and relevant taxes.

[78] Data taken from Internet analysis.

[79] On May 20, 1981, the federal funds rate reached 20.6%. Source: Federal Reserve Website.

[80] This is regardless of the October 1987 stock market crash.

[81] Today's employment problems in the U.S. and other developed countries may be the result of excessive outsourcing of manufacturing and administrative tasks.

[82] You may annoy an expert when you question your financial advisor on how his recommendations will perform if inflation rates climb significantly.

[83] It is important to view accounting issues in the context of the accounting rules of a country. There might be significant differences among different countries and the resulting complexity is beyond the scope of this book.

[84] This is particularly true given that a number of recognized experts warned in great detail of a financial crisis scenario.

[85] The field of systems analysis provides very helpful tools and concepts for these tasks.

[86] I heard of a contract with a builder in which by paying an upfront fee, the builder assumed all repair costs for a five-year period. Unfortunately, the builder defaulted one year after the contract was signed.

[87] Calculated on the basis of Berkshire Hathaway's annual reports for the years 1973 to 1982.

[88] Calculations based on CPI data from the U.S. Department of Labor for the period December 1972 to December 1982.

[89] Internet analysis.

[90] Lowenstein (1995), Chapter 8, pp. 140–161.

[91] Feldman, *The Great Disorder*, p. 606.

[92] The high number of often complex corporate measures (e.g., capital increases with exclusion of minority owners) makes an accurate measurement of share performance difficult.

[93] The key problem in assessing the performance of German equities during that time is the large number of complex capital and corporate governance measures that often favored certain groups of shareholders (e.g., large stake owners) over others (e.g., small investors).

[94] As with any investment topic discussed here, this chart is for illustrative purposes only. Factors such as the respective situational context may have significant influence.

[95] The so-called Hauszinssteuer.

[96] Boeckh (2010), pp. 240-241; in this context, data from Robert Shiller was used.

[97] House price appreciation does not include rental income (for rental properties) or rent equivalent savings if owner occupied.

[98] Keep in mind that higher inflation is typically accompanied by higher interest rates. The latter may have, at least initially, a strong negative impact on real estate prices.

[99] Period covered: January 1983 to December 1999. Calculation based on data from U.S. Department of Labor.

[100] Wikipedia, based on World Council Figures for 2012,

[101] Source: Wikipedia.

[102] Source: Wikipedia.

[103] Assumptions: world population of 7.2 billion, gold content of an average wedding band 4.5 grams.

[104] Assuming a gold price of US$1200 per ounce.

[105] Wikipedia states (on October 6 2015) that about 20% of all gold holdings are held in form of bars and coins as investment vehicles (keyword *"gold as an investment"*). One may double the sum by adding a portion of jewelry to it assuming attractive gold prices may motivate jewelry owner to sell their gold. However, it can also be argued that in an environment of rising inflation fewer people are willing to sell their gold for "paper money."

[106] Based on gold price of US$1200 per ounce as of early May 2015 (assuming 40 percent of all mined gold is available for investment purposes).

[107] Source: Bloomberg article: New York apartments, art top gold as stores of wealth, says Fink, April 21, 2015.

[108] Estimate based on McKinsey Global Institute (2011) data.

[109] This is the case even if we include other precious metals such as platinum or silver.

[110] Source: World Gold Council.

[111] Calculation based on average gold prices in early May 2015.

[112] This excludes the issue of theft protection.

[113] When you calculate the value of the gold of a piece of jewelry, remember that jewelry is not made of pure gold. In the case of 14 karat gold, you will find a little more (14/24) than half of the material is actual gold.

[114] Samuelson (2010), Statistisches Bundesamt (Federal Statistics Office of Germany), Federal Reserve website (historic FX data).

[115] Hammes (2011), based on Deutsche Bank research,

[116] In Germany, this type of crisis was referred to as "Stabilitaetskrise." The Stinnes empire was not the only business that struggled with this problem.

[117] Bresciani-Turroni, p. 319. Administrative costs had to be paid in the new currency while interest rate payments were based on the old (and by then practically worthless) currency.

[118] The book *1913 - Der Sommer des Jahrhunderts* by Florian Illies offers excellent insights into German life prior to World War I.

[119] The author recalls conversations as a youth with older Germans who witnessed this period. In these conversations, the causality between hyperinflation and the rise of the Hitler regime was a recurring theme.

[120] Estimates based on internet research.

[121] A person who was born in 1914 in the former East Germany and continued to live there would have lived with the following domestic currencies: German Goldmark, German papermark (after the abolishment of the German gold standard), diverse forms of "Notgeld", Rentenmark, Reichsmark, East German Mark, Deutschmark (after the reunification of Germany), and the Euro.

[122] Obviously, World War I had a great impact on the German decline. Germany could not afford this war without engaging in significant debt issuance activities.

[123] For example, debt financed share buybacks.

[124] McKinsey Global Institute: Debt and not much deleveraging, February 2015.

[125] Compare to Barclays Wealth and Investment Management Compass November 2014, Figure 1.

[126] Source: Federal Reserve data (website).

[127] Several articles on this topic can be found in newspapers and magazines such as *The Financial Times* and *The Economist*.

[128] Around 2000, Germany was often referred to as the sick man of Europe due to a deteriorating economic situation, poor growth perspectives, lack of structural reforms and its fiscal challenges.

[129] Compare to Allen (1964), particularly Chapter 12, "The Big Bull Market."

[130] Compare Shilling (2013).

[131] Please note that the author relates absolute price stability to the case of mild deflation. This is in contrast to many experts that relate price stability to low rates of inflation. Some central bankers view their goal of ensuring price stability as achieved if inflation stays at or below two percent.

[132] Often referred to as an electronic box or central control unit.

[133] In German, the original name is Roemerbruecke. It bridges the Moselle River, connecting the two parts of Trier and directs traffic to Luxembourg.

[134] For example, in Trier there are two large churches that still use substantial Roman construction. In addition, a 30 meter (about 33 yards) high Roman city gate, the Porta Nigra, is as robust and stable today as when it was built during the second century. Unfortunately, many Roman buildings were destroyed during the Middle Ages to obtain cheap building materials. Otherwise, today's world would have many more examples of extremely robust engineering and construction from Roman times.

[135] Germany's reform program, Agenda 2010, not only improved Germany's economic competitiveness, but also provided its government with record tax revenues a few years after its introduction.

[136] The German dual education system organized by the government and conducted in concert with employers is often cited as a significant advantage of German SMEs over their foreign counterparts.

[137] With the exception of safety-related requirements and regulations.

[138] With the exception of Japan, none of the leading developed countries are among the top ten countries in the most recent PISA ranking (2012) for science, math and literacy.

[139] Obviously, many people criticize the PISA results. Often, the criticism comes from lowly rated countries and claims that specific circumstances were omitted in the test design. While no test of that scope can be perfect, most test results are so striking that criticism regarding the outcomes can be considered as defensive reactions and the unwillingness to face the harsh truth of falling behind. Interestingly, Germany chose a different approach and took the results to heart by introducing structural changes in its education system. While Germany is still lagging Asian countries, it succeeded in narrowing the gap.

BIBLIOGRAPHY

Allen, Frederick Lewis: Only Yesterday, New York 1964 (originally published in 1931)

Bain & Company: A World Awash in Money—Capital Trends through 2020, 2012

Bank for International Settlement: Statistical Release – OTC derivatives statistics at end-December 2014, April 2015

Bernholz, Peter: Monetary Regimes and Inflation, Cheltenham 2003

Bloomberg: U.S. Banks Hoard $ 2 Trillion of Ultra-Safe Bonds, February 22, 2015

Boeckh, J. Anthony: The Great Reflation, Hoboken 2010

Brescianti-Turroni, Constantino: The Economics of Inflation, London 1937

Domberg, Bernhard-Michael; Rahtje, Klaus: Die Stinnes – Vom Rhein in die Welt, Vienna 2009

Ehrlich, Eugen: Amo, Amas, Amat and More, New York 1987

Feldman, Gerald: Hugo Stinnes, Biographie eines Industriellen 1870-1924, Muenchen 1998

Feldman, Gerald: The Great Disorder, Oxford 1997

Fergusson, Adam: When Money Dies, London 2010 (first published 1975)

Financial Times, Risky Debt May Cause Trouble for US Banks, Feb 20, 2000

Greenspan, Alan: The Age of Turbulence, London 2007

Hammes, Wolfgang: The 10 most Dangerous Myths about Inflation for Insurance Companies, Presentation at the Guy Carpenter Insurance Conference, Munich 2010

Hammes, Wolfgang: Impact of Inflation on the (Re-)Insurance Sector, Presentation at the Reinsurance Summit Conference, Zurich, Switzerland, June 28, 2011

Illies, Florian: 1913, Frankfurt/Main 2012

Loomis, Carol: Tap Dancing to Work: Warren Buffett on Practically Everything, New York 2012

Lowenstein, Roger: Buffett, the Making of an American Capitalist, New York 1995

McKinsey Global Institute: Mapping Global Capital Markets 2011, Paper by Roxborough, Charles; Lund, Susan; Piotrowski, John, 2011

McKinsey Global Institute: Debt and Not Much Deleveraging, February 2015

Parsson, Jens O.: Dying of Money, Indianapolis 2011 (First published in 1974)

Reinhard, Carmen; Rogoff, Kenneth: This Time is Different, Princeton 2009

Samuelson, Robert: The Great Inflation and Its Aftermath, New York 2010

Schroeder, Alice: The Snowball—Warren Buffett and the Business of Life, New York 2008

Shilling, Gary: The Benefits of Chronic Deflation, Bloomberg Website, March 25, 2013

Smith, Craig R.; Ponte, Lowell: The Inflation Deception, Phoenix 2011

ACKNOWLEDGMENTS

For several years, I have been deeply concerned about the risks of inflation. What started as a personal research project during a vacation in Venezuela, a country plagued by rising inflation, has turned into countless speeches, presentations, and company workshops on the topic. This book is a further milestone in this journey. I have to thank many people who supported me on this journey.

First of all, I would like to thank my former colleagues at Deutsche Bank, Dr. Stephan Leithner and Jorge Calderon, for their great support, encouragement, and the many critical discussions on this and many other strategic risk and finance topics. In addition, I owe great thanks to my former colleagues Pawel Dela, Axel Seel, Golo Theis, and Henning Schreiber with whom I started the first research project on the topic. I was privileged to have worked with such excellent people.

Also, while at Deutsche Bank, I had support, encouragement, and valuable discussions with the following people: Peter Babej, Dr. Rainer Polster, Dr. Jan Boehm, Dr. Jobst von Hoyningen-Huehne, Melanie Richter, Christoph Rabenseifner, Wilhelm Steinmark, and Stefan Teufer.

Furthermore, I am very thankful for the support and the many critical discussions I had with the following people: Andrew Brandman, Christopher Dennison, Prof. Dr. Alfonso Dufour, Sean Dunlea, Prof. Dr. Martin Fontanari, Dr. Michael Froehls, Dr. Roland Gahn, Michael Hartigan, Bartolomeo Lops, Stefan Maser, Prof. Dr. Niko Mohr, and Nicole Schepanek. I am blessed to have such talented friends who volunteered to support me with their time and feedback.

Over the past years, I have given numerous speeches and presentations to audiences at conferences and to clients. I also moderated many management workshops on the topic. I am particularly thankful for all the critical remarks and the encouraging suggestions that I have received from my audience. Please continue to be outspoken and critical as this is required to advance scientific research and the development of management solutions going forward.

I owe special thanks to my former McKinsey colleague, Dr. Tom Wilson, who not only introduced me to the field of risk management, but also invested a substantial amount of time and patience to explain challenging risk topics to me. I am grateful that I had such an exceptionally qualified teacher and mentor. Also, while at McKinsey I benefited from the guidance of three exceptional individuals, Dr. Ruediger Adolf, Dr. Arnold Gerken, and Dr. Michael Ollmann, who encouraged me to venture into the world of risk management and to always challenge conventional wisdom if rigorous analysis suggests doing so. My ability to translate risk issues into practical reality for companies was greatly improved by working with my former McKinsey colleagues, Oliver Baete and Dr. Michael Muth, and by profiting from their great experience.

Writing a book that pursues a different view than that shared by the majority of people requires both courage and rigorous critical thinking. Not accepting the view of reality that is commonly regarded as the right one and developing an alternative, controversial theory about how reality works and how the future may evolve is a substantial challenge. I am thankful for the following institutions that educated me and enabled me to accept such difficult challenges: Grundschule Trier-Pallien (Germany), Friedrich Wilhelm Gymnasium Trier (Germany), Universitaet Trier (Germany), and Clark University (U.S.). Too often we forget to give thanks to the hard work of our teachers who selflessly spend their lives making their students more successful. The teachers I have experienced were truly amazing. At Trier University, I owe special thanks to Prof. Dr. Walter Schertler, Prof. Dr. Hans Czap, Prof. Dr. Helmuth Milde, and especially the late Prof. Dr. Hartmut Waechter. At Clark University, I owe particular thanks to Professor Jon Chilingerian, Professor Joseph Golec, Professor Ed Ottensmeyer and Professor Maurry Tamarkin, who transferred in an ideal way the University's mission "Challenge Convention, Change our World" into the classroom.

Special thanks are due to Julie Tamarkin and Diane Adams for the difficult task to edit a book written by a non-native speaker and for the many suggestions to make this book easier to read. If some parts of this book are still difficult to read or unclear, it is solely the fault of the author. Also, I owe special thanks to Joanne Sprott for creating the index for this book and for "shepherding" the last steps of this publication.

Finally, I would like to thank my wife Angela and my children Claudia and Maximilian for their patience and support while writing this book and my parents Georg and Hildegard Hammes for being the best teachers in risk and opportunity management.

Let me also thank every reader for spending time with this book. Hopefully, you will gain some valuable insights.

LIST OF ABBREVIATIONS

BV	Book value
CPI	Consumer Price Index
CPI-U	Consumer Price Index—Urban
EMEG Inflation	Emerging Markets Economic Growth Inflation
FPIM model	Four Phases Inflation Management Model
LOFIS Inflation	Loss of Faith in Stability Inflation
PISA	Program for International Student Assessment
OECD	Organization for Economic Cooperation and Development
SWOT	Strengths, Weaknesses, Opportunities, Threats

ABOUT THE AUTHOR

Wolfgang H. Hammes, Ph.D., is the CEO of The Vangi Group LLC in Boca Raton, Florida. Dr. Hammes has been a Managing Director in Investment Banking for both Merrill Lynch and Deutsche Bank in London. He advised clients around the world on strategy and investment banking topics. At Deutsche Bank, he was co-head of the European Financial Institutions Group, advising banking and insurance clients on M&A, capital management, strategy, and risk management topics. Between 1993 and 2000, Dr. Hammes worked as a top management consultant and partner at McKinsey & Co. in New York and Germany. At McKinsey, he was a leader and pioneer of the firm's strategic risk management consulting activities. In early 2000, he was one of the first experts who publicly warned of a major banking crisis in the U.S. due to deteriorating risk management standards in the financial sector.

Dr. Hammes has a Ph.D. (summa cum laude) in business administration from Trier University in Germany and an M.B.A. from Clark University in Massachusetts. He is a member of the board of trustees at Clark University, where he currently heads the strategy and finance committee. He has authored a book on strategic alliances and published many articles on strategy, finance, and risk topics. He is also an active speaker at international strategy, risk management, and finance conferences and company events in North America and Europe.

About The Vangi Group LLC—Consulting

The Vangi Group LLC is a top management consulting boutique that delivers tailor-made services to top decision makers in private and public sector companies. Its expertise is **linking strategy, risk management, and future management** to help achieve successful strategic positioning, "immunization" against major risk events and disruptions, and long-term sustainable competitive advantage. Our goal is to help top management anticipate future challenges and risks and to develop appropriate strategic responses. Our credo is that most risk events are attractive opportunities for those strategically well prepared to deal with them.

We prefer short, interactive, and focused consulting engagements to big and lengthy projects. Often, counselling, a series of targeted workshops, or offsite meetings prove to be more effective than traditional long-term consulting projects.

The Vangi Group Future Lab is our "think laboratory" and our campus for research. This initiative of The Vangi Group focuses on improving our understanding of future risks and opportunities and their strategic implications. It challenges and stress-tests status quo thinking and researches more effective approaches to prepare for future volatility. The Vangi Group Future Lab generates practical, relevant research, develops and tests new management tools and strategies, and organizes conferences and workshops. It publishes our client newsletter, "The Critical Strategist."

INDEX

Note: Page numbers with "n" plus a number following indicate endnotes.

361